LOST
ON THE
LAKES

LOST ON THE LAKES

SHIPWRECKS OF BERRIEN COUNTY, MICHIGAN

Robert C. Myers

ANDREWS UNIVERSITY PRESS
BERRIEN SPRINGS, MICHIGAN

©2003 by Andrews University Press
213 Information Services Building
Berrien Springs, MI 49104-1700
269-471-6134; FAX: 269-471-6224
aupress@andrews.edu
http://www.andrewsuniversitypress.com

Printed in the United States of America
07 06 05 04 03   5 4 3 2 1

Library of Congress Cataloging-in-Publication Data

Myers, Robert C.
    Lost on the lakes : shipwrecks of Berrien County, Michigan / Robert C. Myers.
        p. cm.
    Includes bibliographical references.
    ISBN 1-883925-38-X (pbk. : alk. paper)
    1. Shipwrecks--Michigan--Berrien County. I. Title.

G525.M97 2003
977.4'11--dc21
                                    2003041782

ISBN 1-883925-38-X

Project Director	Ronald A. Knott
Project Editor	Deborah L. Everhart
Copy Editor	Joyce Jones
Data and Clerical Assistants	Eike A. Müller, Jewel Scott
Cover Designer	Saschane Stephenson
Text Designer/Typesetter	Deborah L. Everhart

Typeset 11.5/14 AGaramond

To Candace

Table of Contents

Acknowledgments

M any individuals and organizations contributed to this book, and I tender my sincere thanks to all of them. Michelle Hill, now registrar for the Mackinac Island State Park Commission, suggested the idea for the book when she was a graduate student intern at the Berrien County Historical Association. I have her to thank or blame for tying up endless hours of my spare time in working on this project.

David Swayze and Walter Lewis unselfishly shared the research materials that they have spent years accumulating. Without their enormous generosity this work would not have been possible. Jonathan Wuepper uncovered a wealth of obscure articles during his readings of nineteenth-century Berrien County newspapers. His work helped locate narratives of many a long-forgotten shipwreck, and he shared his findings unstintingly.

All historians owe a great debt to the archivists and librarians who maintain our nation's collections of books and manuscripts. They not only make those documents available for research, but also share their personal knowledge of the source materials that make new books and articles possible. Martin J. Touhy, archivist at the Chicago branch of the National Archives, was of great assistance and gave freely of his encyclopedic knowledge of the Archive's holdings. Robert Graham and his staff at the Historical Collections of the Great Lakes at Bowling Green (Ohio) State University proved ever cheerful and immensely helpful despite my ignorance. Virginia Schwartz and other staff members at the Milwaukee Public Library opened their collections for me and retrieved a seemingly endless stream of documents.

Libraries in Berrien County with their specialized collections are an enormously valuable resource for anyone working on local history. My thanks particularly go to the staffs of the Benton Harbor Public Library, the Niles Community Library, and the St. Joseph Public Library.

As a non-sailor, I had no familiarity with many of the circumstances described in old accounts of ships and shipwrecks or with the terminology then in use. An experienced sailor, Rick Seymour of South Lyon, Michigan, interpreted this foreign language for a landlubber.

Valerie van Heest, a member of the Southwest Michigan Underwater Preserve and of Michigan Shipwreck Research Associates, provided encouragement, research leads, and her own drawings of the remains of shipwrecks lying in the waters off southwest Michigan. Several local genealogists, especially Chriss Lyon and Norbert Cramer, helped track down obscure facts about some of the people and families involved in the area's maritime history.

Special thanks go to Brendon Baillod, Patrick Labadie, David Swayze, and Kenneth Vrana, who read the manuscript. I am deeply grateful for their comments and many thoughtful suggestions.

Deborah Everhart at Andrews University Press has been a delight to work with, making the sometimes aggravating experience of dealing with a publisher a positive joy.

My wife, Candace Seymour Myers, has given me not only the support typical of most writers' spouses, but has been an outstanding research assistant as well. She accompanied me on most of my research trips, took copious notes, ferreted out all sorts of information, and provided many suggestions for the manuscript.

Finally, I thank John H. Frambach, who rescued parts of the manuscript from the Never-Never Land of computer oblivion, and my niece, Jacalyn Odden, who loaned her MacIntosh iBook computer for note taking.

Robert C. Myers
St. Joseph, Michigan

Introduction

A ship amounted to more than a mere assemblage of planks and fittings. To the men who sailed them, Great Lakes vessels were living creatures. Each ship had her own personality, her own quirks, faults, and attributes. She was born, lived, and died; she had her own name. When a captain and crew took possession of a ship, they made her their own. Skippers often commanded a single vessel for years and came to know her intimately. They knew all the sounds she made while underway, turning in a harbor, or creaking softly at her moorings, how her deck felt underfoot, how she rolled and pitched during a storm. If the worst happened and she wrecked, the sailors mourned the ship as much as their lost shipmates.

Most histories of Great Lakes shipwrecks relate the stories of disasters considered significant for one reason or another, an outstanding example of this genre being Mark Thompson's *Graveyard of the Lakes*. A few other works analyze the circumstances surrounding the loss of a single vessel; notable among these are Robert J. Hemming's *Gales of November: The Sinking of the Edmund Fitzgerald* and George W. Hilton's exemplary *Eastland: Legacy of the Titanic*. This study, however, attempts a comprehensive examination of all the shipwrecks pertaining to a small geographic area—namely, Berrien County, Michigan.

Established in 1829 and organized in 1831, Berrien County is located in the extreme southwest corner of Michigan's lower peninsula. It is one of Michigan's "cabinet counties," so called because they were named for members of President Andrew Jackson's cabinet.

2 LOST ON THE LAKES

Berrien County honors Attorney General John MacPherson Berrien of Georgia.

The county has enjoyed a long maritime history. The St. Joseph River rises in Hillsdale County, Michigan, drops south into Indiana, and then flows northward on a meandering path through the towns of Niles, Buchanan, and Berrien Springs before emptying into Lake Michigan at St. Joseph. During the eighteenth century, French voyageurs in their birchbark canoes found the St. Joseph a valuable highway from Lake Michigan to the Mississippi River, via the Kankakee Portage and the Kankakee and Illinois rivers.

In the days of the early republic, keelboats and boxlike arks navigated the river from St. Joseph as far upstream as Constantine, spurring the region's development by allowing settlers to import finished goods and export lumber and agricultural products. After completion of the Erie Canal in 1825, travelers could make the entire journey from New York City to Niles or Constantine without touching dry land: they could ascend the Hudson River to Albany, take a canal boat to Buffalo, then a ship from Buffalo through the Great Lakes to St. Joseph, and head up the St. Joseph River aboard a keelboat or steamer to their final destination. Freight rates plummeted. Settlers poured into southwest Michigan, many of them New Yorkers and New Englanders taking advantage of the relatively inexpensive and comfortable water routes.[1] Ships, typically the cheap and easily sailed schooner, went into operation throughout the Great Lakes to fill the demand for water transportation. Hundreds and eventually thousands of these ships were lost.

Many of those ships and the men who sailed them died for no good reason. Greater caution on the part of owners and masters would have averted the loss of many ships and crews. Prudence dictated that the ships should have laid up for the winter before the storm season set in, but the temptation of good returns on late season runs proved too tantalizing to resist. In November 1879, the Chicago *Inter Ocean* newspaper summed up the situation on the Lakes:

> It is just the time now for owners who have old, worn-out vessels afloat to lay them up before they drown or freeze their crews. So long as freights offer, and harbors are not actually frozen up, these

old traps will probably be kept in commission. Freights being high this fall, vessels will generally be tempted to "go" until the last moment, and more than a few terrible disasters may be looked for.

The *Inter-Ocean* noted that hundreds of worn-out ships were then running in the lumber trade and concluded:

> The vessels are worth, in themselves, little or nothing, so that in case of disaster they [do not] lose heavily, and as to the poor sailors, nobody cares for them—except their families. All steam craft are looked after by the government, but there is no law controlling the grasping, heartless owners of the old hulks run as barges of sail vessels.[2]

Modern weather-forecasting technology has confirmed the *Inter-Ocean's* assessment of lake conditions. Severe weather strikes Lake Michigan during the months of September through April, with the worst storms in October and November. According to the National Oceanic and Atmospheric Administration (NOAA), wave heights on the lake range from five to ten feet about 35 percent of the time. South and southwest winds most frequently generate rough seas in October, while winds from the west and north are responsible during November. From November through March sailors can expect to encounter seas of ten feet or more between 3 to 5 percent of the time, and extreme waves of over twenty feet are not unknown. High seas are rare during the spring, however, and in the summer months the seas reach ten feet or more less than 1 percent of the time.[3]

Gales also strike during the fall and winter. Again according to NOAA, gales sweep through the region frequently and one may expect winds of twenty-eight knots or more as often as one day in five. The strongest measured over-the-lake wind came out of the west-southwest at fifty-eight knots, but Green Bay, Wisconsin, once clocked a ninety-five knot wind in May; NOAA therefore cautions that sailors out on Lake Michigan could conceivably meet with winds of over one hundred knots. Because the fall and winter gales sweep in from the west and northwest, they make harbor entrances on the lake's east shore especially hazardous.[4]

Correlating the frequency of shipwrecks with the seasons of the year over an extended period of time confirms the *Inter-Ocean's* assessment of the dangers of running ships late into the fall. David Swayze of Lake Isabella, Michigan, has spent (at this writing) over fourteen years compiling a comprehensive database of Great Lakes shipwrecks which he has generously posted on the World Wide Web.[5] He has thus far identified more than 4,275 ships that sank, burned, exploded, or were otherwise total losses, beginning with the disappearance of La Salle's *Griffin* in 1679 and continuing through the end of the twentieth century. Swayze's database includes only complete losses (with a few exceptions for notable wrecks, like the capsized *Eastland,* which returned to service after extensive repairs) and does not attempt the almost impossible task of documenting the hundreds of ships involved in less catastrophic accidents every year during the nineteenth and early twentieth centuries.

Of the ships that Swayze describes as total losses, he has determined the month (and usually exact date) of loss for 3,802 vessels. Few ships sank during the winter months of January, February, and March for the simple reason that ships rarely ventured onto the lakes during that season. Iced-in harbors generally prevented ships from sailing regardless of their owner's or master's greed or daring; the small number of ships plying the lakes during the winter correspondingly lessened the possibility of shipwrecks. In over three centuries, only 103 ships—2.7 percent of the total dated losses—became documented sinkings during those three months.

Ship losses naturally mounted after the navigation season opened in the spring, but Great Lakes ships could sail in relative safety during the spring and summer. Only about a third of the total dated losses—1,157 ships, or 30.4 percent—occurred during the spring and summer months from April through August despite the intensive shipping activity. Great Lakes weather turned deadly in the fall. More ships are known to have gone down in November—1,030—than in any other month, and the months of September through December combined to claim 2,542 ships, or 66.9 percent of the total dated losses.

Lake storms did not claim all the lost ships, of course. Boiler explosions, on-board fires, overloading, and even wartime combat sank ships on the Great Lakes, and these calamities occurred in all seasons of the year. Nevertheless, the fact that two-thirds of the total known losses happened during the fall months indicates that prudent masters and owners should have suspended operations much earlier in the season to preserve lives and property.

1. For a description of Michigan settlement in the early nineteenth century, see Willis F. Dunbar, *Michigan: A History of the Wolverine State,* rev. ed. George S. May (Grand Rapids, MI: W. B. Eerdmans Publishing Company, 1980), 193-213.

2. *The Inter Ocean* (Chicago), November 3, 1879.

3. United States Department of Commerce, *United States Coast Pilot 6,* 24th ed. (Washington, DC: U. S. Dept. of Commerce, National Oceanic and Atmospheric Administration, 1994), 232.

4. Ibid.

5. David Swayze, *The Great Lakes Shipwreck File,* January 17, 2002, <http://greatlakeshistory.homestead.com/home.html> (January 28, 2002).

Coastal Development, Harbor Improvements, and the United States Life-Saving Service

L ike most areas, Berrien County developed in relation to its transportation routes. The county's earliest and most important towns all came about because of their convenient links to the outside world. Not only could prospective residents reach the towns with relative ease, but they knew that they could ship goods into and out of the village at comparatively low freight rates.

The village of Niles at the southeastern corner of the county originated in October 1828, when Obed P. Lacey, Samuel B. Walling, and William Justus arrived in the area with their families and settled near the St. Joseph River crossing known locally as "Pogwatique." The spot was located where the Great Sauk Trail, soon to become the Chicago Road, crossed the river and a short distance downstream from the old location of Fort St. Joseph. Walling and Lacey opened a little store in a log cabin built by an early settler, Eli Bunnell. On August 1, 1829, the three settlers, along with Lacey's son, Elijah, platted the village of Niles. They named the new town in honor of Hezekiah Niles, publisher of the *Niles Register,* a famous Whig newspaper in Baltimore, Maryland.[1]

Although situated well inland, Niles enjoyed easy access to Lake Michigan via the St. Joseph River, which was considered navigable by steamboat and keelboat for a distance of over one hundred miles. Niles grew rapidly after the arrival of the Michigan Central Railroad in 1848, which linked the town with Detroit to the east and Chicago to the west. The Michigan Central built a large warehouse at Niles where river vessels picked up and discharged goods for the region upstream, which included the fast-growing town of South Bend, Indiana. A big steamboat named the *John F. Porter*—108 feet in length—was built at Mishawaka, Indiana, to run between Constantine, Michigan, and the Michigan Central warehouse in Niles. For a few years, steamboats and keelboats enjoyed considerable trade along the St. Joseph River above Niles. When the Michigan Southern Railroad completed its line from Toledo to South Bend in 1851, however, it siphoned off most of the river trade in that area.

Despite the decline in river traffic, the Michigan Central remained Niles's trump card in its efforts to attract manufacturing interests and new settlers. The village grew quickly and immediately established itself as the county's largest town and its economic, social, and cultural hub. It was incorporated as the county's first city in 1859, and by 1884 its population had climbed to 4,606 people.[2]

While the proprietors of Niles busied themselves developing their town at the south end of the county, other men created a town at the St. Joseph River harbor. Calvin Britain, a native of Jefferson County, New York, had come to the county in the 1820s as a book-keeper for the Carey Mission, a Baptist Indian school and church founded a few miles west of Niles in 1823. He moved to the mouth of the St. Joseph River in about 1827 and preempted land there with another settler, Augustus B. Newell. Britain and Newell were two of Michigan Territory's innumerable squatters who settled on public land in hopes of purchasing it at a later date. Their hopes were rewarded when the federal government surveyed the area in 1829 and 1830. On September 30, 1830, they bought the land they had preempted.[3]

Britain and Newell's property included the entire area of the town they planned to establish, a place they called Saranac. Benjamin C. Hoyt, another early settler who acted as an agent for the town's proprietors, filed the village plat in Cass County (to which Berrien County was still attached) on April 16, 1831. Britain and Newell named their town Newberryport, apparently in honor of Oliver Newberry of Detroit. The name did not stick, however, and the little village became generally known as St. Joseph, due to its location at the mouth of the St. Joseph River. The Michigan Legislature recognized the town's more popular name by officially changing it from Newberryport to St. Joseph on April 23, 1833.[4]

Manufacturing developed early in Niles because of the transportation advantages offered by the Michigan Central Railroad. Business interests in St. Joseph, however, lagged behind despite government-financed improvements to the harbor. Residents there naturally desired that their town acquire rail connections, too, and launched a variety of schemes to secure a railroad. None of these came to fruition until 1869 when a group of St. Joseph businessmen organized the Chicago & Michigan Lake Shore Railroad Company to build a line northward along the Lake Michigan coast from New Buffalo to St. Joseph. They completed the twenty-eight-mile line on January 28, 1870, and opened it for business on February 2. By 1873, extensions and branch lines connected the Chicago & Michigan Lake Shore to Pentwater, Grand Rapids, Muskegon, and Big Rapids. Its terminus in New Buffalo tied the line to the Michigan Central, linking St. Joseph to Chicago and Detroit. The line reorganized as the Chicago & West Michigan Railroad after the Panic of 1873. Eventually it became part of the famous Pere Marquette system.

The advent of rail transportation and the development of the city of Benton Harbor on the northeast side of the river spurred growth in St. Joseph. A county history published in 1880 noted that "until a few years ago only the common industries were carried on," but that several factories had started up during the past decade.[5] By the end of the nineteenth century, St. Joseph numbered the Cooper, Wells & Company knitting mill, the Truscott Boat Company (specializing in small pleasure crafts), the Compound Door Factory, and the Wells-Higman Company basket factory among its major manufactures.[6]

Although Niles remained the county's largest town, the twin cities of St. Joseph and Benton Harbor quickly eclipsed their upriver neighbor. In 1884, Niles's population (4,606) had exceeded that of St. Joseph (2,623) and Benton Harbor (1,388) combined.[7] The latter two towns both incorporated as cities in 1891. By 1920, St. Joseph's population of 7,251 people nearly equaled the number of people—7,311—living in Niles, and Benton Harbor alone had grown to a population of 12,233 citizens.[8] Economic power had also shifted to the north end of the county. By 1905, some sixty-three factories had located in Benton Harbor and St. Joseph, while Niles had twenty-four.[9]

St. Joseph and Benton Harbor flexed their emerging political and economic muscle when they wrested the prestigious county seat of government away from the town of Berrien Springs. Michigan's legislature had moved the county seat from St. Joseph to Berrien Springs in 1837, largely because of the latter town's location in the geographic center of Berrien County. Niles residents tried and failed to have the county seat moved to their city in 1880, but during the next decade, public discontent grew with Berrien Springs's isolation. A railroad through the town opened twice and went bankrupt both times, leaving only riverboats (which could not run in the winter) to connect it with other communities. St. Joseph, with much help from Benton Harbor, secured the county seat in 1894 after a bitterly fought contest.[10]

While Benton Harbor and St. Joseph grew, Berrien County's other Lake Michigan port town, New Buffalo, languished. Platted in 1835 at the Galien River harbor, New Buffalo was incorporated as a village the following year. The Panic of 1837 hindered the town's development, so much so that only two families remained there during the winter of 1841–1842. A few more settlers trickled in during the following years, however, and the town saw a slow growth in population. Unlike St. Joseph, the town's harbor could not accommodate lake vessels, so most ship captains ignored New Buffalo. The few schooners that did arrive there had to lighten their cargos out from the harbor.[11]

The Michigan Central Railroad reached New Buffalo in 1848, connecting the town with Detroit and Chicago. The railroad company bridged the Galien River and built two piers into Lake Michigan to provide a docking facility for ships that would connect with its trains. Eber B. Ward established a steamship line that met the morning and evening trains and carried their passengers and cargos on the final leg of the journey to Chicago. Residents constructed a hotel, taverns, and other businesses to cater to the increased traffic, and for a short time New Buffalo flourished. Lots in town that had sold for $5 to $25 in 1842 went for as much as $500 after the railroad arrived. Unfortunately for New Buffalo, the Michigan Central kept on laying track around the southern tip of Lake Michigan. When the line reached Chicago in 1852, New Buffalo's boom went bust. Property values plummeted.[12]

The completion of the Chicago & Michigan Lake Shore Railroad in 1870 should have made New Buffalo an important railroad center, but the lack of a proper harbor continued to hinder any major development. No manufacturing enterprises started there. Despite an influx of German immigrants into the surrounding township during the mid-nineteenth century, New Buffalo itself grew slowly. It incorporated as a village in 1836, but by 1884 only 593 people lived there.[13] Its population actually declined afterward, to 496 people in 1920.[14] Not until the late twentieth century, when it became a thriving resort community for tourists from Illinois and Indiana, did New Buffalo grow in stature to become an important city in southwest Michigan.

Developing the St. Joseph Harbor

The mouth of the St. Joseph River, as Nature designed it, did not flow straight into Lake Michigan. Just before the river reached the lake it turned south and swept along parallel to the shoreline until it entered the lake some 1,200 feet south of the present harbor. Ships trying to enter the harbor thus had to sail northward fighting the current, a difficult task that sometimes became impossible when faced with stiff northerly winds during the fall months. Many skippers refused to even attempt to make the harbor under those conditions, instead anchoring outside the harbor and sending passengers and cargo ashore in lighters.

Fatal accidents happened all too frequently. In 1832, lighthouse keeper Thomas Fitzgerald wrote of a tragedy that struck when the schooners *Austerlitz* and *Napolean* anchored at the harbor mouth

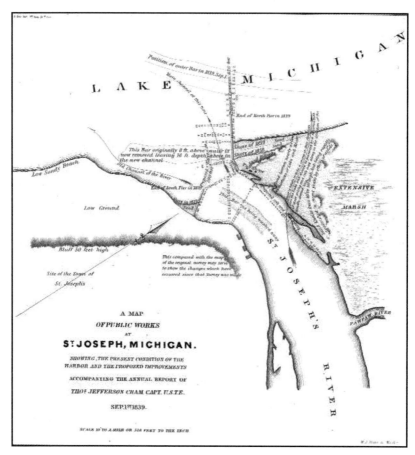

Map of the St. Joseph River harbor, 1839. Drawn by Capt. Thomas Cram of the United States Topographical Engineers, this 1839 map shows early improvements to the St. Joseph harbor, including construction of the north pier. The map depicts the river's original channel and the sandbar that wrecked many ships in the 1830s. *(Courtesy of the Berrien County Historical Association)*

during a November storm. Both ships rode at anchor for two days during the worst kind of weather. When the wind abated somewhat the captain and five men from the *Austerlitz* attempted to reach shore in a boat; it capsized and threw all of them into the freezing water. Thirty villagers waiting on the beach did all in their power to save them, but the captain, two crewmen, and a passenger drowned. Fitzgerald noted that another schooner, the *Free Trader,* had also wrecked the previous year with the loss of two lives.[15]

Within the space of a few weeks during the fall of 1835, the schooner *United States* ran aground at the harbor and several ships lost their anchors while trying to hold position at the harbor. Then the crew of the schooner *Commodore* attempted to land in the ship's jolly boat and capsized; five of the eight sailors died, including the ship's mate. St. Joseph residents who went out in a boat to rescue them also capsized—fortunately, without loss of life.[16]

In response to this succession of shipwrecks, southwest Michigan residents begged the federal government to survey and improve the St. Joseph harbor. In 1834, Lt. John MacPherson Berrien, an engineer with the United States Army at Detroit, led a team of engineers to St. Joseph to survey the harbor. Congress looked over his report and the following year appropriated $26,000 to build a breakwater and make other improvements. This work began in 1836 and straightened the mouth of the St. Joseph River so that it entered directly into Lake Michigan. Various improvements from that time until 1866 resulted in a north pier of 1,100 feet and a south pier of 212 feet. Another government survey in 1863 led to plans for further work, including the extension of the south pier by 200 additional feet. The harbor improvements contributed immeasurably to safe navigation and made St. Joseph an important Lake Michigan port.[17]

The Benton Harbor Ship Canal

The Benton Harbor Ship Canal magnified the importance of the St. Joseph harbor. Unlike most canals, this one did not link other bodies of water; it simply led a short distance inland. Nevertheless, this man-made waterway dug in the early 1860s from the north side of the St. Joseph harbor had an enormous impact on area shipping operations and played an instrumental role in creating the city of Benton Harbor.

While the city of St. Joseph grew up on a high bluff overlooking the harbor, the land on the opposite north bank remained largely uninhabited. It consisted mostly of marshes dotted by a few farms established on higher ground. Sand dunes and steep bluffs running up the lakeshore north of the harbor combined with the marshes that stretched inland to make the north side of the river's mouth unsuitable for settlement and farming. The farmers there had no easy means of bringing in goods or shipping out produce.[18] Area residents built bridges over the river, but this solution proved not altogether satisfactory. The farmers still had to haul their crops in wagons long distances over roads that ranged in condition from bad to abominable. Once the heavily-laden farm wagons reached the river, they still had a long pull uphill to reach St. Joseph, then a descent to the low ground at the harbor itself.[19]

In 1858, floodwaters washed out the Spink's Bridge over the St. Joseph River and left everyone on the north side stranded once more. Farmers in Benton Township tried to persuade St. Joseph merchants to finance the construction of a new bridge, but the economic depression of 1858 was on and the businessmen grumbled and stalled and at last declined to help.[20]

Digging a canal would solve the whole problem. A waterway run northward from the St. Joseph River would let farmers and merchants circumvent the long trip across the river and into St. Joseph to reach ships in the harbor. Instead, they would create their own inland harbor and the ships would come to them. Benton Township residents had already broached the idea during the internal-improvements craze of the 1830s. St. Joseph founder Calvin Britain, Benton Township pioneer Henry C. Morton, and Judge Thomas Conger had stood on the east-side high ground overlooking the harbor in 1837 and pondered the advantages and difficulties of running a canal through the marsh to the river. Nothing then came of their scheme, but the idea returned in full force twenty years later after the flood washed out the Spink's Bridge.[21]

After St. Joseph declined to help rebuild the bridge, three residents of Benton Township—Charles Hull, Morton, and a recent arrival from Indiana, Sterne Brunson—traveled to Chicago in early 1860 to meet with a contractor named Martin Green to review their canal plan. Henry Morton's son, James Stanley Morton (the Morton half of the Graham & Morton Transportation Company) recalled many years later how the three men worked out the canal contract.

Benton Harbor promoter Sterne Brunson. *(History of Berrien and Van Buren Counties, Michigan, 1880)*

Brunson had taken a leading role in pushing the idea forward, but he was "a great talker and in many instances unreasonable, bordering on insanity, and always an unsuccessful man in his business undertakings…" and, therefore, unsuited to working out the particulars of a contract.[22] When they met with Green, Morton and Hull realized that they could never accomplish anything while Brunson was in the way, so they contrived a ruse to divert his attention while they formulated the contract. With the contract terms agreed upon, the three men returned home to set about fund-raising.[23]

A committee asked residents to subscribe to the canal project and Benton Township residents responded with liberal donations of money and land. Construction work commenced that October, and the summer of 1861 found the Benton Harbor Ship Canal already in use. When Green completed the canal in 1862, it stretched about one mile from the St. Joseph River eastward into Benton Township and measured fifty feet in width and ten feet in depth. The canal became an immediate success, and Martin Green accepted contracts to enlarge it in 1864 and 1866, increasing its width to seventy-five feet and its depth to twelve feet with a turning basin at the end of the canal to allow ships to swing around and head back down to the harbor.[24]

The city of Benton Harbor grew up along the ship canal. Originally platted as Brunson Harbor in 1863 (honoring Sterne Brunson), its name became Benton Harbor in 1865; a year later, its

Offices of the Graham & Morton Transportation Company in Chicago.
(Courtesy of the Morton House)

citizens organized it as a village.[25] Main Street in Benton Harbor paralleled the ship canal and the town's business district rose up along its length. During the late nineteenth and early twentieth centuries, untold millions of baskets and boxes of fruit and other farm produce departed Berrien County aboard ships that sailed down the canal. Surviving photographs show downtown streets clogged with farm wagons filled to overflowing with produce from area orchards.

Competition from other modes of transportation, including railroads, trucks, and automobiles, eventually rendered the ship canal obsolete. Ships no longer used it and the canal became a stagnant waterway, an unnecessary part of a changed world. During the 1960s, most of the canal was filled in, ending Benton Harbor's service as a Michigan port city.[26]

The St. Joseph Lighthouse

In 1831, the federal government began construction of one of the first of Lake Michigan's lighthouses on the bluff overlooking the St. Joseph harbor. The structure, like many lighthouses of the time,

Benton Harbor Ship Canal, ca. 1890. *(Courtesy of the Berrien County Historical Association)*

Map of the southern Lake Michigan region, showing Berrien County's transportation network. *(Courtesy of the Fort Miami Heritage Society)*

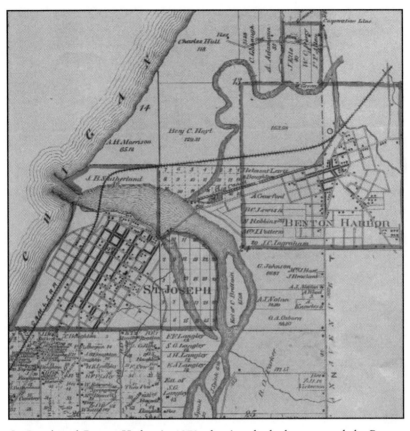

St. Joseph and Benton Harbor in 1873, showing the harbor area and the Benton Harbor Ship Canal. *(Courtesy of the Berrien County Historical Association)*

consisted of a circular stone tower, forty feet tall and eighteen feet in diameter at the base. Thomas Fitzgerald successfully petitioned for the appointment as lighthouse keeper in 1832. He found his new situation less than satisfactory and complained that "The Light House is Completed, but the oil has not yet arrived, and Mr. Reed, in whose charge I found it has been furnishing Sperm Candles to keep it lighted in the place of oil...."[27] It and the Chicago light, which went into service the same year, were the first two lighthouses on Lake Michigan.

Whatever Fitzgerald's misgivings about the operation, a government inspector who visited the lighthouse soon after its construction

Schooners anchored in the Benton Harbor Ship Canal, ca. 1890. The *A. W. Luckey*, in the foreground, was built in Oak Harbor, Ohio, in 1867 and sailed the lakes until abandoned by her owners in 1916. *(Courtesy of the Berrien County Historical Association)*

declared it an excellent facility, with the tower in good repair and the lantern properly cleaned, although the reflectors had deteriorated from heavy use. Maintenance was a chronic problem. The contractors entrusted to keep the lighthouse in good repair had not once come around during the preceding two years, arguing that "the scanty emoluments of the contracts would not allow more frequent calls."[28]

This first lighthouse guided sailors for the next twenty-eight years. A wooden tower built in 1846 at the end of the north pier assisted the lighthouse by shining a white range light out over the water. In 1859, a fine new wooden tower mounted atop an equally fine keeper's house replaced the original stone tower. Like the original tower, this lighthouse stood on Front Street (now Lake Boulevard) on the bluff in St. Joseph. The keeper's house provided lodging for the lighthouse keeper, his family, and an assistant. A woman, Slatira B. Carlton, served as one of the lighthouse's first keepers. After her husband, Monroe, died in 1861 at age twenty-eight, his young widow took over the job, serving from November 18 to December 18, 1861.[29] John M. Enos and his wife Jane also numbered among the new dwelling's first occupants. Between them they served as lighthouse keepers for nearly twenty years. When John died in 1878, Jane took charge and managed the facility for the next three years. She lost her job to the demands of political patronage when President James A. Garfield took office in 1881 and appointed Curtis Boughton, an elderly Civil War veteran, in her place. The *St. Joseph Traveler-Herald* stoutly declared that no accident or mishap ever befell a ship at St. Joseph due to failure of the lighthouse during the time that Jane Enos had charge of the light.[30]

Built in 1859, St. Joseph's second lighthouse stood in the city overlooking the harbor.
(Courtesy of the Berrien County Historical Association)

Ironically, Boughton lost his position to the same political patronage that got him the job in the first place. His successor, Donald R. Platt, had by far the longest tenure of any of the St. Joseph lighthouse keepers. Appointed on August 13, 1883, he served for the next half century. Platt had worked as a government surveyor prior to his employment with the Lighthouse Service, and before that served as a Great Lakes ship captain, employed by the Detroit & Cleveland Navigation Company, among other firms. He won his appointment to the St. Joseph lighthouse through political influence: he numbered among his cousins United States Senator Thomas Platt of New York and the president of the United States, Chester A. Arthur. His appointment caused a near riot in St. Joseph, for residents there greatly desired that Curtis Boughton should retain the post. Their howls of rage eventually quieted down and Platt gained at least a grudging acceptance.[31]

The installation of a fourth-order Fresnel lens in 1889 dramatically increased the illuminating power of the lighthouse. Made in France, Fresnel lenses represented the pinnacle of the glass-craftsman art. One skilled workman assembled each lens by hand, from start to finish, from dozens of perfectly cut glass prisms. The craftsmanship was so exacting that if a workman died while fashioning a lens, Fresnel destroyed it and had a new craftsman start the work over. When the lens was installed in its tower, its light could be seen by ships over seventeen miles away from St. Joseph harbor.

In 1898, the federal government installed inner and outer lights on St. Joseph's north pier. The inner light featured a foghorn powered by its own steam-generating plant. Sailors out on Lake Michigan would listen for the distinctive call of the St. Joseph horn: a three-second blast followed by seven seconds of silence, then another three-second blast and seven seconds of silence. Each foghorn on the lake used a different set interval so sailors could distinguish one harbor from another even if an impenetrable fog obscured the coast. The original wooden outer light tower gave way to a steel one in 1906. The wooden building for the inner light was replaced in 1907 by a square steel structure surmounted by an octagonal tower, completing

The lights on St. Joseph's north pier, 2002. *(Photograph by Anne Odden)*

the range-light system that still exists today. The system consists of two lights, one of which is lower than the other. When ship captains line up the lights, it gives them a perfect guide into the harbor.[32]

The new lights and foghorn on the pier seemingly made the old one on the bluff obsolete, so the Lighthouse Board planned to discontinue its use. Local sailors, however, protested that decision. At a meeting with a representative from the lighthouse board in March 1907, fishermen and steamer captains argued forcefully for the retention of the old lighthouse. From its location high on the bluff, they declared, they could see the light from a distance of eighteen to twenty miles, even farther in especially clear weather. Moreover, the light still could be seen in bad weather when the range lights on the pier disappeared as their ships descended into the troughs of high seas.[33] The Lighthouse Board relented in the face of their arguments and kept the old lighthouse in service; it remained in use until 1924.

New Buffalo's Lighthouse

Lt. John M. Berrien returned to Berrien County in 1835, leading a team of officers from Detroit to New Buffalo to survey the
Galien River harbor and make recommendations for its improvement.
Berrien filed a favorable report, and on July 7, 1838, Congress included New Buffalo in an appropriation of funds to construct lighthouses
and other maritime fixtures. Navy lieutenant James T. Homan select-
ed a site for the lighthouse forty feet from the lake on the south bank
of the river. Jeremy Hixon, who had built the Michigan City, Indiana,
lighthouse two years earlier, won the contract to build the lighthouse
and keeper's dwelling for a total of $4,490 and agreed to finish the
work on or before October 15, 1839.[34]

Hixon set to work building a round brick tower lighthouse. The
contract called for a tower only twenty-five feet high and eighteen feet
in diameter at the base, tapering to nine feet in diameter at the top.
The light itself was to be housed in an octagonal wrought iron frame,
each side of the frame to include an iron window of eighteen panes of
glass. The keeper would climb the tower on a circular stone interior
staircase. Hixon's contract also called for him to erect a little wooden
keeper's house with an attached kitchen wing, a privy, and a water well.

Work on the lighthouse progressed slowly and Hixon missed his
October deadline. He did not complete the work until the spring of
1840, and then the lighthouse dome leaked so badly that rainwater
ran down over the lamp, through the upper flooring, and dribbled to
the base of the tower. A disgusted Stephen Pleasonton, the Fifth
Auditor of the Treasury who had charge of lighthouses, threatened to
make an example of Hixon and Truman H. Lyon, the Superintendent
of Lighthouses on Lake Michigan who had overseen the project, and
sue them both.[35]

Keeper Thomas S. Smith lit the lighthouse for the first time on
June 20, 1840. As it turned out, neither lighthouse nor keeper met
with satisfaction. An official report declared: "The building is very
poor, the lantern leaks badly, and the lamps appeared to have been
made at as little expense as possible....It is altogether a miserable

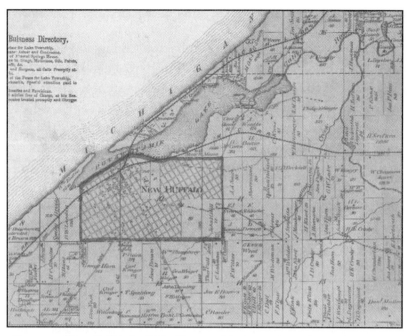

Plat map of New Buffalo in 1873. *(Courtesy of the Berrien County Historical Association)*

concern." Smith lived seventeen miles from New Buffalo and delegated much of his keeper's duty to a deputy, which his contract forbade him to do, so he was dismissed in August 1841.

Smith's successor, Elijah B. Pressey, proved only marginally better as a lighthouse keeper. He evidently kept the tower and dwelling in good repair, but he and his wife lived in a veritable pigsty. The service finally fired him on December 20, 1845. His replacement, Reuben W. Smith, met with satisfaction, and an 1847 report pronounced the facility "an excellent light."[36]

Still, the New Buffalo lighthouse had no great importance for safe navigation. The Galien River was barely navigable and led nowhere, so few ships sailed in or out of the harbor. When the Michigan Central Railroad linked New Buffalo with Detroit in 1849, Capt. Eber Ward established a steamship line to carry passengers from New Buffalo to Chicago. Ward's ships lent the New Buffalo light greater significance, but the steamer traffic ended when the railroad pushed on to Chicago in 1852.[37]

With nothing to justify its expense, the lighthouse closed at the end of the 1858 shipping season and never reopened. The Lighthouse Board officially discontinued its use on August 1, 1859, citing the proximity of the St. Joseph and Michigan City lights and the lack of traffic at New Buffalo as reasons for its abandonment. At first, the government left a man in charge of the property "for the privilege of its use," but later it sold the bricks, metalwork, and keeper's dwelling at public auctions in 1861 and 1862.[38] The tower itself fell victim to lakeshore erosion and toppled into the water.[39]

Lumber Piers

In addition to the natural harbors at New Buffalo and St. Joseph, schooners also took on cargo at the many lumber piers that jutted out into Lake Michigan up and down the length of Berrien County. These piers served the sawmills that sprouted up through the countryside during the mid-nineteenth century. Unlike the region north of Grand Rapids, where lumberjacks floated the logs down the rivers to waiting sawmills in towns like Ludington, Saginaw, Alpena, and Manistee, most of the logs in Berrien County were sawn into lumber well inland and hauled to the coast on horse-drawn tramways. Since the lumber schooners could not run up to the beach to take on their loads, the mill owners built piers that reached far enough into the lake for the ships to tie up alongside.[40]

Many of these logging enterprises developed into sizable operations. At Union Pier in Chikaming Township, at the site of the town that still bears its name, Clement Goodwin and his nephew, Richard M. Goodwin, built a sawmill, a store, and a tramway that extended some three miles inland. Wilkinson's Pier, which eventually became the hamlet of Lakeside, boasted a pier that stretched six hundred feet into Lake Michigan. Three brothers—John W., Joseph N., and James Wilkinson, operating under the name J. N. Wilkinson & Company—bought up several hundred acres of Chikaming Township and built a steam-powered sawmill, a storehouse, the pier, and a boarding house to accommodate some of the fifty to one hundred men in their employ.[41]

A few miles to the north, George Bridgman, Warren Howe, and Charles F. Howe set up the county's largest lumber mill operation at Charlotteville in 1856. The three entrepreneurs constructed a sawmill over a mile away from Lake Michigan that could cut 25,000 feet of lumber per day. A railroad ran through two tunnels under the sand dunes to connect the mill with a five-hundred-foot-long pier. The railroad also wound its way eastward into the woods, giving it a total length of about seven miles. The line's rolling stock consisted of a steam locomotive and thirty-three cars, and the whole business employed between fifty and seventy-five men. The sawmill, railroad, and a boarding house represented an investment of some $90,000—a vast sum for that time. The mill burned in 1863; the company rebuilt twice, lost both new mills to fire, and finally went bankrupt. The village of Charlotteville eventually disappeared, but George Bridgman soon platted a town (which he named, rather immodestly, for himself) a short distance from the old milling operation.[42]

The region's forests consisted of stands of hardwoods: oak, walnut, hickory, poplar, beech, and maple. Sawmills and factories converted the timber into building materials, tool handles, railroad ties, and fuel for steam engines. Although even at an early date a few people railed against the "unpardonable and irreparable destruction" of the county's forests, the logging continued at a breakneck pace.[43] Forests quickly gave way to farmland in the third quarter of the nineteenth century. The sawmills closed when the trees gave out and the lumber companies abandoned their piers. An 1873 atlas of Berrien County depicted numerous lumber piers dotting the coast; by the time publishers produced the next atlas, in 1887, the piers had vanished.[44] The settlements that originated as lumber piers, such as Union Pier, Wilkinson, and Lakeside, exist today as resort communities.

The United States Life-Saving Service

"Regulations say we have to go out, but they don't say anything about coming back."

So went the unofficial motto of the United States Life-Saving Service. It was almost literally true. The Life-Saving Service regulations specified that a station keeper and his crew had to use every means at their disposal to rescue shipwrecked sailors, no matter what the circumstances. A keeper had the option of using a surfboat, breeches buoy, or life car for the rescue attempt and could select the one best suited, in his judgment, for the existing conditions. If the attempt failed, regulations required that he employ the next best option and then, if necessary, the last option. The service would not accept a keeper's statement that the sea or surf was too heavy to launch a boat unless he and his crew had actually made the attempt and failed. No matter how horrific the weather, the life savers had to go out.[45]

No significant government-sponsored organization for aiding shipwrecked sailors existed in the United States until 1848, when losses of ships and lives along the Atlantic coast led the U. S. Congress to establish a series of eight life-saving stations in New Jersey. Prior to that time, wrecking crews often lent assistance to shipwreck victims. American colonies, and later, states, levied taxes against property recovered from shipwrecks that occurred on their coasts. Their governments appointed "wreck masters" or "commissioners of wrecks" to supervise salvage operations and to safeguard the government's interests. Wrecking crews would rescue the passengers and crew of a wrecked ship, if possible, but their primary interest in a shipwreck was

The St. Joseph harbor, ca. 1910. The United States Life-Saving Service facilities are at the base of the north pier. *(Courtesy of the Fort Miami Heritage Society)*

to salvage the ship and cargo. Otherwise, rescue attempts were made by residents who happened to spot a ship in trouble and voluntarily elected to help her crew.

Congressman William A. Newell of New Jersey, appalled by the destruction and loss of life along the coast of his state, persuaded Congress to appropriate $10,000 in 1848 to purchase surfboats, rockets, and other paraphernalia for the New Jersey coast between Sandy Hook and Little Egg Harbor. A year later, fourteen more stations were built on Long Island and New Jersey. Although manned only by volunteers, the stations immediately proved their worth. During the 1849–1850 shipping season, life savers rescued 555 people from wrecks in New Jersey and Long Island, including 201 of 202 persons from the stranded ship *Ayrshire* in January 1850.

No stations were built on the Great Lakes at that time, although in 1854 and 1855 the U. S. Treasury Department sent fifty-one Francis metallic surfboats to various locations on all the Great Lakes except Lake Huron. Built by Joseph Francis of the Novelty Iron Works of Brooklyn, New York, the Francis surfboats cost $450 each, measured 26.5 feet in length with a 6.5 foot beam, and boasted galvanized iron sides and bottom. Integral air tanks made the boats nearly unsinkable, although they weighed in at a hefty 1,500 pounds. The surfboats were entrusted to lighthouse keepers, collectors of customs, or government officials, but they came without any beach wagons or other equipment. Berrien County received two Francis boats—one for St. Joseph and one for New Buffalo—assigned to the care of lighthouse keepers Thomas Fitzgerald and Reuben Smith. Others in the region went to Michigan City, Indiana, and Saugatuck, Michigan. Officials in charge of the surfboats were ordered to use them with volunteer crews to save lives and property from shipwreck.[46]

Volunteer life savers, whatever their courage, could hardly take the place of trained professionals. After a particularly heavy loss of ships and lives on both the Great Lakes and the East Coast during the winter of 1870–1871 (including the schooner *Emma* at St. Joseph), Congress authorized the Secretary of the Treasury to spend

$200,000 to hire crews of experienced surfmen under the auspices of the Revenue-Marine. Secretary of the Treasury George S. Boutwell appointed Sumner I. Kimball as chief of the Revenue-Marine. Kimball reorganized the department and a special Treasury commission recommended the establishment of three classes of life-saving stations: first-class stations, fully manned and equipped, for remote areas; second-class stations with volunteer crews for more populated areas; and a House of Refuge for Florida only. Congress accepted the commission's recommendation, which became law on June 20, 1874. The life savers remained part of the Revenue-Marine until 1878, when they became the United States Life-Saving Service, a separate agency of the Treasury Department.[47]

One of the surfboats at the St. Joseph Life-Saving Station.
(Courtesy of the Berrien County Historical Association)

The Life-Saving Service established three of its twelve districts on the Great Lakes: the Eighth District on lakes Erie and Ontario; the Ninth on lakes Huron and Superior; and the Tenth on Lake Michigan.[48] The service put three life-saving stations and nine lifeboat stations on Lake Michigan. The lifeboat station at St. Joseph went into operation on May 1, 1877, with Joseph A. Napier as the station's keeper.[49] The service equipped stations with everything judged necessary for their operations, from a self-righting lifeboat and oars to paint brushes and shovels; but as lifeboat stations were located at ports or harbors, the service considered the local populace perfectly capable of putting together volunteer crews under the keeper's direction whenever vessels needed assistance.[50]

Rowing out to a wrecked ship was not always possible, so the Life-Saving Service equipped its stations with mortars known as Lyle guns to fire lines out to stranded vessels. Invented by Lt. David A. Lyle of the U. S. Army's Ordnance Department, the Lyle gun was a small, bronze, smoothbore mortar. Life savers loaded their Lyle guns

The St. Joseph Life-Saving Station crew at practice with their Lyle gun, ca. 1900. The Lyle gun itself rests in the sand in the foreground. *(Courtesy of the Berrien County Historical Association)*

with the appropriate charge of powder and a cylindrical-conical projectile which they loaded nose-first into the muzzle. The projectile had an eye bolt screwed into its base, to which was attached a linen shot line. When the mortar fired, the projectile arced through the air and turned nose-first with the line trailing out behind. If all worked properly, the shot soared over the wrecked ship so that the line fell onto it. Sailors aboard the ship drew in the shot line until they reached a heavier hauling line, which they fastened onto their ship. The line also came with a tablet, or tally-board, that had on it instructions for the proper rigging of the lines so that the life savers on shore could set up a breeches buoy and thereby pull the breeches buoy back and forth to the wreck and take off one person at a time. All of this worked beautifully in theory. In practice, firing a line with the Lyle gun involved enormous skill and a degree of luck. Such attempts were often made at night in bitterly cold weather with a howling wind and a freezing spray encrusting men and equipment. Even when everything worked perfectly and the line draped across the ship, the sailors on board—under the same conditions—had to read and follow the instructions on rigging the line. Nevertheless, David Lyle's mortar and the breeches buoy saved countless lives.[51]

The St. Joseph Lifeboat Station almost immediately proved its worth, and its captain his courage, in the epic rescue of the crew of the schooner *D. G. Williams* on October 10, 1877. The *Williams* had stranded on the harbor's outer bar during a heavy gale, and although her crew of six climbed into the rigging to escape the seas breaking over her, they remained in imminent danger of being

The St. Joseph Life-Saving Station crew practicing with the breeches buoy, ca. 1900. *(Courtesy of the Berrien County Historical Association)*

swept off and drowned. Napier organized three volunteers, commandeered a boat, and set off to save them. Their boat capsized in the breakers on their first try, but on their second attempt, they reached the wreck and returned to shore with two of the survivors. The boat filled with water as Napier and his men headed out to the wreck for the third time, but they bailed it out, reached the *Williams,* and succeeded in taking off two more of the stranded crew. With two survivors still remaining on the wreck, Napier and his volunteers headed out through the surf for the fourth time. A vicious surge hurled all of them out of the boat and badly injured one of Napier's legs. One of the volunteers swam ashore while the *Williams's* crew threw a line to another volunteer and pulled him aboard the wreck. The captain and the other man hung onto the boat, managed to right it, bail it out, and then, despite his injuries, Napier brought it alongside the schooner and saved both the remaining two crewmen and his own volunteer. For his daring gallantry at the risk of his own life, Joseph Napier became the first recipient of the Life-Saving Service's highest honor, a Gold Lifesaving Medal, awarded on May 1, 1878.[52]

Crewmen of the St. Joseph Life-Saving Station, 1895.
(Courtesy of the Berrien County Historical Association)

At the beginning of the 1879 season, the Life-Saving Service upgraded the St. Joseph Lifeboat Station to a fully crewed life-saving station. From the station, located near the base of the St. Joseph north pier, the Life-Saving Service crews assisted the crews of scores of ships and saved a great many lives. Joseph Napier resigned his captaincy of the station that December at the end of the 1879 season. His successor, who took over in early December, became one of the service's legends.[53]

William Lyman Stevens was born in St. Joseph on December 5, 1851, the son of James E. and Lucinda Hastings Stevens. James Stevens had emigrated to St. Joseph from Brownsville, New York, in 1842, when the whole of southwest Michigan was little more than forests broken by a few clearings and tiny hamlets. He became a prosperous farmer and merchant, then entered the shipping business. He built and operated the schooners *R. B. King* and *Belle Stevens* and involved himself in one way or another with the management of the steamships *Favorite, Lady Franklin, A. C. Van Raalte,* and *Skylark.* His son, William, helped his father in his various business enterprises and worked in both St. Joseph and Chicago as a dock foreman. Six months after the Life-Saving Service established a full crew at the St. Joseph station, William became its keeper.[54] He devoted the rest of his life to that calling and carried out his duties with such courage and skill that scores of Great Lakes sailors and passengers owed him their lives.

Within a short time after his appointment, Stevens had molded his men into a team that attained an unexcelled degree of proficiency. They had a chance to show off for the head of the service himself when Sumner I. Kimball visited their station in August of 1883. Kimball arrived aboard the U. S. Revenue Service steamer *Andrew Johnson* on an inspection tour with Michigan's U. S. senator, Omar D. Conger, and District Superintendent Nathaniel Robbins. Stevens put his crew through various exercises for these dignitaries. In the line drill, which consisted of shooting a line from the Lyle gun across a spar and bringing in a man, they accomplished their task in three minutes and thirty-seven seconds, beating the old American record by one and one-half seconds and the Great Lakes Service record by three seconds.[55]

The St. Joseph station exemplified the proud traditions of the Life-Saving Service and eventually became part of the United States Coast Guard, the direct descendent of the service. A bill went before the United States Senate in 1913 providing that the Revenue-Cutter Service combine with the Life-Saving Service to form the United States Coast Guard. The bill passed the Senate on March 12, 1914, and the House of Representatives on January 20, 1915; President Woodrow Wilson signed it into law on January 28, 1915. The old Life-Saving Service thereby became part of a military organization; the keeper was given the rank of warrant officer and the surfmen becoming enlisted men. The keepers and surfmen could look back on their service record with pride: from 1876 to 1914, the Great Lakes stations had rendered assistance to 9,763 ships and 55,639 people, and in all those accidents and incidents only 275 people died.[56]

Berrien County Shipwrecks

This book describes shipwrecks that pertain directly to Berrien County, Michigan. The inclusion or exclusion of specific ships was a somewhat subjective decision. With a few exceptions, the narrative only includes commercial vessels that sank or became total losses and

The St. Joseph Life-Saving Station crew in the harbor, ca. 1900.
(Courtesy of the Berrien County Historical Association)

does not include the scores, and perhaps hundreds, of ships that grounded or otherwise sustained serious damage. All of the vessels, however, had strong ties to Berrien County. Most of them wrecked along the county's coast. Others, like all three ships owned by the Israelite House of David religious colony, were locally owned and sailed out of Berrien County ports.

Undoubtedly many shipwrecks have been omitted. Contemporary sources described some ships as sunk or irretrievably wrecked, yet the owners later recovered these same vessels, rebuilt them, and returned them to service. Others wrecked with little or no historical trace. Scant documentary evidence exists for many wrecks, especially those in the antebellum period. Business records do not survive for most of the privately owned schooners and other small ships that plied the lakes. Local newspapers provide an important source of information for minor shipwrecks; few towns, however, had a newspaper until around the time of the Civil War, and even those that began publishing in the 1830s, like the *Niles Gazette and Advertiser,* carried little local news until the 1870s. Many shipwrecks certainly occurred that received little if any notice, particularly if no lives were lost.

Nevertheless, this book presents a fairly complete listing of shipwrecks related to Berrien County. From La Salle's fur trading bark *Griffin* in 1679 to the steamer *City of Cleveland III* nearly three centuries later, the loss of Great Lakes commercial vessels has had a profound and often tragic impact on the county's history.

1. Franklin Ellis, *History of Berrien and Van Buren Counties, Michigan* (Philadelphia: D. W. Ensign & Co., 1880), 154; Walter Romig, *Michigan Place Names* (Detroit: Wayne State University Press, 1986), 399.

2. Gilbert R. Osmun, *Official Directory and Legislative Manual of the State of Michigan for the Years 1887-8* (Lansing: Thorp & Godfrey, 1887), 292.

3. Ellis, 312.

4. "An act to change the names of several townships," in *Laws of the Territory of Michigan,* 3 vols. (Lansing: W. S. George & Co., 1874), 3:242. The village's original name appears in some sources—erroneously—as "Newburyport."

5. Ellis, 319.

6. Orville W. Coolidge, *A Twentieth Century History of Berrien County, Michigan* (Chicago: The Lewis Publishing Company, 1906), 188–89.

7. Osmun, 294.

8. Charles J. DeLand, comp., *Michigan Official Directory and Legislative Manual for the Years 1921 and 1922* (n. p., n. p., 1921), 250 and 260.

9. Coolidge, 54.

10. Jan H. House and Robert C. Myers, "The Berrien County Courthouse Square: A Sesquicentennial History," *Michigan History* 70 (November/December 1986): 21-27.

11. Ellis, 271–72.

12. Ibid., 273–75.

13. Osmun, 294.

14. DeLand, comp., 271.

15. Thomas Fitzgerald to John Tipton, November 21, 1832, *The John Tipton Papers,* comp. and ed. Glen A. Blackboon, Nellie A. Robertson, and Dorothy Riker, 3 vols. (Indianapolis: Indiana Historical Bureau, 1042), 2:716–17. The *Free Trader* apparently survived this disaster, as Harriet Martineau described what could only have been the *Free Trader* wrecked at Sleeping Bear Point in November 1835; see Steve Harold, *Shipwrecks of the Sleeping Bear* (Traverse City, MI: Pioneer Study Center, 1984), 9.

16. *Niles* (Michigan) *Gazette and Advertiser,* October 10, 1835.

17. Ellis, 45. By an odd coincidence, the John MacPherson Berrien who surveyed the harbor was a first cousin (and had the same name) as U. S. Attorney General John MacPherson Berrien for whom Berrien County was named. See Robert C. Myers, *Historical Sketches of Berrien County,* vol. 2 (Berrien Springs, MI: Berrien County Historical Assn., 1989), 13–14.

18. Ellis, 316.

19. James A. Tolhuizen, "History of the Port of St. Joseph-Benton Harbor," (Master's thesis, Western Michigan University, Kalamazoo, MI, 1965), 32–33.

20. Ibid.

21. Ibid., 34; Mary A. Raymond to James Stanley Morton, November 30, 1903, Josephine Morton Memorial House, Benton Harbor, MI.

22. James Stanley Morton to Mary A. Raymond, December 8, 1903, Josephine Morton Memorial House, Benton Harbor, MI.

23. Ibid.

24. Tolhuizen, 34–43.

25. Coolidge, 235.

26. Tolhuizen, 44–45.

27. Thomas Fitzgerald to John Tipton, June 26, 1832, *The John Tipton Papers,* 2:638–39.

28. United States, Serial Set No. 345, 25th Congress, 3rd Session, Executive Document No. 24 (December 13, 1838), 117.

29. Mary Louise Clifford and J. Candace Clifford, *Women Who Kept the Lights: An Illustrated History of Female Lighthouse Keepers* (Williamsburg, VA: Cypress Communications, 1993), 164; Registers of Lighthouse Keepers, 1845–1912, Great Lakes, 1845–1900, Microfilm M 1373, NARA, RG 26, 525.

30. *St. Joseph Traveler-Herald,* April 2, 1881.

31. Ibid., September 8, 1883, and Supplement, September 1, 1883; *The*

Herald-Press (St. Joseph, Michigan), February 12, 1934.

32. United States Lighthouse Board, "Description of Buildings, Premises, Equipment, etc., at Front and Rear Range Lights, St. Joseph Pierhead Light-station, St. Joseph, Michigan," June 8, 1909, Lighthouse file, Maud Preston Palenske Memorial Library, St. Joseph, Michigan.

33. *St. Joseph Evening Herald,* February 16 and March 8, 1907.

34. Patricia Gruse Harris, *New Buffalo, MI, Lighthouse, 1839–1859* (Michigan City, IN: Gen-Hi-Li, 1992), 1–7. Harris's booklet presents a detailed history of the construction and use of the lighthouse.

35. Ibid., 6–9.

36. Ibid., 10–15.

37. Ellis, 275.

38. Registers of Lighthouse Keepers, 1845–1912, Great Lakes, 1845–1900, 526.

39. Ellis, 275.

40. Harvey Franz, "Lumber Piers of Southwestern Michigan," Berrien County Historical Association, Berrien Springs, Michigan. Photocopy.

41. Ibid.; Ellis, 233.

42. Franz, "Lumber Piers"; Ellis, 251.

43. T. G. Turner, *Gazetteer of the St. Joseph Valley, Michigan and Indiana* (Chicago: Hazlitt & Reed, 1867), 75.

44. *Atlas of Berrien County, Michigan* (Philadelphia: C. O. Titus, 1873), 7, 11, 17, 33, and 45; *Atlas of Berrien County, Michigan* (Chicago: Rand, McNally & Company, 1887), 13, 17, 29, 31, and 37.

45. Regulations of the Life-Saving Service of 1899, Article VI "Action at Wrecks," Section 252, 58.

46. Jacob Abbott, "Some Account of Francis's Life-boats and Life-cars," *Harper's Magazine,* 1851; reprint ed., *The United States Life-Saving Service—1880* (Grand Junction, CO: Vistabooks, 1989), 33–44; Frederick Stonehouse, *Wreck Ashore: The United States Life-Saving Service on the Great Lakes* (Duluth, MN: Lake Superior Port Cities, 1994), 8–12.

47. Stonehouse, 13–15.

48. Ibid., 18. The district designations changed later so that, among other regions, Lake Michigan became the Eleventh District in 1877 and the Twelfth District in 1900.

49. Ibid., 18–19.

50. Ibid., 44.

51. Ibid., 121–27; M. J. Lamb, "The American Life-Saving Service," *Harpers New Monthly Magazine* 64 (December 1881–May 1882), 371–72.

52. U. S. Coast Guard, "Gold Lifesaving Medal Awardees," United States Coast Guard Historian's Office, January 2002, <http://www.uscg.mil/hq/g-cp/history/Gold%20Medal%20Index.html> (February 16, 2002).

53. *St. Joseph Traveler-Herald,* December 6, 1879.

54. J. B. Mansfield, *History of the Great Lakes,* 2 vols. (Chicago: J. H. Beers & Co., 1899; reprint ed., Cleveland: Freshwater Press, 1972), 2:246–47.

55. *St. Joseph Traveler-Herald,* August 18, 1883.

56. Stonehouse, 198–99.

Shipwrecks of the Colonial and Antebellum Period

Griffin, 1679

The bark *Griffin* was not only the first sailing ship on the Great Lakes but also became the lakes' first shipwreck.

The *Griffin* was built for René-Robert Cavalier, Sieur de La Salle, the son of a wholesale haberdasher, born in Rouen, France, in 1643. He entered the Society of Jesus, or Jesuits, at age fifteen, and took the vows of the order a year later. Eventually, however, he grew discontented and resigned. His father had died in the meantime, and La Salle's vow of poverty had prevented him from inheriting any of the estate. The year 1665 found the young man penniless and without a career or suitable training for any employment except that of a priest. Seeing no future for himself in France, he set sail for the New World the following spring.

Although the Sulpicians at Montreal granted him a seigneury—a parcel of land—life as a gentleman farmer held no appeal for La Salle. Instead, he found much more alluring the prospect of exploring the western reaches of the colony and establishing himself in the lucrative fur trade. He led an expedition to chart the Ohio River in 1669–1672, and in 1677 received permission to establish a colony in the Illinois country.[1] La Salle promised to explore the lower Mississippi for France, seek out a navigable route to the Pacific, and locate mineral deposits, all at his own expense. In return, La Salle received a land grant and a monopoly on the trade in buffalo hides.

The Crown forbade him, however, to trade with any Indian nations who brought their furs to Montreal.[2]

Upon his return to New France, La Salle promptly violated the last part of this agreement by sending out a party of fifteen men to trade with the Illinois Indians. In the spring of 1679 La Salle put up a shipyard on Lake Ontario, just above Niagara Falls, and constructed the first sailing vessel on the Great Lakes. He named her *Griffin* to honor his sponsor, the Governor General of New France, Louis de Buade, Comte de Frontenac, whose coat of arms bore two of the mythical half-eagle, half-lion creatures. According to Father Louis Hennepin, the Jesuit priest who accompanied La Salle, the *Griffin* was a small bark of about forty-five to sixty tons burthen and carried as armament five small cannon (two of them brass) and three swivel guns.[3]

La Salle envisioned the *Griffin* as a floating trading post, capable of carrying large quantities of trade goods to the western Indians and returning with a cargo of furs. Unlike canoes, she would be invulnerable to attack by the hostile Iroquois. The vessel, with La Salle, Hennepin, Henri de Tonty (La Salle's lieutenant), two missionaries, and some thirty other men crammed aboard, weighed anchor on August 7, 1679, and sailed across Lake Erie and headed north on Lake Huron. Upon reaching Michilimackinac, La Salle discovered that his advance party had deserted and stolen his trade goods. He found four of the deserters at Michilimackinac, and when he learned that two others were at Sault Ste. Marie, he sent Tonty and six men to capture them. Thirteen men remained at Michilimackinac to await Tonty. They had instructions to bring their combined party to a rendezvous point at the mouth of the St. Joseph River. La Salle and the rest of the crew set sail in the *Griffin*. They reached Green Bay in early September, where the *Griffin* took on a cargo of furs.[4]

La Salle decided to send the *Griffin* back to Niagara while he, Hennepin, and several men proceeded to the St. Joseph River. After the *Griffin* had discharged her cargo and taken on another load of trade goods, she would rendezvous with La Salle. On September 18, the *Griffin* fired a salute from one of her cannon and sailed out into the lake. La Salle and his men watched until her sails dipped below the horizon, then they set out in four heavily laden canoes down Lake Michigan's western shore.

On November 1, 1679, La Salle and his men reached the St. Joseph River—or the River of the Miamis, as it was then called, for the Miami Indians who lived along its banks. Displaying a keen understanding of Indian psychology, La Salle refused to continue south into the Illinois country, saying that the Frenchmen would be "expos'd to their Mercy and Scorn, if we offer'd to enter their Country with so few Men."[5] Instead, he called his men together and announced that he had decided to await Tonty's arrival at the river's mouth. La Salle well knew that the charms of running away to live with the Indians held an irresistible appeal for his men, so he resolved to keep them too busy to contemplate that option. To that end, he proposed that they construct a fort and a house for the security of the *Griffin* and the goods she would bring, as well as a shelter for themselves.[6] The men grumbled and complained, but their leader was nothing if not persuasive and at length they agreed to follow his orders.[7]

La Salle immediately commenced work on the fort, the first such structure in Michigan's lower peninsula. According to Hennepin, they built the fort, which La Salle christened Fort Miami, at the river's mouth on a high, steep bluff, defended on two sides by a ravine. The men built a "Redoubt of forty Foot long, and eighty broad, with great square pieces of Timber laid one upon the other; and prepar'd a great Number of Stakes of about twenty five Foot long, to drive into the Ground, to make our Fort the more unaccessible on the River side."[8]

Construction continued through November. Hennepin and Father Gabriel de La Ribourde took turns preaching to the men in a rude cabin each Sunday, choosing texts that were "suitable to our present Circumstances, and fit to inspire us in Courage, Concord, and brotherly Love."[9]

Meanwhile, La Salle stared out over Lake Michigan in hopes of spotting the *Griffin.* He had the harbor sounded and found to his great consternation that a sandbar obstructed its entrance. His men sank posts into the harbor floor and fastened bear skins onto them as primitive marker buoys to warn the *Griffin's* pilot away from the dangerous bar—the first of many efforts over the next three centuries to make the St. Joseph River entrance safe for navigation. As a further precaution, he dispatched two men to Michilimackinac to meet the *Griffin* and guide her into the harbor.

Tonty arrived at Fort Miami on November 20 with the devastating news that the *Griffin* and her entire cargo of furs had vanished. Since La Salle's men could not winter at the fort without additional provisions, he had no choice but to push inland, but to do so he wanted as large a force as he could muster. Tonty had left a few men about seventy miles northward to hunt game and La Salle sent him to bring them down. In the meantime, he kept the men working on Fort Miami, which they finally completed about the end of November.[10]

After Tonty and his men arrived at Fort Miami, a late thaw and rains melted the river ice and on December 3 the thirty-three men started up the St. Joseph River in eight canoes.[11] They then portaged to the Kankakee River, which flowed into the Illinois. La Salle built another post, Fort Crevecoeur (Heartbreak), on the Illinois and set his men to work on a ship which he evidently intended to use in exploring the Mississippi. Hoping to learn what had happened to the *Griffin,* La Salle returned to Fort Miami on March 24, 1680. There he found the two voyageurs he had sent to Michilimackinac the previous fall, but they could tell him nothing about the *Griffin's* fate.[12] La Salle set out on an epic winter journey to Niagara, traversing Michigan's lower peninsula by land and water. He and three companions reached Niagara more dead than alive, only to find that the *Griffin* had vanished en route from Green Bay.[13]

The *Griffin's* disappearance remains one of the Great Lakes' most intriguing mysteries. She probably went down in a severe storm that sprang up the day after her departure, although other theories include the ship's capture by Indians or being scuttled by her own crew.[14] Whatever the cause, La Salle suffered financial disaster in the *Griffin's* loss.

Upon reaching Montreal, La Salle managed to secure enough credit to procure supplies and men for a new expedition. When he returned to Fort Frontenac, however, he received a crushing message from Tonty. A ship carrying twenty-two thousand livres' worth of his merchandise had been wrecked in the St. Lawrence River. Nor was that all. Tonty also told him that the men at Fort Crevecoeur had deserted and destroyed not only that post but had also burned Fort Miami and stolen all his supplies at Michilimackinac.

Undeterred, La Salle left Fort Frontenac with an aide, William de La Forest, and twenty-four men on August 10, 1680, for a second expedition to the Illinois country. They arrived at Fort Miami's burned ruins on November 4. Leaving La Forest and several of the men behind, La Salle set off for the Illinois River in search of Tonty. The search was unsuccessful, and by now La Salle was concerned for the life of his trusted lieutenant. Returning from the Illinois country, he reached Fort Miami on January 26, 1681. He found that the energetic La Forest had not only rebuilt the fort and cleared the ground for cultivation, but had also begun the construction of a new ship.[15]

La Salle wintered at Fort Miami and then, determined to locate Tonty, set out for Michilimackinac, where the two finally reunited. From there he proceeded to Montreal, where Governor General Frontenac authorized what would be his final expedition, a trading and exploration voyage down the Mississippi River. The expedition reached Fort Miami in December 1681. Tonty pushed on ahead with an advance party, while La Salle paddled up the St. Joseph River with a score of men and six canoes filled with supplies.

La Salle never returned to Fort Miami; the post fell into disrepair after he abandoned it and by 1689 it had vanished entirely.[16] La Salle himself turned his attention to the development of the lower Mississippi River valley, an area he dubbed Louisiana. His ruthless pursuit of his own ambitions ultimately led to his assassination by his own disaffected followers in present-day Texas in 1687.

Pioneer, 1834

The steamboat *Pioneer* inaugurated steam navigation at St. Joseph in 1831 when she arrived at the harbor.[17] Her owners had sent her from Lake Erie to Lake Michigan to run between Chicago and St. Joseph, although Berrien County's early settlers did not recall her making regular trips to the latter town.[18]

The *Pioneer* was launched at Black Rock (later Buffalo), New York, on June 11, 1825, and first enrolled at Buffalo that August under the ownership of Augustus S. Porter. When she reached Detroit on her maiden voyage on August 20, the *Detroit Gazette* hailed her as a "truly elegant steam-boat." The *Pioneer* had made the run from Buffalo to Detroit, a distance of 250 miles, in thirty-three hours—a fine turn of speed for the day. "Her machinery," the *Gazette* declared, "is in good order, her cabins, though small, are convenient and elegant, and the furniture new and in excellent condition." The *Pioneer's* skipper, Capt. William T. Pease, put her on a weekly run between Buffalo and Detroit.[19] Residents of the rapidly growing Michigan town pronounced the *Pioneer* a shining example of the progress evident in the state's expanding commerce and population, and a promise of even more robust growth to come.[20]

The *Pioneer* had met with near disaster before her voyage to St. Joseph when she beached in a storm at Black Rock on October 17, 1825. Her crew and passengers all made shore safely but thought that the extensive damage to her hull and machinery left the steamer an unsalvageable wreck.[21] The *Pioneer,* however, was then less than a year old and consequently a valuable ship, so she was quickly repaired and returned to service.

Capt. John F. "Bully" Wight, who had commanded the *Pioneer* on her first voyage to St. Joseph, bought her in 1833 and was the captain in early July 1834 when she towed the riverboat *Davy Crockett* from Lake Erie to the St. Joseph. The *Pioneer* completed her mission but grounded on the bar at the harbor entrance. A sudden gale blew up and pummeled the stranded steamer until she became a total wreck and finally went to pieces.[22] The schooner *Marengo,* captained by Mason Dingley, rescued the crew and passengers.[23] The *Pioneer* was reincarnated in a much altered form when Curtis Boughton of St. Joseph salvaged her and used some of the timbers to build the schooner *Drift,* which he ran from St. Joseph to Chicago for several years.[24]

Bridget, Swan, and *Chance,* 1835

A ferocious November storm that swept through the Great Lakes region in 1835 spread destruction everywhere, roaring in from the west-southwest with a sound like the approach of a gigantic freight train. In Buffalo, New York, a creek rose to a depth of twenty feet, floating ships onto streets and crushing canal boats under bridges; on the west side of the harbor, the storm tore houses from their foundations and drowned their occupants.[25]

The storm wrecked three schooners along the Berrien County coast. The new schooner *Bridget,* owned by merchants at Detroit and Michilimackinac and commanded by Capt. Peter Druyea, arrived at the St. Joseph harbor from Chicago on the evening of November 10, 1835, dropped anchor outside the harbor, and sent part of her cargo ashore. Druyea intended to proceed northward through the Straits of Mackinac and on to Detroit, but he never made it. The storm that hit that night swept the *Bridget* northward along the lake, carrying her fifteen passengers and crew with her. She eventually foundered with all hands some eighteen miles north of St. Joseph.[26]

At any rate, that is how the story went as recounted by a local newspaper, the *Niles Gazette and Advertiser.* Other sources related the tale with slightly different particulars. The *Buffalo Whig & Journal* reported that the *Bridget* had discharged her passengers in Chicago, her first stop, before heading for St. Joseph. Her skipper, Capt. Charles H. Ludlow, was at first reported lost with his ship, but it later developed that he had disembarked in St. Joseph and was not aboard when the storm hit.[27] The *Chicago Democrat* identified the Bridget's skipper as "Capt. Drouillard" and reported that all hands, including the captain, his wife, and all aboard (fifteen in all), including two female missionaries bound for Michilimackinac, perished in the disaster. The

Democrat reported the *Bridget* floating keel upward, moored by her anchor, about eight miles (not eighteen) from St. Joseph.[28]

The same gale that wrecked the *Bridget* also sank the schooners *Swan* and *Chance*. The *Swan* had apparently arrived safely at her destination of St. Joseph, but slipped cable during the storm and drifted down Lake Michigan until she foundered off New Buffalo with the loss of all aboard.[29] Little documentation exists as to the fate of the *Chance*. Contemporary accounts reveal only that residents of St. Joseph found her offshore with only the masts protruding above the water, and that seven people lost their lives in the disaster.[30]

Delaware, 1836

The steamer *Delaware* was built in 1834 for merchants Oliver Newberry of Detroit and Richard Sears of Buffalo, and first skippered by Chelsey Blake. Capt. George J. King bought her in 1836 and in June sailed her to St. Joseph.[31]

Harriet Martineau, the famous English author and commentator on America, was at that moment en route from Niles, Michigan, to Chicago on her grand tour of the new republic. She and her party debated whether they should make that leg of their journey by stagecoach or on board the *Delaware*. At length they decided on the overland route because no one knew what time the *Delaware* would set sail and also because they wished to skirt the southern tip of Lake Michigan to see the settlements then springing up along its shore. On June 22, as Martineau's group followed the winding road through the dunes, someone called to them to halt the stagecoach and run up a bank to see a shipwreck. They scrambled to the top of a dune and looked down. Below them near the shore lay the *Delaware*. "She had," Martineau recalled, "a singular twist in her middle, where she was nearly broken in two."[32]

The *Delaware* had steamed out of St. Joseph for Chicago on June 19 but encountered a ferocious nor'easter that lasted for the better part of three days; she ran ashore at about ten o'clock that evening a few miles west of Michigan City, Indiana, and went to pieces.[33] The passengers had stood in water up to their necks for twenty-four hours before they were rescued, but all of them survived. A bemused Martineau reported that as soon as the passengers had dried themselves out they drafted a letter to the *Delaware's* captain, which afterward appeared in all the region's newspapers, thanking him for all the comforts they had enjoyed aboard his ship. "It is to be presumed," Martineau chuckled, "that they meant previously to their having to stand up to their necks in water."[34]

Davy Crockett, 1836

Built at Erie, Pennsylvania, the stern wheel riverboat *Davy Crockett* came to the St. Joseph River in July 1834 in tow of the steamboat *Pioneer* and Capt. John F. Wight of the firm John Griffith and Company. Named for the famed frontiersman—already an American legend—she entered service with Pitt Brown of Berrien Springs as captain and Joseph Smith as pilot. The *Crockett* featured a remarkable figurehead, described as a half-horse, half-alligator. A small tube connected the engine's exhaust pipe to the figurehead so that the beast's mouth expelled a jet of steam at every piston stroke.[35]

The *Davy Crockett* ran in competition with the *Matilda Barney*, a flat-bottomed sternwheeler built in 1833 at St. Joseph by the firm of Edward P. Deacon and William McCaleb. When the *Matilda Barney* hit a snag on the river in 1834 and broke her wheel, she suffered the indignity of being tied to her rival and hauled to St. Joseph. As both riverboats were sternwheelers, the *Matilda Barney* had to be lashed alongside the *Davy Crockett* for the trip, which prompted eccentric Berrien Springs poet Nathan Young to pen a few lines of doggerel to the tune of Yankee Doodle:

> Now Davy Crockett came to town
>   All dressed up like a dandy;
> From Presque Isle, he has come around
>   To spark Matilda Barney.
>
> Now Davy he approached near,
>   With her began to blarney,

"Your company not wanted here,"
    Replied Matilda Barney.

"O how can you treat me so,
    My dearest Miss Matilda,
Since you have got no other beau,
    And I love you so dearly."

"You appear to be a nice young man,"
    replied Matilda Barney.
"You are also an obliging friend,
    More than I would wish to have you."

At length Matilda she grew lame,
    And Davy made toward her,
She soon consented for him
    To see her safe to the mouth of the river.

It was hand in hand they both locked arms,
    And down they came together,
Delighted with each other's charms,
    Like a sister and a brother.

It is now they are in St. Joseph Bay,
    Beneath the storms and weather,
But whether they are married or no,
    It is there they lie together.[36]

Although the *Davy Crockett* enjoyed little trade in 1834, she returned to the St. Joseph the following year with Benjamin Putnam as captain and Joseph W. Brewer and Moses D. Burke as pilots.[37] Apparently the skippers were changed rather frequently; in 1835, one John Rosmond signed a petition as "Master, Steamer Davy Crockett."[38]

The *Niles Gazette and Advertiser* praised the *Davy Crockett* as a fine steamer, "handsomely refitted and repaired," but Samuel Tudor, a pioneer resident of Berrien Springs, remembered her differently. Writing years later, Tudor recalled that although the *Crockett* boasted the most powerful engine of any boat on the river, the vessel herself proved "a poor model, very logy." Her engineer, James Watson, found that the boat's builders had set her paddlewheels too far aft, which raised the stern and plunged the bow deep into the water.[39] Business improved steadily regardless of the *Crockett's* quality, but in early August 1836, luck ran out. The *Davy Crockett* struck a rock in the river some seven miles above Berrien Springs, broke in two, and sank. For decades afterward, local residents referred to the spot in the river that proved its undoing as "Crockett's Defeat."[40] The *Davy Crockett's* machinery was salvaged and installed in a new riverboat, the *Patronage,* which ran for a few years on the St. Joseph until it went to the Grand River in 1841.[41]

The little riverboat had survived her namesake by only five months—Davy Crockett had died in Texas with the other defenders of the Alamo the preceding March.

Post Boy, 1841

Most shipwrecks have little long-term effect save for the passengers and crew directly involved. The unlucky schooner *Post Boy,* however, helped found a whole town.

The *Post Boy* was built in Portland Harbor, New York, in 1832 and was owned by Augustine Eaton, Morgan L. Faulkner, Eliphalet L. Tinker, George Mount, and her captain, Gilbert Knapp. She had hardly begun her career on the Great Lakes when she capsized near the Manitou Islands in 1833. The owners recovered her, and sometime during that year a new skipper took command: Capt. Wessel Whittaker of Hamburg, New York. Whittaker was a Great Lakes veteran. From 1824 until he came aboard the *Post Boy,* he had captained the schooners *Marie Antoinette, Fair Play, Good Intent, William,* and *Governor Cass,* and the brig *Union,* all out of Buffalo.[42]

In the fall of 1834, a sudden storm caught the *Post Boy* as she sailed southern Lake Michigan. Whittaker elected to run for safety to the mouth of State Creek, near present-day Michigan City, Indiana. Despite his best efforts, the *Post Boy* beached herself; Whittaker and his crew braved the bitter cold and walked to St. Joseph to report the accident to the insurance underwriters.[43]

The crew's route took them past the mouth of the Galien River and Whittaker made a mental note of the place which struck him as a likely spot for a shipping harbor and town. After he finished his business in St. Joseph, he went to a government land office and bought the property he had admired. He then returned to Buffalo, New York, where he cornered Jacob Barker and Nelson Willard, part owners of the *Post Boy,* and sold them a half interest in his property for $15,000. In March 1835, Whittaker and three other men—Truman A. Clough, William Hammond, and Henry Bishop—set off overland from Buffalo and Hamburg for Michigan. They stopped at the hamlet of Bertrand, near Niles, and procured the services of surveyor and old acquaintance Alonzo Bennett, who accompanied them to their land and surveyed the town. They named the place New Buffalo, in honor of the city in New York, and went to work selling lots in the village.[44]

So went the story. The particulars may be suspect, however, for Whittaker actually bought the Galien River property in November 1833, a year before the *Post Boy's* accident.[45] The exact sequence of events may have differed from later recollections, or perhaps Whittaker had designs on the property before the *Post Boy* came to grief there. An advertisement in the *Buffalo Whig* newspaper reported that he planned to sail the schooner *Indiana* out of Buffalo for Michilimackinac, St. Joseph, Michigan City, and Chicago in July 1834, suggesting that he was at least reasonably well acquainted with the area at that time. Whatever the true story, Whittaker brought his wife and four children to New Buffalo in June of 1835, where they took up residence as one of the village's first families.[46]

Dr. Lyman A. Barnard, a pioneer of Berrien County, later recalled that Whittaker raised the money for his land purchase in a rather unorthodox manner. Barnard in the early 1830s found employment running goods up and down the St. Joseph River for the firm of Britain & Feeland of St. Joseph. One evening shortly before the *Post Boy* incident, Barnard returned to St. Joseph to find Feeland engrossed in an intense, and losing, gambling session with Whittaker. Whittaker cleaned out Feeland just as Barnard walked in, so Feeland turned to his employee and asked under his breath whether Barnard had had any luck collecting money from customers upriver. Barnard handed Feeland about five hundred dollars but admonished his boss not to risk it, for he knew of Whittaker's abilities at the gaming table. Feeland could not be dissuaded, however, and returned to the game. Both men arose from the table shortly thereafter, Whittaker with full pockets and Feeland with empty ones. Soon after that, the *Post Boy* went aground and Whittaker bought the property at New Buffalo. Barnard always believed that Feeland's lost money had financed the purchase.[47]

The *Post Boy* recovered from her wreck at State Creek and went back to sailing the lakes. Jeremy Hixon, Jr., of St. Joseph (builder of New Buffalo's lighthouse) became owner and master when he bought her in 1841, but the *Post Boy's* service ended catastrophically in October of that same year. When she sailed out of Chicago on that last voyage, she carried a keg of gunpowder in her hold. No one ever saw the *Post Boy* or the ten passengers and crewmen again, and people theorized that the powder exploded and blew her to pieces.[48]

Wessel Whittaker did not survive the *Post Boy.* New Buffalo residents remembered him years later as a man of "untiring energy and great perseverance," but also recalled that during his rough life on the Great Lakes "he had acquired habits which in those days were common, and which were greatly to his disadvantage"—perhaps a coy hint at his taste for gambling. He died in New Buffalo in 1841, leaving his wife and four children to mourn his passing.[49]

Edward Bancroft, 1842

A snowstorm blew up on the Great Lakes on Thursday, November 17, 1842.[50] Two days later the continuing storm caught the schooner *Edward Bancroft,* owned by the firm of Wheeler & Porter and Capt. Curtis Boughton, as she neared St. Joseph harbor. The *Bancroft* had sailed out of Buffalo, New York, laden with five hundred barrels of apples, five hundred barrels of salt for Wheeler & Porter, and some furniture and general merchandise. Just after daybreak on November 19, the howling wind and driving snow caused decreased visibility as Boughton tried to enter the harbor. The *Bancroft* struck

the sandbar outside the north pier, swung about, and finally grounded below the south pier. The crew escaped to the shore, but the
Bancroft wound up a total wreck, lying on the beach with several feet
of water in her hold.[51]

Jefferson, 1844

Capt. William Dougal sailed the schooner *Jefferson* out of
Chicago on March 16, 1844, bound for St. Joseph with a cargo of
stone. A northwesterly gale hit when they were still twenty miles
from their destination and a vicious snowstorm soon raged around
them. Dougal and his crew tried desperately to bring the schooner
into port the following day, but the *Jefferson* finally succumbed to the
elements and sank in fourteen feet of water a half mile from the St.
Joseph harbor. As the waves closed beneath them, the *Jefferson* crew
scrambled into the gaffs and rigging which rose above the lashing
water. They clung to their perch like a family of treed cats as the wind
and snow swirled around them.[52]

Dougal and his men knew that rescue was an almost impossible
hope and that their sanctuary could only forestall their inevitable
fate. Eventually the bitter cold would seep through their clothing,
stiffening their muscles until they could no longer maintain their
hold and, one by one, they would plunge into the frigid waves. Death
would come almost instantly. A few might maintain their grip to the
end until they died of exposure while still holding tightly to a rope
or spar. The half mile of water separating them from safety might as
well have been an ocean.[53]

At that very time, Capt. Nelson W. Napier was in St. Joseph fitting out the brig *Scott*. Seeing the *Jefferson's* predicament, he enlisted
a crew of volunteers, loaded the brig's smallboat onto a cart, and
hauled it down the beach to the point nearest the wreck. Napier and
his group launched the little craft and set out into the lake through
the surging breakers. One of the *Jefferson's* crewmen, eighteen-year-
old John Prindiville, never forgot the hope and gratitude he felt as he
watched his rescuers approach in their cockleshell boat. Somehow
Napier reached the wrecked *Jefferson,* took off the half-frozen crew,

and paddled back to shore. The schooner's men suffered greatly from their eight-hour ordeal, but all survived.[54]

Experiment, 1855

The Napier family of St. Joseph made the Great Lakes an intimate part of their lives. They lived—and in many cases died—on the lakes. Over the years, the Napiers met with an unusual share of tragedy, which they first encountered in 1855 with the schooner *Experiment.*

Nelson W. Napier was the patriarch of the Napier family, most of whom sailed the lakes. In the summer of 1855, his wife Henrietta and two of their five children went to Chicago to visit the family of Capt. Charles Harding, who was then away on a voyage. Mrs. Napier begged Mrs. Harding to accompany her on a return trip to St. Joseph, but because Mrs. Harding anticipated her husband's imminent return, she finally decided not to go.[55]

Henrietta Marie Napier and her children—fifteen-year-old Edward and ten-month-old Hardin—embarked on the small schooner *Experiment* commanded by Capt. William Jennings.[56] The *Experiment* had nearly made St. Joseph when a sudden gale roared across the lake. Henrietta Napier knew a thing or two about sailing and told Captain Jennings that he was carrying too much canvas, but the captain refused to listen, so Mrs. Napier and her children finally went below to seek refuge from the storm in the ship's cabin. Nevertheless, the schooner's crew handled the storm well, and as they approached the harbor began hauling in the sails.[57]

At that moment the *Experiment* suddenly capsized and rolled completely bottom-up in the lake. As the schooner rolled over, the quick-thinking Edward reached out a window, grabbed a sailor named Tom Prosser, and pulled him inside. The rest of the crew washed overboard and drowned. An air pocket kept the survivors alive, and a table in the cabin served as a makeshift life raft. Using the table, Edward managed to keep his mother's head above water during the succeeding hours. Henrietta Napier grasped her baby tightly, but in the frigid, pitch-black cabin the infant Hardin slipped from his mother's grasp and drowned.[58]

The following morning, a full day after the wreck, the *Experiment*, floating upside down and missing her spars and rigging, drifted ashore on a sandbar near the harbor entrance. Several St. Joseph residents, intrigued by the wrecked ship, strolled down to the beach to examine it, assuming that no one remained aboard. A few people, more curious than their fellows, scrambled up onto the ship to examine the hull's condition. The wreck survivors, still trapped in the cabin, heard the people walking up above. Edward pounded on the cabin, sending the astonished people racing off for axes with

The schooner *Experiment* with a heavy deck-load of lumber. *(Courtesy of the Historical Collections of the Great Lakes, Bowling Green State University)*

which they chopped a hole through the planking and freed Prosser and the Napiers.[59] Curtis Boughton of St. Joseph maneuvered a small boat up to the wreck and transported the survivors back to shore.[60]

Bad luck dogged the Napier family for the next half century. In 1859, Jack Napier, Nelson's brother and also a ship captain, touched off a six-pounder cannon in St. Joseph to celebrate the Fourth of July; the thing blew up and killed him.[61] Nelson Napier drowned when his ship, the *Alpena*, went down in 1880. Five more of Henrietta Napier's children also predeceased her. Until she died at age eighty-seven, the memory of the *Experiment* wreck and her drowned child haunted the clan matriarch. Henrietta died on February 28, 1908—killed when she broke her hip in an accident.

The *Experiment*, however, like Mrs. Napier, survived the cata- strophic wreck in 1855. Resurrected and repaired, she went on to sail Lake Michigan for another forty-seven years until she wrecked again, this time completely.

Thomas Bradley, 1856

Saltwater sailors often pooh-pooh the Great Lakes. Accustomed to the dangers of the vast oceans, they see the lakes as mere millponds and liken sailing the inland seas to transiting a sheltered bay, with land never more than a few score miles distant. Time after time, the Great Lakes prove them wrong—i.e., witness the case of the schooner *Thomas Bradley.*

The *Bradley* had sailed up and down the Atlantic Ocean and Caribbean Sea prior to visiting the Great Lakes. She made five voy- ages to South America, three to the West Indies, and one to Central America. Each time she returned safely to her home port of Fishburg (later Vineyard Haven), Massachusetts.[62] In the fall of 1856, she sailed into New York City and took on a four-hundred- ton cargo of machinery and general merchandise. The machinery included two steam engines, four boilers that measured five by twenty-nine feet, and all the mechanism for a gristmill and a sawmill, destined for South Haven, Michigan. Under the command of Capt. Nathaniel Robbins, she sailed up the Atlantic Ocean and ascended the St. Lawrence River, crossed Lake Ontario and the Welland Canal to Lake Erie, headed up Lake Huron and through the Straits of Mackinac, and started down Lake Michigan.[63]

On November 4, a storm of wind and snow struck just as the *Bradley* reached her destination and drove her onto the beach seven miles south of St. Joseph. Residents of St. Joseph braved the elements to help rescue the crew, and during the following weeks, Robbins managed to salvage almost all of the cargo. Six weeks later, the Niles, Michigan, newspaper reported optimistically that the *Bradley* was a staunch vessel and that Robbins would get her off the beach, but he never did. The wreck, however, did give Robbins his first taste of life saving, and the experience had a lasting effect: *Bradley's* skipper settled in St. Joseph and later became the district superintendent for the United States Life-Saving Service.[64]

Antelope, 1857

A late November storm in 1857 tore into ships all across Lake Michigan. Schooner after schooner went ashore along the Berrien County coast: *Bell City, Col. Glover, Triumph, H. Rand,* and *Hirandell.*[65]

The schooner *Antelope,* out of Oswego, New York, ran aground with a cargo of wheat near Andrew's Pier, south of St. Joseph. The captain and three crewmen drowned, but people on the shore came to the rescue and pulled off five of the *Antelope's* remaining six crewmen. In the end, one man remained aboard, frozen into the rigging where he had climbed for safety. Those on the beach called to him and asked if he could help himself, but the unfortunate sailor could only shake his head. He remained there, iced into the rigging like an insect in a spider's web. Those on shore could only watch as he slowly froze to death.[66]

The *Antelope* did not die with her crew. Despite suffering heavy damage in the stranding, the schooner was recovered the next year and rebuilt at great cost. She continued to sail the Great Lakes until at least 1879.

Sunshine, 1859

Four years after Henrietta Napier miraculously escaped death in the overturned schooner *Experiment,* an almost identical accident befell another St. Joseph family. This time the wreck took place on Lake Erie and involved the bark *Sunshine.*

Of all the Great Lakes, Erie displays the greatest treachery. The shallowest of the Great Lakes, Erie has a maximum depth of only 210 feet and an average depth of 62 feet. Because of these shallow depths, storms that sweep across from either the southwest or northeast can whip up enormous seas in an astonishingly short length of time. Storms ordinarily strike in November and December, but the strongest wind on record—87 knots—occurred in July 1969.[67] It was one of these rare summer storms that wrecked the *Sunshine.*

On June 30, 1859, Cornelius McNeil of St. Joseph and the *Sunshine* set sail from Buffalo, New York, carrying a cargo of four tons of general merchandise for Saginaw, Michigan. There he intended to take on a load of lumber for Chicago. The *Sunshine* was nearly new, a big bark of 594 tons, owned by Jesse R. Bentley of Buffalo and Jesse Hoyt of New York City. The *Sunshine's* complement included McNeil's wife, Persilla, their three children, and eleven crewmen.[68]

Persilla McNeil got seasick and took to her cabin. On Saturday, July 2, a small, furious squall swept through Buffalo and out over Lake Erie. Captain McNeil and his crew saw it coming and hauled in their sails, but a wild gust of wind from the southwest struck the *Sunshine* and capsized her. The spars struck the shallow lake bottom and tore away the bark's fore main top-mast and mizzen-mast, but the *Sunshine* eventually righted herself and remained on her beam-ends. Several crewmen—Jeremiah Sweeney, Marshall Logan, Frank Larkin, and the cook, Joseph Watson—went overboard and disappeared into the lake when the ship capsized. Captain McNeil and First Mate Mark Graham clung to the rigging until a huge wave washed them off and sent them to their deaths. Persilla McNeil and her children had vanished, too, and the surviving crewmen supposed that they had all drowned.[69]

Unbeknownst to them, Mrs. McNeil was still very much alive. Thrown from her bunk as the ship went over, she found herself trapped with her children in her dark cabin as the water boiled up around them. A table was fastened to the floor, which had become the cabin's ceiling, so she lifted her children up onto the table and climbed on after them. The sudden lurch as the *Sunshine* righted herself threw all of them back into the water, which continued to pour into the cabin.[70]

Above, the surviving crewmen—Second Mate Alexander Elton and seamen John Gordon, John Wilkinson, James Martin, Dennis Daley, and John Cossick—heard knocking coming from the cabin below. They tore away the bulkhead of the break to the deck and found Persilla McNeil in the galley, which she had somehow reached after falling from the table. Her children had drowned in the darkness, and the surviving crewmen pulled her out clad only in her nightclothes. Each sailor gave her an article of clothing to wear and tried to protect her from the elements as best they could. At eight o'clock the next morning, they caught the attention of the schooner *Nebraska,* whose crew picked them up and carried them to Fairport, New York, and safety. Some three weeks later, the tug *Relief* towed the wrecked *Sunshine* into Buffalo, completing her voyage.[71]

The owners thought the *Sunshine* well worth salvaging, and over the succeeding weeks they resurrected her from ruin. The propeller *Buffalo* towed the wreck back to its birthplace in East Saginaw, Michigan, where shipyard workers repaired the extensive damage and rebuilt the *Sunshine* as a three-masted schooner. By early October 1859, newspapers reported her "thoroughly overhauled, repaired, newly rigged, sparred, and fitted with a new set of sails," and nearly ready to head out to sea.[72] The old *Sunshine* went on to a long life on the Great Lakes. She was converted to a barge in 1871 and burned to a total loss at her mooring at the foot of Fisher Avenue in Detroit on November 28, 1906.[73]

Hurricane, 1860

On Saturday, November 24, 1860, a large, black, fore-and-aft schooner went ashore about eight miles north of St. Joseph during a wild gale that destroyed or damaged over sixty ships on the Great Lakes. The storm had hit the area on the Thursday before and lasted until the following Monday, wreaking havoc with bitter cold and a fierce northwesterly wind.[74]

The shipwreck spread 14,000 bushels of rye along the shoreline and left a crewman's body washing back and forth in the waves, but the vessel's identity remained unknown to the local residents who retrieved the unfortunate corpse. The first people on the scene after the storm slackened on Sunday afternoon reported that the mystery ship had already gone to pieces. They observed that she had had a new foresail and an old mainsail, but could learn nothing of her identity from the bits and pieces of flotsam that drifted ashore.[75]

Eventually locals discovered that the schooner was the *Hurricane,* owned by the firm of Sears and Clark of Buffalo, New York, and bound from Chicago to her home port under the command of Capt. William Walch. She had carried a crew of nine, and all were dead.[76]

The loss of the *Hurricane* raised little comment or concern in St. Joseph; the schooner was neither locally owned or crewed, and area residents had far more interest in the weekly newspaper headlines describing the threat of secession in South Carolina than a shipwreck involving no one they knew. The unlucky sailors had drowned in a November storm, but they were strangers and their fate, while tragic and regrettable, was commonplace for men in their line of work. One by one, the bodies of all nine victims washed ashore near St. Joseph a week or so after the wreck. Captain Walch's young widow arrived in town shortly afterward to recover her husband's remains.[77] What little concern people in southwest Michigan felt about the loss of the ship faded quickly with the outbreak of the Civil War.

1. Céline Dupré, "René-Robert Cavalier, De La Salle," in *Dictionary of Canadian Biography,* 12 vols. (Toronto: University of Toronto Press, 1866; reprint ed., 1979), 1:173.

2. Willis F. Dunbar, *Michigan: A History of the Wolverine State,* rev. ed. George S. May (Grand Rapids, MI: Eerdmans Publishing Co., 1980), 43.

3. Louis Hennepin, *A New Discovery of a Vast Country in America,* trans. and ed. Reuben G. Thwaites, 2 vols. (London: 1698; reprint ed., Cambridge, MA: John Wilson & Son University Press, 1903), 1:73.

4. Ibid., 136.

5. Ibid.

6. *Relation of the Discoveries and Voyages of Cavalier de La Salle from 1679 to 1681,* trans. Melville B. Anderson (1682; reprint ed., Chicago: The Caxton Club, 1901), 71.

7. Hennepin, 1:137.

8. Ibid., 138. Fort Miami probably stood on a site corresponding to the present-day location of the corner of Ship and Front Streets in St. Joseph, although this location does not agree in all respects with Hennepin's description.

9. Ibid.

10. Henri de Tonty, *The Journeys of Rene Robert Cavelier Sieur de La Salle,* trans. and ed. Isaac Joslin Cox, 2 vols. (New York: Allerton Book Co., 1922; reprint ed. New York: AMS Press, 1973), 1:4.

11. Hennepin, 1:140.

12. *Relation of the Discoveries...La Salle,* 157.

13. George N. Fuller, *Historic Michigan,* 3 vols. (National Historical Assn., n. d.), vol. 3, Southwest Michigan and Berrien County, ed. Charles A. Weissert, 29–30.

14. George Irving Quimby, *Indian Culture and European Trade Goods* (Madison: The University of Wisconsin Press, 1966), 57–62. Although modern-day searchers have uncovered pieces of several wrecks that are each claimed to be the *Griffin's* remains, none of these has ever been confirmed to be the *Griffin.*

15. Fuller, 30-31.

16. Dunning Idle, "The Post of the St. Joseph River during the French Regime, 1679–1761" (Ph.D. dissertation, University of Illinois, 1946), 101.

17. Ellis, 41.

18. Ibid.; Mansfield, 1:619.

19. *Detroit Gazette,* June 14 and August 23, 1825.

20. *Black Rock* (New York) *Gazette,* August 30, 1825.

21. *Detroit Free Press,* October 25, 1825.

22. Ellis, 41.

23. Mansfield, 1:619.

24. Ellis, 41.

25. Mansfield, 1:619.

26. Ibid., 47; *Niles Gazette and Advertiser,* November 21, 1835; *Chicago Democrat,* November 18, 1835. The *Democrat* reported that the *Bridget* was found capsized six miles off Michigan City, Indiana. Mansfield, 1:620, states that sixteen lives were lost in the wreck. The fact that all three wrecks occurred almost simulta-

neously in the same area may have confused newspaper editors and caused them to mix up details of their accounts.

27. *Buffalo Whig & Journal,* November 25 and December 2, 1835.

28. *Chicago Democrat,* November 25, 1835.

29. *Niles Gazette and Advertiser,* November 21, 1835; *Chicago Democrat,* November 18, 1835.

30. *Niles Gazette and Advertiser,* November 21, 1835; Mansfield, 1:620.

31. Mansfield, 1:621.

32. Harriet Martineau, *Society in America,* 2 vols. (New York: Saunders and Otley, 1837), 1:248 and 258. The *Detroit Democratic Free Press* of July 6, 1836, gave the wreck location as eight miles south of St. Joseph. Martineau, an eyewitness, wrote that she and her group encountered the wreck after they had left Michigan City on their way to Chicago.

33. *Detroit Democratic Free Press,* July 6, 1836, reprinted from an article in the *Chicago American.*

34. Martineau, 1:258.

35. Ellis, 42–43.

36. Otto M. Knoblock, *Early Navigation on the St. Joseph River* (Indianapolis: Indiana Historical Society Publications, 1925), 196; Edward B. Cowles, *Berrien County Directory and History* (Buchanan, MI: Record Steam Printing House, 1871), 284-85.

37. Ellis, 42-43, 318.

38. "Petition to Congress by Inhabitants of the Territory and Others," November 1835, in Clarence Edwin Carter, comp. and ed., *The Territorial Papers of the United States,* vol. 12, *The Territory of Michigan, 1829–1837* (Washington, DC: United States Government Printing Office, 1945), 1044.

39. *Niles Gazette and Advertiser,* November 7, 1835; *Berrien Springs Era,* June 10, 1920.

40. *Niles Gazette and Advertiser,* August 10, 1836; Ellis, 318.

41. Ellis, 318.

42. Jay C. Martin to the author, August 18, 1989; Ellis, 271; *Buffalo Whig,* July 9, 1834.

43. Ellis, 271.

44. Ibid.

45. United States Land Sales Tract Book, Berrien County Register of Deeds Office, St. Joseph, Michigan, 130. Whittaker bought a little over 179 acres of land in New Buffalo Township from the federal government on November 26, 1833, listing his residence as Erie County, New York. He bought another 560 acres in the township in April 1835, this time giving his residence as Berrien County, Michigan.

46. *Buffalo Whig,* July 9, 1834; Ellis, 271.

47. Cowles, 282–83.

48. Mansfield, 1:637.

49. Ellis, 274.

50. *Detroit Free Press,* November 30, 1842.

51. Ibid., December 7, 1842.

52. *St. Joseph Traveler-Herald,* November 27, 1880; Mansfield, 1:645. *History of*

the Great Lakes dates the *Jefferson's* loss as March 27.

53. Ibid.

54. Ibid.

55. *St. Joseph Traveler-Herald,* November 27, 1880.

56. Ibid.; *St. Joseph Evening Herald,* September 13, 1902.

57. *St. Joseph Evening Herald,* September 13, 1902; *The Chicago Tribune,* October 21, 1880.

58. Ibid.

59. Ibid.

60. *St. Joseph Saturday Herald,* May 16, 1896.

61. *St. Joseph Traveler,* July 6, 1859.

62. *St. Joseph Traveler-Herald,* February 24, 1883.

63. Ibid., August 19, 1882; *Niles Republican,* December 20, 1856.

64. *St. Joseph Traveler-Herald,* August 19, 1882 and February 24, 1883; *Niles Republican,* December 20, 1856.

65. *Niles Republican,* November 28, 1857; *Allegan* (Michigan) *Journal,* November 30, 1857.

66. Ibid.

67. United States Department of Commerce, *United States Coast Pilot* 6, 134–35.

68. *Detroit Free Press,* October 18, 1854; *St. Joseph Traveler,* July 13, 1859; Petition for the Appointment of Administrator, August 3, 1859, Berrien County Probate Court, Deceased Files, File No. 236, Cornelius McNeil, Berrien County Historical Association, Berrien Springs, MI.

69. *St. Joseph Traveler,* July 13, 1859.

70. Ibid.

71. Ibid.

72. *Detroit Free Press,* July 31, August 2 and 16, October 5, 1859.

73. Swayze, "Sunshine," <http://greatlakeshistory.homestead.com/home.html> (March 14, 2000).

74. *St. Joseph Traveler,* November 28, 1860.

75. Ibid.; *Chicago Tribune,* November 26, 1860.

76. *St. Joseph Traveler,* December 19, 1860.

77. Ibid., December 5 and 19, 1860; *Detroit Free Press,* December 15, 1860.

The *Hippocampus*
and Other Shipwrecks

L. B. Britton, 1861

The propeller steamer *L. B. Britton* headed out of St. Joseph harbor on the evening of July 9, 1861, bound for Chicago with a cargo of 1,200 railroad ties and eight boxes of fresh fish. The *Britton* had an odd lineage for a Lake Michigan ship, for she had originated as a steamer built for the Erie Canal: specifically to tow canal boats up the Hudson River between New York City and Albany. As the first steam-powered vessel of its kind, she created such a sensation that no less a personage than New York's first Republican governor, John A. King, took passage on her maiden voyage.[1]

The *Britton's* master, Capt. John Quincy Adams, also hailed from Albany. He had on board his wife and three children plus a crew of four or five men when he steamed out of St. Joseph for Chicago. A gale that blew up that afternoon continued through the evening, and the *Britton* disappeared into it. After several days passed with no word, Capt. Nathaniel Robbins of Benton Harbor, who owned her cargo, traveled to Chicago to seek information about the missing ship. No one in Chicago had any news of the *Britton* either, so Robbins returned home under the assumption that the ship had sunk with all aboard.[2]

The *Britton*, although wrecked, had not gone down. Battered by the storm, driven off course and disabled, she was finally stranded on the beach in Illinois about six miles from the point where the

Calumet River emptied into Lake Michigan. All her passengers and crew reached shore safely.[3]

Whip, 1865

At the United States Naval Academy in Annapolis, Maryland, instructors drill into cadets the order of responsibility for officers: in times of crisis they must place the welfare of their ship first, their shipmates second, and themselves last. Capt. Nelson H. Blend of the schooner *Whip* never attended the Naval Academy, but the veteran of twenty-five years on the Great Lakes followed that school's dictum when disaster overtook his ship.[4]

The Milwaukee, Wisconsin, skipper had invested everything he owned in the sixteen-year-old schooner, even mortgaging his house to buy her. On Tuesday, March 21, 1865, Blend and his crew headed out of St. Joseph for Chicago with a load of lumber from the firm of Hopkins & Company. The *Whip* ran headlong into a storm soon after leaving port, so Blend turned his ship about and ran back to St. Joseph. Captain and crew had lashed themselves to the rigging and sent the ship's female cook below to take shelter, but they managed to keep control of the schooner as they neared the harbor. As the *Whip* approached the tricky harbor entrance, however, waves swept her too far to the north; she grounded about a quarter mile beyond the north pier and began to break up as the furious gale pounded her.[5]

Realizing that the rising water in the hold would trap and drown the cook, Captain Blend gallantly untied himself and started across the deck to rescue her. An instant later, the waves swept him away and into the lake. His crew watched helplessly as their captain grasped at floating pieces of lumber until the storm knocked him off and he vanished into the angry water. The mate went overboard as well, but he managed to grab a floating plank and rescuers pulled him safely ashore. Sailors watching from shore spotted the *Whip* and went to her aid in a yawl. They found the cook still in the cabin, exhausted and submerged to her chin in the bitterly cold water, but alive. They somehow succeeded in taking off all on board, but Capt.

Blend had drowned in his attempt to save the cook, leaving a widow and six children to mourn his passing.[6]

Anna, 1865

The scow schooner *Anna,* of Benton Harbor, was found floating upside-down off St. Joseph on the morning of October 13, 1865, her entire crew missing.[7] The bodies of two of her crewmen, Trimble and Black, washed ashore near New Buffalo soon afterward and were returned to Benton Harbor for interment.[8]

Hippocampus, 1868

A few ships earned fame not for their contributions to commerce but for the calamities that befell them. Vessels sailing from a single port often carried a sizable number of crew and passengers from one town; a single disaster could devastate an entire community. The loss of a good-sized ship frequently cost many lives and left every resident of the home port to grieve for a lost friend or relative. Until 1868, shipwrecks had made only a minimal impact on Berrien County, but that changed with the sinking of the propeller steamer *Hippocampus.*

The *Hippocampus* was built in St. Joseph in the summer of 1867 and was owned by Curtis Boughton, Allen Brunson, and the captain, John Morrison. After her launch in July 1867, the steamer *Lady Franklin* towed the unfinished vessel to Chicago where she received the new machinery that the Vulcan Iron Works of that city had crafted for her. *Hippocampus* is the Latin name of the whimsical-looking seahorse. It is also a creature from Greek and Roman mythology with a horse's head and forequarters and the tail of a dolphin or fish. The fish's namesake was a wooden-hulled steamer with an overall length of eighty-two feet, a beam of eighteen feet, and a depth of hold of seven feet.[9]

The 1868 shipping season began auspiciously for the *Hippocampus*—she was the first vessel out of St. Joseph harbor that spring, and the *St. Joseph Herald* reported that the "sonorous tones of its ponderous whistle…made the ice bound denizens of St. Joseph leap for joy." A week later, an advertisement in the *Herald* announced proudly that "The Propeller Hippocampus—The newest, Safest, and most Seaworthy Steamer now on the line between Chicago, St. Joseph and Benton Harbor, solicits the patronage of the Public. Fare reduced to one dollar."[10]

During the summer, the *Hippocampus* made daily runs between St. Joseph and Chicago. Berrien County's orchards yielded a bumper peach crop that year, and a steady parade of fruit-laden wagons (locals dubbed them "berry schooners") trundled along the country roads bound for the Benton Harbor fruit market. Ships could hardly carry the produce to city markets fast enough. By September, seven steamships—the *Hippocampus, Comet, St. Joseph, George Dunbar, Skylark, Benton,* and *Fanny Shriver*—plied the lake from Benton Harbor to Chicago, Michigan City, and Milwaukee, each carrying five thousand to eight thousand baskets and boxes of peaches on every voyage. Even so, on Monday evening, September 7, 1868, thousands of baskets of peaches still filled the Benton Harbor warehouse of fruit dealer Alvin Burridge. Captain Morrison had driven himself to the point of exhaustion sailing back and forth to Chicago to haul the perishable fruit to market until he fell too ill to make another voyage. He turned command of his steamer over to another ship captain, Henry M. Brown.[11]

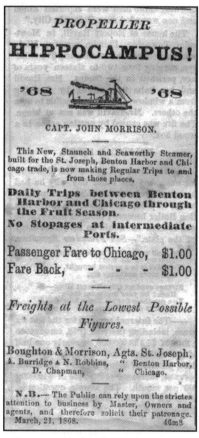

PROPELLER

HIPPOCAMPUS!

'68   '68

CAPT. JOHN MORRISON.

This New, Staunch and Seaworthy Steamer, built for the St. Joseph, Benton Harbor and Chicago trade, is now making Regular Trips to and from those places,

Daily Trips between Benton Harbor and Chicago through the Fruit Season.

No Stopages at intermediate Ports.

Passenger Fare to Chicago, $1.00

Fare Back,   -   -   - $1.00

Freights at the Lowest Possible Figures.

Boughton & Morrison, Agts. St. Joseph,
A. Burridge & N. Robbins, " Benton Harbor,
D. Chapman, " Chicago.

N.B.— The Public can rely upon the strictes attention to business by Master, Owners and agents, and therefore solicit their patronage.
March, 21, 1868.   46m8

Advertisement for the *Hippocampus* in the *St. Joseph Herald*, September 12, 1868. *(Courtesy of the Berrien County Historical Association)*

Brown, then three weeks shy of his thirty-fifth birthday, had sailed Lake Michigan since he was fifteen years old. He had helped build the schooner *Experiment* in 1854 (the same ship that almost cost the Napier family their lives the following year), then nearly lost his own life during the Civil War when he fell wounded in the Battle of Resaca while serving as an officer in the 19th Michigan Infantry. Although a capable skipper, Brown did not know the *Hippocampus* as well as Morrison and felt pressured to take on as large a cargo as possible. When the ship left port at ten o'clock that evening she had on board 7,001 boxes and baskets of fruit and forty-one passengers and crewmen, yet still left five hundred packages of fruit in the warehouse. Peaches filled the ship's hold and covered her promenade deck, and one hundred more containers lined the hurricane deck from bow to stern. Because of the steamer's short depth of hold, much of the cargo went above, on the decks. Captain Brown claimed later that the fruit baskets did not fill the ship's lifeboat, but his statement may have amounted to a half-truth at best. Deckhand Thomas E. Johnson had helped load the *Hippocampus,* and while he left the small boat on the hurricane deck empty, he filled the lifeboat itself on the promenade deck with boxes of peaches.[12]

The *Hippocampus* attempted to leave her dock on the Benton Harbor ship canal after loading was finished at about 9:30 P.M., but the cargo's weight grounded her on the bottom and she refused to budge. At last, the tug *Daisy Lee* arrived and struggled to pull the grounded ship away from the dock. The tug pulled so hard that the *Hippocampus* listed over until water ran in at the after bunker, but finally the steamer broke free and the two ships started down the canal toward the harbor. The *Daisy Lee's* towline ran to a cleat on the *Hippocampus's* promenade deck some twelve to fifteen feet above the waterline. The downward tension on the line, coupled with overloading, caused her to pitch and roll during the trip down the canal. She often strayed too close to the bank and grounded, but at last she reached the harbor entrance. Although the seas were not heavy at the harbor's bar, the *Hippocampus* listed and lurched drunkenly from side to side as she crossed over.[13]

The steamer's gyrations worried Thomas Johnson. The African-American deckhand ran into one of the wheelsmen, Charles D. Morrison (a son of the ship's regular skipper), on the promenade deck and confided that from the way the boat acted he feared she would never reach Chicago. The seventeen-year-old Morrison grumbled that "he had nothing to say about it, but if he had his way, or if his father were in command, the deck-load would be thrown overboard."[14] Once the *Hippocampus* crossed over the bar and headed into the lake under her own power, however, the wallowing ceased and she handled normally.

As the night wore on, the wind picked up and started to churn Lake Michigan into heavy seas. Officers of the heavily laden side-wheeler *Comet,* also en route to Chicago that night, reported that gale-force winds threw their ship so far onto her side that one paddlewheel lifted completely out of the water; she ran over twenty miles in that attitude before the crew could right her. The nearby propeller *Benton* listed so badly that several baskets of fruit toppled overboard.[15]

At about 2:30 A.M., and thirty miles out of St. Joseph, the *Hippocampus* began to roll badly in the heavy seas. Captain Brown spoke to the on-duty wheelsman, Charles Russell, and ordered the ship "hauled up half a point to the windward, to bring her head more to sea," seeking to put the ship more bow-on into the waves and expose less broadside to the storm. Soon afterward, Brown went below to check the engine room and fire hold for water. He found everything dry. He then rounded up wheelsman Charles Morrison and inspected the forepeak, but found everything there secure as well. The ship's roll grew violent enough to frighten Brown, and when he and Morrison came back on deck, he told the wheelsman that they would have to throw cargo overboard from the promenade deck to lighten the ship.[16]

The *Hippocampus* now had only a few seconds of life remaining. Morrison called out the captain's order to lighten the load, and baskets and boxes of peaches began to sail over the side. Passengers overheard the commotion and rushed on deck in a panic.

Deckhand Thomas Johnson, sure he knew what was coming, jerked off his shoes and overcoat and tossed them over the side. Captain Brown ordered the wheelsman, Charles Russell, to put the wheel hard aport.[17]

At that moment the *Hippocampus* careened over onto her port side and began sinking by the stern as water poured into the after gangway. Brown cried to the panicked passengers to help launch the lifeboat, but "Not one stirred. They seemed paralyzed with fear." Charles Morrison and Thomas Johnson, assisted by Captain Brown, scrambled atop the pilothouse and made a futile effort to launch the lifeboat. Although Johnson sawed away at the ropes with his knife, they found that the lifeboat was lashed in so tightly that they could not loosen it. It was filled with peaches anyway, so they gave up. Brown climbed back down and started forward; Johnson and Morrison leaped into the water together.[18]

The waves closed over the *Hippocampus* two minutes after she rolled over. Some passengers and crewmen leaped or were swept overboard; others went down with the ship.

Thomas Johnson swam to a floating mast and caught hold of the rigging. As he started to climb onto it someone grabbed his legs and pulled him under water. Johnson fought his way to the surface and kicked his assailant loose, great scratches furrowing his legs where the terrified man had clawed at him. The other man sank beneath him and disappeared into the depths. The hard-won mast quickly sank as well, however, so Johnson swam to a forty-foot-long section of the hurricane deck. He scrambled onto it and sat there about five minutes, but other survivors saw it, too, and soon eight or ten others had climbed aboard, overcrowding it. Johnson spotted another piece of the cabin floating about eighty feet away, so he slipped off the deck and swam to that. He hoisted himself onto the cabin section and drew a floating door onto it after him, then spotted the ship's clerk, John Bloom, struggling in the water nearby. Johnson called Bloom over to him and pulled him aboard. The half-dead clerk vomited water, and Johnson was sure that he would have drowned in less than a minute.[19]

Johnson and Bloom paddled off by themselves, using a board from the cabin as an oar. Desperate men struggled in the water on every side, "drowning, gasping, shouting for help, and calling on God to save them." They saw the mate, Robert Richardson, and a fireman, David Taylor, trying to climb onto the floating pilothouse, but it rolled over and over like a log as they tried to climb up its sides. Both men drowned.[20]

Capt. James Trimble, a passenger, plunged into the water on the weather side of the ship when she rolled over. He and Charles Morrison both tried to pull off wooden fenders to have something to hold onto, but the fenders were too tightly fastened and they had to give up. Trimble crawled out on the weather rigging and dropped onto a floating door. He used the door to buoy himself up while he swam to the piece of hurricane deck that already supported several men. While swimming to this makeshift raft, he spotted Captain Brown struggling in the water and called to him to grab a nearby box. Brown on the box and Trimble on the door both swam to pieces of floating deck and clambered aboard them.

As Trimble lay on the raft, he became aware of people struggling in the water in every direction, moaning and begging for help. Screams of "Oh God, what shall I do," and "God help us" rose from the darkness all around. Those on the raft could neither see them nor go to their assistance, so they lay there and listened as the voices faded out one by one.

Like Thomas Johnson, passenger Edward N. Hatch of St. Joseph nearly drowned when a fellow passenger clung to him as the ship went down. Hatch tried to kick him loose but they both went under together. As he sank deep into the water and the pressure closed around him, Hatch wondered how far it might be to the bottom of the lake—it seemed to him as though he had gone forty feet deep. Then, "while under the water he let go and I came up." Somehow Hatch fought his way to the surface and clung to the rigging of one of the steamer's spars as he gasped for air. He found his friend James Trimble, who called him over to join the captain and Charles Morrison. The four of them hung onto the raft-like portion of the hurricane deck that Johnson and Bloom had abandoned and picked up other survivors until eleven men floated together on the wreckage.[21]

The ship's steward, Cyrus Rittenhouse, had fallen asleep in his bunk the minute the *Hippocampus* left port. The listing ship and cargo shifting awakened him, and he raced out of his cabin half dressed. The *Hippocampus* was already going down stern first, partly on her side, as passengers screamed "Oh, my God! what shall I do, what shall I do!" Rittenhouse saw a door float past and leaped overboard after it. Just as he caught the door, a panic-stricken passenger grabbed him from behind and began to choke him. "If you won't choke me you can have the door," Rittenhouse cried. His assailant let go and Rittenhouse went under. He came up once and got entangled in some floating twine, went under again, and for a second time fought his way up. He found Johnson and Bloom aboard their little raft, too small to support three men, so he swam to the drifting section of hurricane deck that then had three other survivors on it. One of them helped Rittenhouse aboard.[22]

Eventually almost all the survivors except Bloom and Johnson lay on the floating piece of deck. One man, however, drifted alone in the darkness. Joseph Riford, an elderly passenger from Benton Harbor, had thrown a chair from his stateroom into the lake and leaped overboard after it. He sat astride the chair all night until the other survivors spotted him at dawn and pulled him aboard the raft.

Not all passengers were as cool-headed or lucky as Riford and the others. Al Palmer, who with his father and two brothers ran a general store in Benton Harbor, had taken the *Hippocampus* to Chicago to buy goods for his shop. He made no attempt to flee his stateroom as the *Hippocampus* sank. A witness recalled that Palmer "just spun 'round and 'round and seemed to be too excited or bewildered to get to the door before the sinking *Hippocampus* made her last lurch and went down."[23]

The *Hippocampus* had passed the schooner *Humboldt* about ten minutes before she sank. Soon after the steamer disappeared beneath the waves the *Humboldt* came sliding through the darkness past the

James Trimble, Cyrus Rittenhouse, and Edward N. Hatch, three survivors of the *Hippocampus* sinking, posed for their photograph on September 8, 1911—the disaster's forty-third anniversary. *(Courtesy of Robert Hatch)*

survivors. The men in the water cried out for help, but the wind blew from the wrong direction and carried their voices away into the night and the *Humboldt* disappeared into the storm.[24]

Wind and waves nearly swept the survivors off their makeshift raft, but the storm quickly died out and a thick fog drifted in. Three times during the night they saw ships pass by without spotting them. "We all felt gloomy and discouraged," Edward Hatch recalled. The next morning, Captain Brown asked Joseph Riford to lead the others in prayers for deliverance. Everyone sat quietly during Riford's prayer, and "all promised to be better men and Christians if they reached shore."[25]

The *Hippocampus* schedule called for her to arrive at Chapman's Dock in Chicago around four o'clock on Tuesday morning. Word that the ship had gone missing stunned people in St. Joseph and

Edward N. Hatch commissioned a painting of the *Hippocampus's* survivors clinging to wreckage after their ship went down. The artist painted the scene on the seat of a wooden stool that Hatch had used to buoy himself in the water that night. *(Courtesy of Debbie Green)*

Benton Harbor. Apprehension turned to grief when the steamers *Comet, Benton,* and *George Dunbar* passed through floating wreckage on their way back from Chicago and the *Dunbar* brought in part of the pilothouse, crushing any remaining hopes that the ship might only be delayed.[26]

The *Hippocampus's* owners sent word to Chicago to call out the big, powerful tug *George W. Wood* to search for survivors and definitive evidence of the ship's loss. The *Wood* found little on the first day's search, but on September 10 her crew began to find bits of wreckage. A little later they encountered a floating box of peaches, then another and another. At first they hoisted the boxes on board, but soon they found so many that they gave up. The *Wood's* crew stopped their work and stared out across Lake Michigan. A trail of hundreds of boxes of fruit drifted for a distance of two to three miles on water that had become as smooth as a millpond. The captain's desk with one drawer still intact was among the wreckage pulled aboard the *Wood;* the drawer contained various ship's papers, including bills of lading, index books, and Captain Morrison's personal correspondence.[27]

While the *George W. Wood* searched for survivors, deckhand Marshall Robinson tried to keep a delirious boy alive. Robinson, a Chicagoan, could never remember how he escaped the sinking *Hippocampus,* but he found himself alone on a piece of floating deck. A few minutes later the ship's teenaged porter swam to Robinson's raft and climbed aboard. The two survivors drifted on it through the

Receipt from the owners of the tug *George W. Wood* for searching for survivors of the *Hippocampus,* 1868. *(Courtesy of the Berrien County Historical Association)*

night, and as dawn broke on Tuesday morning, Robinson could see both the large raft with Riford and the others and the small piece of wreckage with Bloom and Johnson floating in the distance. Robinson kept them in sight through the day.[28]

The boy's condition worsened through the next night until by early Wednesday morning, Robinson thought that he was dying from exposure and internal injuries. Robinson tried to talk to him, but the young porter shook violently and made no reply. Robinson held onto him to keep him from falling off the raft until, about 6:00 A.M., the boy died. Robinson decided to save the body for the boy's relatives. As he dragged it to the center of the raft to keep it from falling off, he sighted a scow schooner, the *Trio,* headed directly for him. He hailed her and watched with joy as the schooner "bore straight down and took me up."[29]

Robinson quickly told Alexander Johnson, the *Trio's* captain, of his ship's loss and added that other survivors remained afloat on the lake. He asked Johnson if they could not hoist the porter's body aboard, but Johnson replied that he would waste no time with the dead while the living remained to be saved. The *Trio* immediately set off in search of other survivors.[30]

With Robinson's guidance, the *Trio* soon located the remaining survivors. When the men on the raft saw the ship's light coming toward them, they waved their arms in the air, flapped a tablecloth that Captain Brown had found, and "hallooed" frantically. A sharp-eared lookout on the *Trio* heard them and soon they were safe aboard the schooner, warmed up and togged out in dry clothing. A famished Thomas Johnson reported that the *Hippocampus* survivors got "a splendid hot smoking breakfast of coffee, hot biscuit, fried salt pork, etc. It was the best meal of victuals I ever ate."[31]

The *Trio* continued to search for more survivors and eventually spotted an object about two miles off, which proved to be passenger Joseph Cooley of Chicago. Cooley had lashed himself to a section of the pilothouse and had grown so weak that he could not speak, but only wave his cap feebly to his rescuers. The *Trio's* crew lifted him aboard, then retrieved the *Hippocampus's* smallboat, which they found floating keel up, and set sail for Saugatuck, Michigan, where they arrived at about six o'clock Friday morning.[32]

All the survivors went into Saugatuck to find clothing. Thomas Johnson was nearly overcome with gratitude to the *Trio's* skipper, who spent money from his own pocket to buy the deckhand a new pair of shoes. Messages streamed forth to Chicago, St. Joseph, and Benton Harbor announcing the rescue of part of the ship's company. Captain Brown's brother, William S. Brown of Chicago, received a curt message from St. Joseph, drafted on Friday evening: "Capt. Brown and 14 others saved. Just arrived from Saugatuck—26 lost." Anxious friends and relatives crowded the telegraph office and the docks in Chicago, begging for news of their loved ones.[33]

For the lucky few, grief turned to joy that Friday as the men everyone feared lost hurried through the streets of St. Joseph. Some people cheered, others cried for joy, and church bells pealed out. Those less fortunate could only watch in bitter disappointment and pain as their neighbors welcomed home the living and they realized that their own loved ones would never return. They had feared the worst, had their hopes buoyed at the news that some men had survived the disaster, then had those hopes crushed when the final tally of those saved came in. The list of dead included Alvin Burridge of Benton Harbor, lost with his cargo of peaches.[34]

What caused the loss of the *Hippocampus?* Almost unquestionably, she sank due to overloading.

In a statement published a few days after the disaster, Captain Brown denied that he had overloaded his ship, declaring that the vessel had carried heavier loads in the past without difficulty. The evidence, including his own actions on the night of the disaster, suggests otherwise. Almost all the survivors agreed that the *Hippocampus* left Benton Harbor dangerously overloaded. Cargo lined the promenade and hurricane decks and (if Thomas Johnson's account is accurate) boxes of peaches even filled the lifeboat. The ship had grounded at her dock and required the services of a tug to pull her free, repeatedly lurched into the canal bank on her way out of the harbor, and rolled drunkenly as she left the harbor and crossed the bar. The

Benton Harbor fruit dealer Alvin Burridge went down with his load of peaches in the sinking of the steamer *Hippocampus.* *(Courtesy of the Berrien County Historical Association)*

Hippocampus clearly handled poorly that evening. Responsibility for the ship's safe loading fell on the chief engineer, Robert Eustace, particularly since Captain Brown was not well acquainted with the *Hippocampus,* but both Eustace and the second engineer, William Brown, perished in the disaster and could not render an account of the loading. Captain Brown and Charles Morrison both agreed that their inspection of the hold just before the ship capsized determined that she had not taken on water, and on returning topside the captain ordered the cargo thrown overboard—a curious action if he did not think her overloaded.

In all likelihood, the *Hippocampus* left port in an unsafe condition, with her metacentric height at or approaching the neutral point.[35] A ship's metacentric height is the measure of her transverse stability—in other words, the ability to recover from a roll to one side or the other. A ship with a positive metacentric height will tend to roll back and right herself when heeled to port or starboard, while a ship with a metacentric height of zero possesses a neutral equilibrium and will tend to remain in whatever heeled position she is placed. A ship with a negative metacentric height is in an unstable condition and will tend to capsize when acted on by external forces—such as the *Hippocampus's* situation when caught in the storm on September 6. The *Comet's* metacentric height was apparently also at or near the neutral point that night, judging from the description of her running for an extended time with one paddlewheel out of the water, and the

Benton's severe list during the storm suggests that she, too, left port in a similar condition. The approaching end of the annual shipping season, customers' demands to get perishable produce to market, and the shipping companies' keen sense of profits led owners and captains to overload their ships even beyond the point of rashness.

Residents of Benton Harbor/St. Joseph and the surrounding area held a special ecumenical memorial service for the lost passengers and crew of the *Hippocampus* on Sunday, October 18, at the First Congregational Church in Benton Harbor. The organizers of the service invited all clergymen, regardless of denomination, to take part.[36]

Thus ended the public observance of the *Hippocampus* disaster. Private mourning of lost loved ones would continue for years, as would the economic difficulties the losses engendered. Memorial services like that at the Congregational Church helped survivors and family members cope with their grief, but communities did little to help families with the financial struggle they faced in the aftermath of losing a breadwinner. Government-assistance programs did not then exist, and a man's income usually stopped the moment he died or could no longer work. Bereaved widows had to find other means of support in a world that offered them few employment opportunities. As a sad example, the widow of Robert Richardson of St. Joseph who was lost with the *Hippocampus* advertised in the *St. Joseph Herald* that she needed to take in four to six boarders so she could provide for her family.[37]

A. P. Dutton, 1868

A ship's sinking represented not only the loss of vessel and crew, but also the loss of her cargo. Such a loss often caused considerable inconvenience to those who eagerly anticipated the cargo's arrival, as in the case of the small schooner *A. P. Dutton* and her load of schoolhouse furniture.

Benton Township residents were, in 1868, completing the construction of a new one-room schoolhouse on Britain Avenue, just east of Benton Harbor. They had ordered for the building (School No. 14, the Boynton School) a brand-new set of "patent school room furniture" from Chicago and engaged the *A. P. Dutton* to transport it to Benton Harbor.[38]

Capt. Joseph McLeane of Chicago, who commanded the *Dutton* and co-owned her with Benton Harbor businessman Patrick M. Kinney, sailed the schooner out of Chicago on the evening of December 8, 1868. The wind blew perfectly for a quick lake crossing—a light breeze from the southwest. Midway across Lake Michigan, however, the wind turned into a northwesterly gale that howled for several days. No one ever saw the *A. P. Dutton* again.[39]

Besides the captain and two crewmen, the *Dutton* had carried one passenger: James Campbell, of Benton Harbor. All four went missing with the ship. Campbell, a Scottish immigrant just getting established in America, left a widow—thirty-two-year-old Sarah—and a pile of debts.[40] The St. Joseph newspaper, however, evinced greater concern over the township's loss of the school furniture, noting that it "will delay the opening of their school in the most important season of the year, besides the loss of the property."[41]

William Tell, 1869

The little schooner *William Tell,* named for the legendary Swiss patriot, set sail from Chicago on Friday morning, August 20, 1869, bound for her home port of St. Joseph. Down in the hold rested a lethal cargo of one hundred and fifty barrels of lime and fifty barrels of salt.[42]

White powdery lime, an ingredient in mortar and wall plaster, might seem an innocuous substance, but mixing it with water sets off a chemical reaction. A chemist would explain that quicklime, or calcium oxide, when treated with water becomes hydrated lime—calcium hydroxide—and in the process generates an enormous amount of heat. A less formally schooled sailor would liken it to sailing atop a sleeping volcano.

While the *William Tell's* crew enjoyed a peaceful sail across Lake Michigan, water seeped insidiously through the schooner's hull and into the wooden barrels of lime. In the hold the barrels of lime began to smolder unnoticed, until flames suddenly burst through the schooner's deck. Within minutes the cargo had turned the *William Tell* into a floating inferno. Capt. Hugh Keenan and his terrified crew barely had time to escape in the ship's smallboat before flames completely engulfed the schooner and she sank into the lake. Luckily the weather was fair, and only twenty miles separated the men from St. Joseph, so the *William Tell's* crew had no trouble reaching port safely.[43]

Union, 1870

The scow schooner *Union*, of South Haven, succeeded in riding out a Lake Michigan storm on Sunday, October 30, 1870. Then, in a supreme bit of irony, disaster struck the ship just as she reached safety. The storm had blown hard all day Sunday and continued through the night; it finally abated on Monday morning. Having survived the elements' best efforts to destroy her, the *Union* sailed into St. Joseph harbor only to smash into a pair of submerged pilings near the base of the north pier. Water poured in through the holes in her hull. Within ten minutes the ship's stern had sunk in eighteen feet of water and left her impaled on the pilings. One of the pilings soon worked free, but the other held the ship fast. Just after dusk that evening, the other piling came loose and the schooner careened over and sank from sight.[44]

The wreck of the *Union* lay in the river channel athwart the current. Someone had tethered it securely with a strong, new hawser, but later that same evening the line parted and the current pushed the wreck out to the end of the south pier. The *Union* lay there, a hazard to any ship trying to enter the harbor, until Merwin Barnes exercised his own initiative and went out with his tug, the *Daisy Lee*, and pulled the wreck to pieces.[45]

Emma, 1871

A frown creased Jacob Kissinger's face as he looked across Lake Michigan. The weather had turned foul and there would be no more fishing that day. The twenty-six-year-old master of the fishing schooner *Emma* ordered his crew of three to haul in the nets and set sail for St. Joseph.[46]

The *Emma* was one of seventeen fishing boats operating out of St. Joseph that spring. Like Kissinger, most of the town's commercial fishermen owned only one boat, although a couple of them owned two or three vessels. A typical fishing boat and its equipment represented an investment of around $25,000. Like the *Emma,* most were schooner rigged, open, with a centerboard, and built for stability to counter rough waves and the sudden storms that sprang up like a flash on Lake Michigan. Many fishing boats were built right in St. Joseph; for example, Charles P. Hayward of that village had earned a reputation for building the staunch little craft.[47]

The fleet set sail every morning for the fishing grounds outside the harbor which began about six miles from shore and extended out twenty or thirty miles to the west. Each boat carried about 180 nets made of strong linen thread. These the crews buoyed and anchored in the lake to create a barricade some four and one-half feet high and 275 feet long. A typical boat would lay down a gang of about twenty nets for a total length of over a mile. Most boats had a crew of about five or six men, each of whom earned a tolerably good wage of forty to sixty dollars per month during the seven-month fishing season. St. Joseph's newspaper estimated that the fishing industry of the village directly or indirectly employed about 150 men.[48]

Spring storms on the lake made for dangerous fishing early in the season, but the profits made the risk worthwhile. People longed for fresh fish after a long winter of preserved food, and fishermen could sell even such ordinarily worthless catches as sturgeon, lake suckers, and dog fish. The fishermen's catch also made a valuable export for St. Joseph: during 1870, the village shipped out 3,408 boxes of fish.[49]

Jacob Kissinger, a Prussian emigrant, had settled briefly in Wisconsin before bringing his family to Berrien County's St. Joseph Township around the end of the Civil War. Now a fisherman with a wife and four children to support, Kissinger had looked forward to the 1871 fishing season. St. Joseph's fishing fleet had started working the lake just a week or two earlier and had enjoyed good success with hauls of trout and whitefish. On March 20, 1871, luck ran out on Jacob Kissinger and the *Emma*.[50]

As the storm gathered strength, the *Emma* joined a small flotilla of fishing boats fleeing for the shelter of St. Joseph harbor. A raging southwest wind drove them onward and the boats thudded through rough seas. One by one they reached safety, but people on the bluff overlooking the harbor watched as the *Emma* pounded up and down through the troughs and crests of the waves. The schooner *Guide* preceded the *Emma* on her race for the harbor, and the spectators looked on in silent tension as the two vessels struggled onward. A mile of frothing water separated the *Emma* from the harbor when she suddenly disappeared from view. Those on the bluff thought the *Guide* had taken her in tow, but as the *Guide* drew close to the harbor's mouth, they realized that she was alone and that the *Emma* was gone. No one saw the *Emma* go under, but it was obvious that in one instant a big wave had capsized and swallowed her.

Over the next few days, the sad evidence of the shipwreck slowly washed ashore around St. Joseph: bits of wreckage, the *Emma's* hull, and finally the bodies of two of her crew. Lake Michigan had claimed both the *Emma* and Jacob Kissinger, and with the schooner's master went fishermen Peter Broderick, Charles Ott, and John Meicher.[51]

J. Barber, 1871

Capt. Selah Dustin had plenty of luck, and too much of it was bad.

Born in Claremont, New Hampshire, in 1817, Dustin left home at age nineteen and moved to Detroit where he became a sailor. By the early 1850s, he had his own ship, the steamer *Dart,* which he placed on a route between Detroit and Port Huron with stops at all points between. For two years all went well, for the *Dart* had no competition and the money rolled in. Trouble soon appeared in the person of Detroit ship owner Eber B. Ward, who saw no reason why the money flowing into Selah Dustin's bank account could not just as easily fill his own. In 1856, Ward put his own ship on Dustin's route and ignited a price war.

Dustin met Ward's challenge by dropping the price of a ticket to Port Huron to two bits. Ward countered by dropping his fare to twenty-five cents, too, and hired a band to entertain his passengers. Dustin brought in his own musicians and made his twenty-five-cent ticket good for a round trip. The two shipping magnates fought and tusseled until both had reduced their ticket prices to a dime for a round trip with meals thrown in. By that time, the two men were in a race to see who would go broke first, and Dustin lost. He retreated from the fight bruised and bloodied and with most of his fortune gone. With the last of his hopes and money, he bought the steamer *J. Barber.*[52]

Built in Cleveland, Ohio, in 1856 for the lumber trade, the *Barber* had spent several years plying a route from Milwaukee to Manistee and Muskegon. Businessman Nathan Englemann of Milwaukee bought her in 1865 and had her rebuilt at considerable expense at the shipyard of Allen & McClelland. The work included repairs and improvements to the upper works, cabins, lower deck, and part of the hull as well as an overhaul of the engine and boilers, all to the tune of over $14,000. Afterward, she carried lumber and passengers between Milwaukee and Manistee with such success that within three years Englemann had a fleet of six steamers running back and forth across Lake Michigan.[53]

Englemann sold the *Barber* to Dustin in 1871, and he, in turn, chartered her to James Paxton and Curtis Boughton of St. Joseph. By that time the *Barber* had seen better days. Despite the extensive renovations of a few years before, she carried only a B 1 rating and many sailors considered her unseaworthy. A September gale in 1866 damaged her badly and forced the crew to throw some of the cargo overboard to keep the ship afloat. Chicagoans remembered that her boiler had exploded while she was in port, and soon afterward, in March 1867, a steam pipe burst and scalded a man to death. The *Barber* risked a December run from Manistee to Milwaukee later that year, ran into a wild gale, and nearly sank: waves smashed in her port side, carried away a portion of the engine room, and dampened the boiler fires so that she could not keep up steam. Only the crew's desperate work with bailing buckets and the jettisoning of 10,000 feet of lumber from the deck load saved the ship. The *J. Barber* survived all these mishaps, and on the evening of July 18, 1871, like the *Hippocampus* three years before, had her decks crammed with peaches from Berrien County orchards destined for market in Chicago. The *J. Barber's* two passengers turned in for the night soon after leaving St. Joseph, as did many of the eighteen crewmen. Capt. James F. Snow retired to his cabin to read, leaving the ship in command of the first mate, George Germain.[54]

At about 12:30 A.M., flames suddenly burst out on the deck near the smokestack. Ship's porter J. C. Nesbitt and steward Harrie Wachter were asleep in their cabins near the smokestack when First Mate Germain pounded down the hallway yelling "Fire!" Both men toppled out of their bunks and tried to pull on their clothing, but the fire spread so quickly they had to abandon their cabins before they could fully dress.[55]

Captain Snow ran onto the deck at the first alarm. He ordered the *J. Barber's* engines stopped, but the flames raced so rapidly through the vessel that no time remained to organize fire-fighting efforts. Instead, Snow gave the order to abandon ship and called on the crew to lower the lifeboats. Nesbitt and Wachter went to help, but the lifeboats hung on davits near the smokestack, and the men had to give up when flames erupted through the deck by the boats and set them afire.[56]

Now desperate, Captain Snow called on his crew to toss overboard anything that would float to act as makeshift life rafts: furniture, boards, and doors. The ship's cook caused amusement in the midst of terror. He wielded an ax to cut away some doors and threw them overboard. When he leaped into the lake after them, he landed directly on a door and broke through to his waist. The sight of the uninjured cook paddling about in the water, stuck halfway through the door and wearing it like a life preserver, tickled Wachter's funnybone.

The cook was the only object of amusement that evening. Two crewmen, watchman Pat Washington and deck hand Charles Brown, never made it to safety. They disappeared, either drowned or trapped in the spreading inferno, and their bodies were never recovered.

The fire lit up the night sky for miles around and drew rescuing ships like moths to a candle. Two Goodrich Transportation Company steamers, the *A. C. Van Raalte* and the *Corona,* were near the *Barber* when the fire flared up, and both immediately hove to and came to her rescue. The *Van Raalte,* being much closer, arrived on the scene first and pulled a dozen survivors out of the water. The *Corona,* two miles away when the flames were spotted, steamed up a little later but in time to rescue six more people.[57]

The fire burned the *J. Barber* nearly to the waterline. About an hour after the blaze first broke out, the hulk slipped beneath the surface of Lake Michigan and settled to its grave in eighty feet of water some ten miles from Michigan City, Indiana. The Goodrich propeller *Skylark,* a few miles ahead of the *J. Barber,* had also spotted the fire and turned around to help. She came too late to aid in recovering survivors

The steamer *J. Barber* burned and sank off Benton Harbor in 1871.
(Courtesy of the Historical Collections of the Great Lakes, Bowling Green State University)

but patrolled the area until daylight that morning in a fruitless search for Washington and Brown, the two missing crewmen. The *Van Raalte* and *Corona* completed their voyages to Chicago, delivering the *J. Barber's* survivors to the Windy City on July 19.[58]

When Selah Dustin learned about the loss of the *J. Barber,* something inside the old New Hampshireman's mind snapped. The steamer had been worth $12,000 and her cargo $7,500; she was insured for exactly two-thirds of that amount. Dustin, therefore, had lost the enormous sum of $6,500.[59] He became, in the quaint term of the day, "an eccentric." He abandoned his family and business interests and took up the humble occupation of an express wagon driver. For many years the odd, weather-beaten, and ragged man was a familiar sight on the streets of Detroit. His only friend seemed to be the sinewy little mare that pulled the wagon. He brooded over the fortune he had lost in the shipping business, and now and then erupted in violent outbursts when fits of rage overcame him. His peculiarities finally resulted in an attempt to have the courts declare him mentally incompetent. The judge deemed the old man legally sane, but Selah Dustin's final victory was short-lived. He suffered a stroke that summer and died at St. Mary's Hospital in Detroit on August 13, 1888, at age seventy-one.[60]

Magnolia

The bones of the riverboat *Magnolia* may—or may not—lie in the St. Joseph River near Berrien Springs. Details of the *Magnolia's* presumed loss remain unknown.

Lorenzo P. Maxfield built the *Magnolia* in Pentwater, Michigan, in 1867 with the intention of running her on the Manistee River to supply the area's logging camps. The construction and operation of the boat appears to have amounted to a family enterprise: the first crew included Joseph P. Maxfield as captain and pilot, Greg Maxfield as chief engineer, Charles Maxfield as second engineer, with John Alley serving as mate, and Milt Chambers as cook. Unfortunately for the Maxfield clan, the Manistee River proved too difficult to navigate, being rather crooked and filled with floating logs, so the operation did not succeed. The *Magnolia* was pulled off the Manistee and sent to run on the St. Joseph River.[61]

The *Magnolia* arrived in St. Joseph on July 17, 1868, with the plan of running on tri-weekly trips to Niles with stops at the many landings along the way, competing for business with two other riverboats. Hiram Barnes, an experienced riverboat pilot, bought the *Magnolia* and set out to make her a success. The *Niles Democrat* newspaper hailed her arrival, proclaiming her "a beautiful little steamer."[62]

Guy Bunker, then an eight-year-old boy living near Buchanan, later recounted how his father had pulled him out of bed early one Sunday morning in 1868 to watch a race between the *Magnolia* and one of her rivals, the *Kalamazoo*. As Bunker reached the riverbank, he saw the two boats tearing down the river under full steam, the *Kalamazoo* hugging the inside track as they swung around the bend. A bridge over the river marked the finish line. Although considered the slower of the two boats, the *Kalamazoo's* position gave her the advantage, and as they rounded the bend and headed straight for the bridge, everyone could see that she would reach the center of the span first, where only one boat had room to pass. The *Magnolia* had to slow down while the *Kalamazoo* chuffed triumphantly across the finish line.[63]

The lost race may have been an ill omen, for the *Magnolia* did not prosper. She was put up for sale in February 1869, and although the owners declared her "well adapted to the river trade between St. Joseph and Niles, and can run in the lowest stage of water," no prospective buyer could have failed to notice that the owners would sell her for five hundred dollars less than the purchase price.[64] The Buchanan newspaper noted that November that the *Magnolia* had tied up for the season, but from that point on she disappears from the historical record.[65]

In 1908, St. Joseph's newspaper printed a small article reporting on the interest of a group of antiquarians in raising the *Magnolia* from its grave in the St. Joseph River near Berrien Springs where many years earlier it had sunk after striking a sandbar.[66]

Unfortunately, the paper did not relate the details of the loss, not even the date, and searches of contemporary newspapers reveal no further clues.

1. *St. Joseph Traveler*, July 17, 1861.

2. *The Chicago Tribune*, July 16, 1861.

3. Ibid.

4. *Niles* (Michigan) *Republican*, March 25, 1865; *St. Joseph* (Michigan) *Traveler*, March 25, 1865.

5. Ibid.

6. Ibid.

7. *St. Joseph Traveler*, October 14, 1865.

8. Ibid., October 28, 1865.

9. *St. Joseph Traveler-Herald*, September 12, 1868; *Detroit Post*, July 20, 1867; *The Chicago Times*, September 13, 1868.

10. *St. Joseph Traveler-Herald*, March 14 and 21, 1868.

11. Ibid., September 12, 1868.

12. James Pender, *History of Benton Harbor and Tales of Village Days* (Chicago: The Braun Printing Company, 1915), 10; *St. Joseph Traveler-Herald*, September 19, 1868; *Saugatuck Commercial*, September 26, 1868; *St. Joseph Saturday Herald*, May 22, 1897; *The Chicago Times*, September 10, 1868.

13. Statements of Thomas E. Johnson and Charles Morrison, in *The Chicago Times*, September 13, 1868.

14. Statement of Thomas E. Johnson, ibid.

15. Ibid., September 10, 1868.

16. Pender, 8; *Saugatuck Commercial*, September 26, 1868.

17. Statements of Thomas E. Johnson and Charles Morrison, in *The Chicago Times*, September 13, 1868.

18. Pender, 8–9; statement of Thomas Johnson in *The Chicago Times*, September 13, 1868.

19. Statement of Thomas Johnson in *The Chicago Times*, September 13, 1868.

20. Ibid.

21. Pender, 6.

22. Ibid., 8–9.

23. Ibid.

24. Statement of Capt. Henry Brown in the *St. Joseph Traveler-Herald*, September 19, 1868; statement of Thomas Johnson in *The Chicago Times*, September 13, 1868.

25. Pender, 8-9.

26. *St. Joseph Traveler-Herald*, September 12, 1868.

27. *The Chicago Times*, September 11, 1868.

28. Statement of Marshall Robinson in ibid., September 13, 1868.

29. Ibid.

30. Ibid.

31. Statement of Thomas Johnson, in ibid.

32. Ibid.

33. Ibid; *The Chicago Times,* September 12, 1868.

34. *St. Joseph Traveler-Herald,* September 12, 1868.

35. For a clear explanation of the complicated subject of metacentric height, see George W. Hilton, *Eastland: Legacy of the Titanic* (Stanford, CA: Stanford University Press, 1995), 27–29.

36. *St. Joseph Traveler-Herald,* October 10, 1868.

37. Ibid., September 26, 1868. Workmen's compensation remained a thing of the future and employers large and small could be remarkably callous about unfortunate hirelings. Wages of crewmen on the RMS *Titanic,* for example, stopped at 2:20 A.M. on April 15, 1912—the precise moment the doomed ship slid beneath the North Atlantic.

38. *St. Joseph Traveler-Herald,* January 2, 1869.

39. *Benton Harbor Palladium,* January 8, 1869.

40. Petition for Appointment of Administrator, May 3, 1869, Berrien County Probate Court Deceased Files, File No. 484, James Campbell, Berrien County Historical Association, Berrien Springs, Michigan.

41. *St. Joseph Traveler-Herald,* January 2, 1869.

42. *St. Joseph Traveler-Herald,* August 28, 1869. *The Detroit Free Press* of August 25, 1869, stated that the *William Tell* was bound from Milwaukee.

43. Ibid.

44. *St. Joseph Traveler-Herald,* November 5, 1870.

45. Ibid.

46. *St. Joseph Traveler-Herald,* March 25, 1871; Ninth Census of the United States (1870), St. Joseph Township, Berrien County, Michigan.

47. *St. Joseph Traveler-Herald,* March 11, 1871.

48. Ibid.

49. Ibid.; Cowles, 349.

50. *St. Joseph Traveler-Herald,* March 25, 1871; Ninth Census of the United States (1870), St. Joseph Township, Berrien County, Michigan.

51. *Benton Harbor Palladium,* March 24, 1871; James L. Donahue, *Steaming Through Smoke and Fire 1871* (Holt, MI: Thunder Bay Press, 1990), 14. Berrien County death records list the deaths of Jacob Kissinger and Charles Ott, but not those of Peter Broderick or John Meicher, suggesting that only the bodies of the two former men were recovered.

52. Mansfield, 2:339.

53. *Milwaukee Sentinal,* April 12, 1866 and March 27, 1868.

54. Donahue, 49–51; *St. Joseph Valley Register* (South Bend, IN), August 3, 1871; *The Chicago Times,* July 20, 1871; *Detroit Free Press,* December 19 and 23, 1866, December 20, 1867; *Milwaukee Sentinal,* December 9, 1867; *Classification of Lake Vessels and Barges* (Buffalo: Warren, Johnson & Co., 1871), 10.

55. Donahue, 49-51; *The Chicago Times,* July 20, 1871.

56. *St. Joseph Valley Register,* August 3, 1871; *The Chicago Times,* July 20, 1871.

57. Ibid.

58. *The Chicago Times,* July 20, 1871.

59. Marine Casualties, 1871, Marine Casualties on the Great Lakes, 1863–1873, Microfilm Publication T 729, RG 26, NARA.

60. *The Detroit Free Press,* August 15, 1888; Mansfield, 2:339.

61. *St. Joseph Evening Herald,* February 24, 1908.

62. *Niles Democrat,* July 25, 1868 and June 26, 1869; *St. Joseph Herald,* Saturday, 25 July 1868.

63. *Berrien County Record* (Buchanan, Michigan), August 16, 1934.

64. *St. Joseph Herald,* February 27, 1869.

65. *Berrien County Record,* November 11, 1869.

66. *St. Joseph Evening Herald,* February 24, 1908.

Shipwrecks of the Mid-Nineteenth Century

E. B. Perkins, Sea Gull, and *St. Joe Doll,* 1875

Lake Michigan inflicted all of its deep cruelty on Wilhelmina Groenke. Her husband Frank, like she, was a German emigrant who eked out a living from the lake. Frank plied the hard, dangerous trade of a fisherman, finding but meager reward for his labor; he and his family, like many other fishermen in St. Joseph, struggled on the edge of poverty. Groenke and Henry E. Grimm co-owned the fishing boat *St. Joe Doll.* Groenke served as the captain, but income from selling the fish that Groenke and his crew pulled from the lake barely supported Frank, Wilhelmina, and their two daughters, eleven-year-old Augusta and seven-year-old Helena.[1]

Early on Thursday morning, April 29, 1875, St. Joseph's fishing boats raised their canvas sails against the gray half-light of dawn and then, pushed on by a northwest wind, headed out of the harbor as a single flotilla en route to the fishing grounds. Cold weather had hung on through April and chunks of ice still dotted the lake. Dreary dark clouds obscured the morning sky and rain commenced to fall at about 7:00 A.M., but the fishermen lowered their nets and hoped for a good catch. They knew that profits from a nice take of whitefish and trout would support their families, so they went at their work with vigor, one eye on the nets and the other on the sky.[2]

As the fishermen lifted their nets that morning, the northwest wind suddenly shifted to the north and in an instant a fierce squall struck the boats. The fishermen lost no time in setting sail for home. Early in the afternoon one boat after another reached the harbor and safety, some bearing scars from collisions with ice floes.[3]

Not everyone made port that day. The *Planet,* skippered by Willie Gennette and crewed by three men, went ashore near Bridgman, and the *Sea Lion,* with Capt. John Springsteen and three crewmen, met a similar fate at Grand Mere. The wind tore all the sails off the *General Hooker* and drove the helpless boat, with Capt. Fred Myer and three men, onto the beach four miles south of St. Joseph. Even so, they were the lucky ones that day, for every man aboard stepped safely onto the shore.[4]

Three other boats went down in the storm and every crewman aboard perished in the cold Lake Michigan waters. Fred Dahlke's wife and five children lost their husband and father when he went down with his boat, the *E. B. Perkins;* his crewmen, Jimmy Fagan, Augustus Schwichtenberg, and another man who had moved to St. Joseph so recently that no one could remember his name, died with him. The *Sea Gull* sank with the loss of captain and half-owner Joseph Clamfoot and crewmen Charles Witte and Frank Bear. Clamfoot left a wife and three children, Witte a wife and two children; Bear was unmarried. Frank Groenke went down with the *St. Joe Doll;* lost with him were his fellow crewmen, John Horntasch, Charles Erdmann, and the other man whose name no one could recall.[5]

The sudden loss of eleven men in one morning stunned St. Joseph. Quick, violent death was no stranger to nineteenth-century Americans. In the days before government safety regulations and workplace inspections, one catastrophe or another occurred almost weekly. A factory boiler might explode one day and a piece of machinery tear a farmhand in two the next, but eleven deaths at once in a small town like St. Joseph still struck a staggering blow. Steamers and sailing vessels in the harbor flew their flags at half-mast the day after the disaster, and that afternoon several fishing boats and the steamer *Corona* headed out into the lake to search for the missing ships. The fishing boats found nothing, but the *Corona* located two wrecks about six miles south of St. Joseph: the *Sea Gull,* close to shore, and Groenke's boat, the *St. Joe Doll,* floating farther out in the lake.[6]

Recovery work began almost immediately. The *Corona* towed in the *Sea Gull* and left her by the Wells & Company basket factory on Water Street. The next day Capt. Samuel Langley took out the steamer *Messenger* and brought the *Planet* back from Bridgman, and the tug *Daisy Lee* towed in the *Sea Lion* from the beach at Grand Mere. The following Tuesday the *Daisy Lee* brought back the *St. Joe Doll.* The *E. B. Perkins* had gone to the bottom of the lake and searchers could find no trace of it. The following March, fisherman William Lessing and his crew discovered the boat's grave about five miles out from the St. Joseph harbor when their nets hauled up one of the *Perkins's* spars and part of its hull.[7]

A committee in St. Joseph circulated a subscription paper in the days after the tragedy, asking people to dig into their pockets for donations to help the fishermen's families. Many did so, enough to raise several hundred dollars. Chicagoans contributed heavily, perhaps because many families there knew firsthand all about death on the lakes or perhaps because many of the fishermen were immigrants and the ethnic communities in Chicago wanted to aid their fellow countrymen.[8]

At any rate, the committee collected money and doled it out to the victims' families who went about the business of trying to put their lives back together. Wilhelmina Groenke had as hard a task as anyone, a widow trying to raise two girls in an era with few employment opportunities open to women. The county probate court appointed Henry Grimm, her late husband's partner, guardian of Augusta and Helena that September, and it was probably through Grimm that Wilhelmina found a new husband, a provider for her family and a second chance at happiness. Grimm owned the fishing boat *Sarah;* one of the boat's crewmen, Robert Miller, married Wilhelmina on September 12, 1875.[9]

Three weeks after Robert and Wilhelmina's marriage, on Monday morning, October 4, the *Sarah* capsized as she tried to enter St. Joseph harbor and tossed Capt. August Habel and crewmen

Charles Gennett, Garret Walters, and Robert Miller into the lake. Capt. John Langley of the nearby steamer *Messenger* saw it happen and immediately lowered one of his ship's lifeboats. His quick work saved three men clinging desperately to the overturned fishing boat, but Robert Miller had disappeared beneath the waves before the rescuers reached him. Searchers found his body the day after the accident, and salvagers soon recovered the *Sarah,* but Lake Michigan had widowed Wilhelmina Groenke twice within six months. For the young widow, life would offer no third chance at marriage and no happy ending; she died in St. Joseph on March 31, 1880, five years after her first husband disappeared in the wreck of the *St. Joe Doll.*[10]

Grace Greenwood, 1876

Spectators heaped praise on the bark *Grace Greenwood* when her builder, G. R. Rogers, launched her at Oswego, New York, on September 1, 1853. The bark represented Rogers's first attempt at shipbuilding, and he seems to have succeeded magnificently. The local Oswego newspaper crowed that "the vessel has all the modern improvements, her cabin is large and commodious, and all in all we have seldom seen a more beautiful craft in Oswego harbor."[11] She was probably named for the popular poet and essayist (and native New Yorker) Sara Jane Clarke Lippincott (1823-1904), who wrote under the pseudonym Grace Greenwood.[12]

The *Greenwood's* owners converted her to a schooner some time after 1869. On her final voyage in 1876, she carried 511 tons of iron ore out of Escanaba, Michigan, bound for her home port of Michigan City, Indiana. Her crew of five men had all signed on for the trip in Michigan City on September 25: Second Mate Frederick Meares and sailors Charles Clark, Frank Campbell, Seth Baldwin, and a man named Dutcher. She ran into a storm on Thursday afternoon, October 5, and her skipper, Capt. F. O. Berryson, decided to take shelter in the St. Joseph harbor. She ran aground two thousand feet north of the north pier at 6:00 P.M., but all her crewmen escaped death.[13]

The *Grace Greenwood* went to pieces offshore during the week after her stranding and the waves spread large sections of her up and down the beach. By the time she wrecked, the twenty-three year-old former pride of Oswego harbor had aged badly and her owners did not think her worth salvaging; the *Benton Harbor Palladium* noted that they had insured her for $5,000, "a good price for an old boat."[14]

L. Painter, 1877

Capt. William R. Johnson scuttled the scow schooner *L. Painter* at Union Pier when a storm caught her on Monday, October 8, 1877. She had just taken on a cargo of cordwood and set sail for Chicago when the storm hit and drove the schooner ashore.[15] After repairing and refloating her the following day, Johnson and his crew headed north up Lake Michigan. The storm struck again that evening, and although Johnson used every trick in his repertoire, the screaming wind carried away the *Painter's* sails, chains, and anchors and sent her deck load overboard. When she finally ran aground about seven miles north of St. Joseph, Johnson scuttled the ship again.[16] Captain and crew spent a desperate night holding onto the rigging as the waves pounded the hull; they finally escaped safely to the shore.[17] On Thursday the ship lay abandoned with four feet of water in its hold.[18] Around the end of October, the U. S. Revenue Service steamer *Andrew Johnson* arrived on the scene and attempted to pull the *Painter* free but to no avail. The *Johnson* retired in defeat after breaking all her lines.[19]

Col. H. C. Heg, 1877

Hans Christian Heg was born on December 21, 1829, in Lier, near Drammen, Norway. Like so many Norwegians, he emigrated to Wisconsin, where he became a major in the Fourth Wisconsin Militia and was elected State Prison Commissioner. Wisconsin's governor commissioned Heg as colonel of the Fifteenth Wisconsin Volunteer Infantry soon after the outbreak of the Civil War in 1861. He served with distinction, enough so that Gen. William Rosecrans appointed him a brigade commander, but he fell mortally wounded in the Battle of Chickamauga on September 20, 1863.[20]

Heg's namesake, the *Col. H. C. Heg,* was a 149-ton schooner built in De Pere, Wisconsin, in 1868. By 1876 she was owned by the firm of Porter & Parker of Chicago and carried a rating of B 1. The *Heg* went ashore near the north pier in St. Joseph on November 9, 1877, and was completely wrecked.[21]

City of Tawas, 1877

The *City of Tawas,* hauling five hundred tons of iron ore to St. Joseph, tried to make port during a northwest gale on the night of October 30, 1877. Capt. George Manning did his best, but the *Tawas* struck the outer bar at the harbor entrance and tore a hole in her hull; by two o'clock the next morning, she had drifted ashore about one hundred and fifty feet south of the piers.[22]

The life-saving-station keeper, William L. Stevens, walked down to the piers at midnight but failed to spot the *Tawas.* The ship's crew awaited rescue for some time until one of the sailors, either more courageous or desperate than the rest, stripped off his clothes and, braving the freezing water and waves, plunged into the surf. He carried a line ashore which his fellow crewmen used to gain the beach and safety.[23]

The *City of Tawas* was valued at $10,000 and carried $6,000 in insurance. Railroad trains hauled two steam pumps to St. Joseph so the ship's owners could pump out the ship and pull her off the beach after the storm let up. However, the gale continued and by November 2 her captain reported the *Tawas* was breaking up and the cargo was washing out of her. A day later she was gone with little left of her but bits and pieces scattered along the beach.[24]

Mary, 1878

Nothing went right for the crew of the schooner *Mary,* but they had only themselves to blame. The Great Lakes are unforgiving and the crew's carelessness cost most of them their lives.

At about midnight on September 7, 1879, Capt. Frank Bartlett and his crew of five sailed out of Chicago bound for Pike's Pier, nine miles north of St. Joseph. An uneventful trip brought them to the 800-foot-long lumber pier at about ten o'clock on Sunday morning after an uneventful trip. After resting on their holy day, the crew started taking on a cargo of lumber at sunrise on Monday.[25]

Captain Bartlett neglected to supervise the loading himself. Instead, he went off in search of a "stick" for a new top-mast and left the loading in charge of his first mate, Joseph Campbell of Saugatuck. Campbell grew careless in the captain's absence. Like most lumber schooners, which typically had little cargo space in the hold, the *Mary* carried much of her cargo on the deck. Instead of spreading dunnage (protective material) over the deck to cushion it, Campbell and the other sailors tossed the lumber down from the high pier and managed to punch several holes in the deck. By the time Captain Bartlett returned to his ship, the cargo concealed both the deck and the damage.

The crew completed loading the schooner and pulled away from the pier at about 6:30 P.M. with the wind to the south. They had only made about three miles toward Chicago when a squall blew up from the northwest. If loading had been done in the typical fashion with the decks piled high with lumber and the schooner weighted down under the load, the water would have come within a few feet of the *Mary's* gunwales even in calm seas. When the squall hit from the northwest, it sent waves sloshing over the *Mary's* starboard side. Water flowed through the holes in her deck into her bilge.[26]

By the time the schooner was about fifteen miles off St. Joseph, the crew discovered that she was rapidly taking on water. Bartlett "shortened her down," probably dropping some sails and reefing others, and kept her on course. The storm continued unabated, sending more and more water over the side as the *Mary* sank lower and lower into the lake. With Chicago still twenty-five miles distant, Bartlett found the water gaining so fast that he altered course for Michigan City to run with the storm. The new heading put the wind behind the *Mary* and greatly reduced the amount of water coming over her decks from the waves. By now the ship was in serious trouble, and

Bartlett ordered his crew to jettison the schooner's deck load. Despite his best efforts, the water continued to gain, and with the schooner's decks awash Bartlett took all the sail off except the stay-sail. The *Mary* remained in that condition for an hour, sailing on course for Michigan City with the deck half-submerged; then she capsized onto her beam's end. The crewmen scrambled into the rigging.[27]

The men kept their hold for three or four hours, but exposure and exhaustion inevitably took their toll and one after the other the hapless sailors fell into the lake and drowned. Michael Kelley, whom Bartlett described as a "boy," went first, followed soon after by James Tiffney, and a half hour later by the steward, Patrick Donavan. Twenty minutes after Donavan's death, the mate, Joseph Campbell, slipped from the rigging and disappeared beneath the lake's surface. By then it was about one o'clock on Tuesday afternoon, the wreck drifting in the lake some seven or eight miles off New Buffalo with Captain Bartlett and one sailor, Frank Wheeler, still holding onto the rigging. They somehow maintained their precarious perch through-out that day and all the next night. On Wednesday morning, the *Mary* finally floated ashore two miles north of New Buffalo, where local residents spotted her and helped the two survivors ashore. They left the *Mary* on the beach a total wreck.[28]

The ordeal left Captain Bartlett and Frank Wheeler half dead from exhaustion and exposure, but both men recovered. Negligence in loading coupled with the storm had cost Frank Bartlett his ship, his cargo, most of his crew, and very nearly his life.

Ithaca, 1879

The schooner *Ithaca,* of Chicago, began its final voyage in Muskegon, where she loaded a cargo of high quality lumber. Michigan's white pine, fed into the sawmills in a frenzy of deforestation, built houses throughout the Midwest during the late nineteenth century. The forests of the Great Lakes state also produced marvelous hard-wood, and it was the latter that the *Ithaca* picked up to carry to Michigan City, Indiana, where the manufacturing firm of Haskell & Barker planned to mill it into opulent, railroad passenger-car interiors.[29]

Halfway to her destination, the *Ithaca* ran into one of the horrific November gales that wrecked hundreds of Great Lakes vessels. A northwest wind and a blinding snowstorm churned up heavy seas as Capt. William Sullivan steered the *Ithaca* for the safety of St. Joseph harbor. Entering the harbor on a calm day presented little challenge to a capable skipper, but in high wind and wild waves it was like threading a needle. The elements swept the *Ithaca* too far to the north. Before the crew could recover, the ship struck the outer bar beyond the harbor entrance, broached to, and ran aground just above the north pier, where the heavy seas pounded her until she broke in two.[30]

Ithaca's crew might well have met the same fate as had so many sailors in the same straits, but their luck was in: St. Joseph now had a fully crewed life-saving station. The Life-Savers were heading out to lunch when the *Ithaca* ran aground, but a sharp-eyed surfman spotted the wrecked schooner when the snowstorm momentarily lifted; the crew ran back to the station, loaded a surfboat onto the wagon and started for the beach. Station-keeper William Stevens was sick in bed, but the crew rounded up twenty-five volunteers in town and pulled the wagon and boat to the beach. They took off the *Ithaca's* captain, five crewmen, one passenger, and the captain's St. Bernard dog.[31]

Although the survivors were chilled through and through, a warm fire and a strong dose of brandy at the life-saving station quickly restored the men's health and spirits. The *Ithaca's* crew managed to salvage most of the $2,000 worth of cargo, but the schooner herself went to pieces on the shore.[32]

Alpena, 1880

The Goodrich Transportation Company sidewheel steamer *Alpena* went down in one of the worst storms in Great Lakes history. For decades people around the lakes spoke of the storm in awed tones as "The Alpena Storm," and its mere mention reminded sailors of the terrible power of Great Lakes weather in full fury.

If any man possessed the skill to bring a ship safely through the "Alpena Storm," it was the *Alpena's* own skipper, Nelson W. Napier of St. Joseph. A native of Ashtabula, Ohio, Napier moved to St. Joseph as a youth and began a career on the lakes, winning one promotion after another until he held command of his own ship at age twenty-one. Lake Michigan afforded him a living, but Nelson Napier knew its dangers firsthand. He and his crew had survived a shipwreck when his schooner, the *Florida,* went to pieces near South Haven during a fierce Lake Michigan gale in November 1842; he had rescued the crew of the schooner *Jefferson* in 1844; and he had lost an infant son in the wreck of the *Experiment* in 1855. Over the years Napier commanded an assortment of schooners, brigs, and steamers on Lake Michigan, and finally he went to work for the Goodrich Transportation Company.[33]

The *Alpena's* owner, Albert E. Goodrich, grew up in New Buffalo, Michigan, where he started a maritime career as clerk aboard the sidewheel steamer *A. D. Patchin.* In 1856, Goodrich went into partnership with George C. Drew to form Goodrich's Steamboat Line, sailing out of Chicago and Milwaukee. The Goodrich Line prospered, and in 1861 Goodrich bought out his partner's share and became sole owner.[34] Goodrich added the *Alpena* to his fleet of ships in 1868. Thomas Arnold had built the *Alpena,* a wooden-hulled sidewheeler, in Marine City, Michigan, in 1866. The *Alpena's* machinery was built by the Detroit Locomotive Works and included a single-cylinder vertical beam engine with a forty-four-inch by eleven-foot stroke that turned a pair of sidewheels. Goodrich bought her from the firm of Gardner, Ward & Gallagher for $80,000.[35] A few days after he bought the *Alpena,* Goodrich incorporated his business as the Goodrich Transportation Company with himself as president and his elder brother Joseph as vice president. The new corporation boasted six steamships: *Alpena, Comet, G. J. Truesdell, Manitowoc, Northwest,* and *Ottawa.*[36]

Goodrich poured $20,000 into the *Alpena* to rebuild her during the winter of 1876-1877. Workmen installed new arches, deck frames and decking, a gallous frame, ceiling and planking wherever needed, and a completely new stern, among other repairs. The rebuild left her stronger and in better condition than at any time since her maiden voyage. In the spring of 1880, Goodrich placed the *Alpena* under Nelson Napier's command.[37]

Friday, October 15, 1880, began as the kind of gorgeous Indian summer day which graces only the Great Lakes region. The sun shone warmly all day, thermometers hovered between sixty and seventy degrees, and a light southerly wind whispered through the dry beach grass as the *Alpena* steamed out of Grand Haven at 9:00 P.M. She had left Muskegon earlier that day, then put in at Grand Haven to pick up two carloads of apples and more passengers. Somewhere between sixty and one hundred passengers and crew were aboard as she headed across Lake Michigan to Chicago.[38] Several ships spotted the *Alpena* that evening during her lake crossing. Although the wind had begun to pick up and whip across Lake Michigan, they reported the *Alpena* making good progress and keeping to her course.

That night the temperature plummeted below freezing and gale-force winds thundered across the lake. Enormous waves lashed into ships and hammered the shoreline, churning Lake Michigan into a wild, frothing frenzy. Lake Michigan got the worst of the weather, although Lake Huron also felt the storm's fury. Out on both lakes, scores of ships fought for their lives. The schooner *Challenger* caught sight of the *Alpena* that night, some thirty miles east of Kenosha, Wisconsin, blowing distress signals as she waged a desperate battle with elements. The *Challenger,* herself in peril, could do nothing to aid the *Alpena.* No one ever saw the Goodrich steamer again.[39]

The sidewheel steamer *Alpena* in 1876.
(Courtesy of the Historical Collections of the Great Lakes, Bowling Green State University)

The Graham & Morton steamers *Skylark* and *Messenger* left St. Joseph shortly after the *Alpena* sailed out of Grand Haven. Both encountered the storm in all its fury: waves dashed over the ships, penetrating every open space and soaking clothing, bedding, cargo, and passengers. The *Messenger* completed the lake crossing unassisted, but the *Skylark* broke down a few miles from Chicago and nearly became another victim of the storm. Fortunately, a tug came to her rescue and brought her safely into Chicago harbor. Unbelievably, both vessels returned through the howling storm on Sunday. Risking the ships and all aboard stretched audacity to folly. Even the St. Joseph newspaper, which usually lent uncritical support to local entrepreneurs, opined that the Sunday voyage "being unnecessary and dangerous, did not reflect any credit upon those who ordered or made the venture."[40]

Some big storms blow out quickly, but the "Alpena Storm" raged unabated through Saturday and Sunday. As the wind finally let up on Monday, telegraph wires began humming across the Midwest. Clicking telegraphers' keys carried report after report of wrecked ships all across the Great Lakes: this schooner aground, that steamer missing, another schooner sunk, and still another afloat but battered to pieces. All through Monday and Tuesday, friends and relatives of those aboard the *Alpena* haunted telegraph and newspaper offices or sat numbly in railroad stations, praying that the steamer had weathered the storm; that she would arrive safely in Chicago or some other port; that the storm had only delayed, not defeated, her.[41]

Bad news trickled in on Monday afternoon. Telegrams coming into St. Joseph and Chicago reported that a portion of the *Alpena's* upper deck had washed ashore near Montague, and that searchers had found a stair railing and a pail marked "Alpena" off Holland. Even so, ships often lost part of their upper works in bad blows and came through battered but unbroken. Those who waited still kept hope alive.

Late Tuesday afternoon a tapping telegraph key destroyed all hope. Railroad telegrapher Fredrick Nye of Holland wired Superintendent Charles M. Lawler of the U. S. Life-Saving Service at

St. Joseph that flotsam from a wrecked steamer was fast washing ashore at that point; no doubt remained that the wreckage came from the *Alpena* and that she was gone. Would anyone, Nye asked, care to ride up on the 7:15 train that evening to be on hand to identify bodies as they, too, washed ashore?[42]

As the Napier family's last hopes vanished, Nelson's son-in-law, Dr. Luther I. McLin, boarded the train for Holland with Don Morrison and Frank H. Platt to identify bodies. Two of Napier's sons, Edward and Arthur, followed by team along the beach the next day; two other sons, Jackson and Ned, went north by train on Thursday.[43] Other families did likewise. As the news spread through western Michigan and Chicago that the *Alpena* had gone down, special trains filled with the friends and families of the passengers and crew chugged into Holland. Hotels and hack drivers enjoyed a thriving business as a result of the tragedy, and rumors circulated that unscrupulous innkeepers and drivers took advantage of the demand for their services and gouged the bereaved. Searchers combed the shoreline during the weeks after the wreck, but only a few bodies ever washed ashore.[44]

The *Alpena* wreck sent southwest Michigan into mourning. Flags flew at half-staff in towns and on ships in harbors. No one survived the sinking, and many of the area's most prominent citizens numbered among the missing. Whitman S. Benham, editor of the *Grand Haven Herald,* and his wife, Sarah, had been aboard. So had thirty-one-year-old Neal A. McGilvary, son-in-law of St. Joseph businessman Alexander H. Morrison, who left a young widow and child. Second Mate Eldridge Van Patten, Wheelsman Lester Shaw, and the ship's second porter, Peter Eggert, all young men of Berrien County's Lincoln Township, went missing, as did Arthur E. Haynes, the clerk, a young man engaged to a St. Joseph woman.[45]

No one ever knew how many people went down with the *Alpena,* as the only copy of her passenger list went with the ship when she sailed out of Grand Haven. The exact circumstances of her loss remain a mystery to this day. Where did she sink, and when? What finally proved her undoing? Did towering waves capsize her, leaks flood her hull, or engine breakdown leave her helpless? What desperate actions did Nelson Napier take to save his ship, and how did he and his passengers and crew meet their end? Whatever acts of heroism, cowardice, or desperation took place on the *Alpena's* decks that night will remain forever unknown.

Large pieces of the *Alpena's* wreckage washed ashore from Holland to Grand Haven that fall. Parts of the ship's superstructure, the piano, cabin doors, two small boats, and a piece of her main deck with the capstan attached were recovered, and hundreds of apples bobbed in the surf. A couple of weeks after the storm, the ship's flag, bearing the name *Alpena,* turned up on the beach near White Lake Channel, far from where the steamer probably went down. In January 1909, nearly thirty years after the wreck, the *Alpena's* paddlewheel box nameboard washed ashore at Alpena Beach, near Holland.

"Wreckers" scoured the coast. Many wanted souvenirs and hauled off every piece of *Alpena* debris that they could carry, sometimes selling their treasures to other curiosity seekers and sometimes refusing substantial sums of money for the choicest items. The more practical minded hauled home barrels of apples and even the coffins

A contemporary artist's conception of the *Alpena* laboring through heavy seas on the night of her loss. *(Courtesy of the Holland Museum Collection)*

that, ironically, had been among the *Alpena's* cargo. Other scavengers dug through packing trunks that washed ashore and robbed the contents. The worst elements of society prowled the shore at night equipped with long pikes with which they dragged bodies out of the lake to loot of money and valuables.[46]

Even the most hardened wrecker could not remain entirely unmoved by the grief of those who had lost friends and family members in the disaster. Most poignant of all was the story of Farrell Hart of Chicago. The thirty-one-year-old church pastor had recently graduated from the Presbyterian Theological Seminary in Chicago and taken a job as editor of Sunday school publications for the publishing house of David C. Cook & Company of Chicago. On the preceding Thursday he had married Miss Lottie T. Davis in White Pigeon, Michigan; the newlyweds took passage home on the *Alpena* and died together before their married life could even begin.[47]

In St. Joseph, Henrietta Napier advertised a one-hundred-dollar reward for the recovery of her husband's body, but the money went unclaimed. On December 5, 1880, seven weeks after the *Alpena's* loss, St. Joseph held a Sunday memorial service in the city's Congregational Church for Nelson Napier, Neal McGilvary, and Arthur Haynes.[48]

Albert Goodrich pieced together what bits of information he could glean from other ship captains and concluded that the *Alpena* had foundered some twenty-five miles east of Kenosha, Wisconsin. He withdrew his ships from the Chicago-to-Grand Haven route and did not resume operations on that line for two years. Goodrich Transportation, however, survived the *Alpena's* loss and went on to enjoy a long, prosperous history on Lake Michigan.

Public interest in the disaster waned gradually over the succeeding weeks, but the enormous loss of life ensured that the *Alpena* story would live on for years afterward. Only a few Great Lakes shipwrecks claimed more lives than the *Alpena* wreck and none had a greater impact on the people of Michigan's southwest coast.

Nina Bailey, 1880

The *Nina Bailey,* a little thirty-five-ton schooner of Milwaukee, headed out of Chicago on Halloween, 1880, two weeks after the "Alpena Storm."[49] A storm struck while she was part way across the lake, and as the strong north-northwest wind and heavy seas swept around her, she began to fill with water. The *Bailey's* skipper and owner, John Johnson, and his single crewman, Dick DeCondason, battled valiantly against the elements, but she went out of control as she entered the harbor at 2:45 A.M. on November 1. The *Bailey* slammed into the north pier and capsized. Her crew went overboard, but both men struggled to the surface, clambered onto her hull and clung desperately to her keel.[50]

William L. Stevens and the St. Joseph Life-Saving Station crew immediately launched a surfboat and rowed out of the harbor to rescue the sailors. They pulled up to the overturned craft and found the *Bailey's* crew half frozen from the icy waves that washed over them. The life savers reached Johnson first, but the *Bailey's* captain refused to get into the boat until DeCondason, who could not swim, was rescued. A change of dry clothing and a warm fire at the life-saving station soon thawed out the two crewmen. The entire rescue, from launching the surfboat to the return to the station, had taken fifteen minutes. The *Nina Bailey,* however, was beyond saving and quickly broke up on the beach.[51]

W. H. Willard, 1880

Nineteenth-century Great Lakes ships sailed in a commercial ocean of big and little fish. Well-established big fish like the Goodrich Transportation Company or the Graham & Morton Transportation Company could afford to own and insure several big steamers. Many vessels, however, were owned by the little fish—men who personally sailed the ships they owned, carrying cargoes from one port to another, going without the insurance they could not afford, and living only a storm or sandbar away from catastrophe.

The *W. H. Willard* belonged to the latter class. Built in 1856 and named for the managing owner, W. H. Willard of Cleveland, Ohio, she sailed in 1880 under the ownership of her captain, S. Peter Lawrence, of Milwaukee, Wisconsin. The Association of Lake Vessel Underwriters, which assessed the condition of ships for insurance purposes, had listed her as "unseaworthy" in 1876 and "uninsurable" in 1879. However, the prospect of late-season profits tempted Captain Lawrence to take her out as winter began to settle in on the Great Lakes.[52]

In November 1880 the *Willard* headed out of Muskegon with a cargo of 108,000 board feet of lumber for the firm of Eldredge & Robbins of Benton Harbor.[53] Captain Lawrence, like so many skippers, risked his ship and his life on a late-season run. Great Lakes captains knew the hazards of sailing in October and November when the weather often turned from fair to foul in an instant, but an idle ship earned no income.

Bad weather caught the *Willard* as she neared her destination about midnight on Saturday evening, November 6. Life-Saving Service surfmen Charles Lysaght and Lew Matthews were on their regular patrol when they saw her coming in shortly after 1:00 A.M. and realized that she was in trouble. Captain Lawrence had not sailed into St. Joseph for twenty years, and in the storm and darkness he mistook the placement of the pier rangelights. Lysaght and Matthews watched helplessly as the *Willard* smashed into the pier and went hard aground. The two surfmen ran back to the station and alerted the life-saving crew, who raced down to the north pier. They lit a torch and held it aloft to signal the schooner that help was on the way.[54]

By good fortune the *Willard* came to rest with her jib-boom projecting two feet over the pier. Captain Lawrence and his crew of three scrambled across the jib-boom to safety. The life-saving crew helped them onto the pier, and escorted them to the station for food and shelter.[55]

Peter Lawrence immediately set to work and salvaged all of the *Willard's* cargo. His ship, which was all he owned, lay wrecked beyond repair. Although valued at $5,000, Lawrence carried no insurance on her and he suffered a devastating financial loss in the disaster. During the next few days, Lawrence removed and sold what materials he could salvage from the schooner, but the *W. H. Willard* was a total loss.[56]

Industry, 1882

Capt. John King of St. Joseph followed the sea all his life. Born in Kirkwall on Scotland's Orkney Islands on September 15, 1823, he made his first voyage at the age of sixteen.[57] He emigrated to America in 1850 and began sailing the Great Lakes, returned to his native Kirkwall just long enough to marry Miss Elizabeth Isbister, and immediately returned to the United States with his new bride. After landing at New Orleans, the young couple spent a few months in St. Louis, Missouri, then moved to St. Joseph, Michigan, in 1853. There he and Elizabeth raised six children, two of whom—James and Ebenezer—followed their father's career on the lakes.

Captain King sailed many different vessels out of St. Joseph, and at various times held a part or whole interest in the schooners *Tri-Color, Two Brothers,* and *John Hibbard.* Finally, he bought the little 44-ton schooner *Industry.* About nine o'clock on Saturday morning, June 1, 1882, he set off from St. Joseph harbor with a load of lumber, bound for Muskegon, Michigan. His crew consisted of his twenty-one-year-old son, Ebenezer, and a seventeen-year-old sailor named Eddie Calendar.[58]

A summer storm blew up, and the seas began to run so heavily that when the *Industry* was off Saugatuck, Captain King decided to put about for South Haven. James L. Donahue, the lighthouse keeper at South Haven, watched her sail into view from the north at about 4:45 P.M., carrying a jib and close-reefed foresail.[59] By that time Lake Michigan was running what Donahue described as "a very heavy sea from the northwest" as a forty-mile-per-hour gale shrieked through the schooner's rigging. "She made good weather of it," Donahue wrote, "until she was about eighty rods from this harbor."

At 6:15 P.M., the *Industry* pitched down at the bow just as a heavy sea broke over the stern. As Donahue watched in horror, she broached to and headed to the west, rolled over to the south and capsized onto her port side. For an instant the little schooner vanished from sight, then struggled to the surface with her bow heading northeast. John and Ebenezer King and Eddie Calender went overboard into the lake but finally scrambled onto the hull, the captain on the stern and the other two sailors amidships.[60]

The *Industry* drifted toward the beach as the waves pushed her southward, and the sailors gestured to Donahue for help as they swept past the lighthouse. Donahue grabbed a large white towel which he waved back in reply to indicate that everything possible would be done to save them. One of the men got up and walked back and forth on the ship's bulwarks; all three sailors slapped their arms about them to keep warm.[61]

Word of the wreck spread through South Haven. People came running with life-lines and life preservers and men waded into the water up to their chests in a vain effort to reach the schooner. Men, women, and children crowded the shoreline, anxious to do whatever they could to help *Industry's* crew. No one even tried to launch a boat, knowing that the seas would swamp them in an instant. Donahue watched three men struggle through water up to their necks, taking "some close chances" in desperate attempts to save the sailors. One of them, grasping a line, waded and swam through the thundering waves to within fifteen to eighteen rods of the crew, but at last he had to give up and return to shore. At one point the *Industry* drifted tantalizingly close to the beach, lying only four seas out, but then the waves cruelly snatched her back into deeper water. Donahue thought her anchor must have fallen away and caught on the bottom, for she stopped drifting and lay with her bow pointing into the wind. "Then," Donahue reported, "the deck and spars went out of her and she rolled over, bottom up...."[62]

Twice the waves washed Captain King from his hold and twice he scrambled back aboard, but the third time he went over and never came up. His son and Eddie Calender followed him to their deaths about five minutes later. Waves swept the wreck south along Lake Michigan until the *Industry* finally grounded against Ludwig's Pier, about five miles south of South Haven.[63]

John King's son, Capt. James King of the *Lizzie Doak,* had the heartbreaking task of searching for the bodies. He and a fellow sailor, James McDonald, trekked north by horse and wagon the following Saturday. They located the wrecked schooner and by Wednesday had pulled its rigging ashore, thinking that the lost sailors might be caught in it, but found nothing. On June 17, James King finally received word that a body had washed ashore a mile south of Paul's Pier, four miles south of the spot where the *Industry* had grounded, and that same evening the tug *Louis Wallace* returned to St. Joseph bearing the bodies of both John King and Eddie Calender. James and some friends started up the coast again in another search for his brother's body, but found nothing. Not until June 26 did he receive a telegram from Capt. Leighton of the tug *Cupid,* of South Haven, that a man's body had floated ashore on the beach near Hannah's Pier, some eight miles below South Haven. That evening James King returned in the *Louis Wallace* with the body which had proved to be that of his brother Ebenezer.[64]

The schooner *Industry* eventually went to pieces on the shore; her gallant crew all rest today in St. Joseph's City Cemetery.

R. G. Peters, 1882

Few disasters are more horrifying than a fire at sea. The safe haven of a ship's deck suddenly becomes a furious inferno as flames threaten to devour the vessel and every living thing aboard. Usually a fast-acting crew can extinguish the fire and save the ship, but sometimes the fire gains too quickly and the only refuge is the dubious safety of the cold water below.

Just such a disaster overtook the steam barge *R. G. Peters* soon after she headed out of St. Joseph on a run to Manistee on December 2, 1882. The 175-foot *R. G. Peters,* a nearly new vessel built in Milwaukee just two years before, lay in port in St. Joseph and in the Benton Harbor Ship Canal during late November. On the first day of December she steamed out of the harbor with the old schooner *A. W. Luckey* in tow as a barge, bound for Manistee. A winter storm blew up out of the north and pummeled the two ships. In the midst of the storm and about twenty-five miles off Milwaukee, flames sprang up aboard the *Peters.* Horrified crewmen on the *Luckey* tried to save the steambarge's crew, but the driving gale made the attempt impossible. They could only watch as fire engulfed the steambarge and burn her out until she sank beneath the waves, taking her captain and twelve crewmen with it.[65]

The storm swept the *Luckey* southward toward Chicago. A tug spotted the schooner "in a dilapidated condition" about ten miles from Chicago and towed her into port. The *Luckey's* crew, grateful to be alive, recounted the evening's events—especially the tragic story of First Mate John Larson of Manistee. Larson had come through five shipwrecks unscathed, only to die aboard the *R. G. Peters.*[66]

Arab, Protection, and *H. C. Akeley,* 1883

Had the owners just abandoned the *Arab* on the beach at St. Joseph, two other ships and their crews would have been better off.

The one-hundred-foot schooner, already nearly thirty years old, set sail from Starke's Pier, near Frankfort, Michigan, on Monday, October 29, 1883, bound for her home port of Milwaukee with a load of lumber, piles, slabs, and cordwood. Soon afterward she ran into foul weather. Capt. Charles Starke ordered his crew of four to toss part of the deck cargo into the lake, but when the *Arab* lost her centerboard, Starke elected to head for the safety of St. Joseph harbor. Just as she neared safe shelter at 7:30 P.M. on Halloween Eve, the *Arab* struck the bar as she entered the harbor.

The Life-Saving Station lookout saw her heading for disaster and lit a torch as a warning signal, but it was too late. Unmanageable, the *Arab* went onto the beach near the foot of the south pier. The crew lashed her to the pier and received assistance from the U. S. Life-Saving Station men, who helped them safely onto the pier and took them to the station to warm up. "They had been out 3 days and were all worn out," Station Keeper William L. Stevens reported. "They seemed very grateful to get to the station."[67]

Thursday morning found the *Arab* stranded and filled with water. During the next week, workmen twice pumped the *Arab* dry with a steam-powered pump brought over from Chicago; but while they succeeded in moving her fifty feet closer to the end of the pier, she twice filled with water and sank. On Friday, November 9, the tug *Protection* arrived with a larger, more powerful pump. By setting both pumps to work the men managed to empty out the *Arab* on Saturday morning.[68]

The *Protection* towed the *Arab* into the harbor between the piers and secured her to the south pier. Workmen fashioned temporary patches to stop up the leaks and loaded her with green hemlock lumber. At about seven o'clock on Saturday evening, the *Arab* started off for Milwaukee under the *Protection's* tow. The sailors and wrecking crew looked forward to a gorgeous Lake Michigan evening: bright moonlight shone down on the lake's gentle swells as a delicate westerly breeze fanned across from Wisconsin. Engineer William Kelley, an assistant, and two firemen kept a steam pump knocking away, sending a steady stream of water over the side. The pump stayed ahead of the leaks, and with a second pump aboard as a backup, the *Arab's* crew and engineers felt confident that they could bring the schooner safely into Milwaukee the next morning.[69]

The *Protection's* crew were enjoying the pleasant early morning hours when a sudden commotion erupted aboard the *Arab*. The schooner's crew raced onto its decks and rushed aft as the *Arab* rolled over and pitched down at the bow, sinking until only ten feet of her port quarter remained out of the water. Kelley, unable to keep steam up in the pump, had decided to start the second pump. While tinkering with that, he failed to notice the amount of water gushing into the schooner until too late. The weight of the water, coupled with that of the two iron pumps, pulled the *Arab's* bow under the surface. It all happened so fast that the larger of the pumps toppled over and crushed Kelley, who went down in the *Arab's* bow.[70]

The astonishing chain of events electrified the *Protection's* crew. They immediately cast off the towline, but in his excitement and haste to help the *Arab's* men the *Protection's* skipper ordered the engines full back instead of full ahead. The *Protection* backed over the floating line and reeled it up into her propeller until it jammed and the engine shuddered to a stop, leaving her disabled and helpless. The tug's crew quickly lowered a boat, rowed over to the *Arab* and took off her sailors and the salvage crew.[71]

As the Life-Saving Service noted in its official report of the incident, "it is not without some show of reason that the idea of perfidy is attached to the sea," and that Nature's elements seem to lie in wait to make cruel sport of helpless sailors.[72] No sooner had the fouled towline crippled the *Protection* than the wind picked up and the swells began to rise. The crew quickly set to work to free the snarled line. They labored all morning without success, until the water grew so rough that they had to give up. By 10:00 A.M., the once-peaceful lake had become a swollen, angry ocean and the gentle breeze had turned into a stiff northwest wind.[73]

To the crew's immense relief, the big bulk freighter *H. C. Akeley,* ploughing through the seas bound for Buffalo out of Chicago with a cargo of corn, hove into view. Hearing the *Protection's* whistles of distress, the *Akeley* altered course and drew up alongside the crippled tug, threw her a line and took her in tow. Together the two vessels headed north up Lake Michigan toward the Manitou Islands.[74]

As the day wore on the wind blew harder and harder and the seas grew worse and worse. By afternoon, the wind had become a terrific gale, with Grand Haven recording wind velocities of fifty-two miles per hour. The *Akeley* had a hard time of it; her cargo shifted and threw the steamer out of trim so that it began rolling heavily. The seas washed completely over her every time she rolled. At seven o'clock that evening her steering gear broke. Soon afterward a feed pipe

The steambarge *H. C. Akeley* under construction in Grand Haven, Michigan.
(Courtesy of the Tri-Cities Historical Museum)

burst, rendering the port boiler unserviceable. Chief Engineer John Driscoll's attempts to feed the port boiler from the starboard boiler failed, and just before midnight the *Akeley* lost power. Completely crippled, she drifted helplessly with the storm. The steamer's crew hoisted sails in an desperate attempt to regain some control, but the howling wind ripped them to shreds. The waves swept one of the lifeboats overboard during the night, and the next morning the funnel tore loose and crashed over the side.[75]

Throughout this ordeal, the *Protection* trailed behind the big steamer on the towline. The *Protection's* crew, in fact, had an easier time of it, for they kept their little tug on the *Akeley's* lee side, thereby pointing her bow into the seas. Both vessels survived the day and by early evening the storm had moderated. The *Protection's* crew found that the tow rope had disentangled itself from the propeller and that her engine worked; thinking that only about thirty miles separated them from South Haven, they cast off the towline and set off for Grand Haven, intending to coal up and return to help the *Akeley*.[76]

Shortly after casting off, however, the tug's crew found that the towline was still entangled in the propeller and that the *Protection's* engine would only run in reverse. They had no choice but to let her drift with the waves. The storm drove the vessel eastward and along the lake until she finally dropped anchor about a half-mile north of the harbor at Saugatuck. The crew hoisted a piece of awning on an upright oar as a distress flag and began signaling frantically on the whistle.[77]

The *Protection's* distress whistle summoned a great throng of people down to the shore, but huge breakers at the harbor mouth precluded any attempt to bring the tug in or take any rescue boat out to her. Several of Saugatuck's leading residents convened a council on the beach and concluded to send for help from the Life-Saving Station at Grand Haven. When word came back that the Grand Haven crew had already left to assist another wreck, they telegraphed the St. Joseph crew.[78]

Life-Saving Station keeper William L. Stevens received the telegram from Saugatuck at 11:00 A.M. He quickly assembled the station equipment and with a crew of seven men caught the 12:55 P.M.

train for Grand Haven, leaving surfman James Flynn behind in charge of the station. Boarding the train posed obstacles of its own. Stevens had to ferry the Lyle gun, its cart, and all the rescue apparatus across a churning harbor, pulling the boat along on a safety line, then load everything into a baggage car in the ten minutes that remained before the train pulled out. He and his men managed the feat, however, and were soon racing up the rails to Saugatuck.[79]

The St. Joseph crew disembarked at the Richmond depot and took the tugboat *Ganges* down the Kalamazoo River, arriving in Saugatuck at about 5:00 P.M. They hauled their equipment down to the beach and began setting it up for the rescue. The *Protection* had held out through the long delay although the waves tossed her about fearfully. Some local fishermen and sailors had made two attempts during the day to reach her with a large Mackinac boat, but the wind and waves beat them back both times.[80]

The St. Joseph life savers considered firing a line from the Lyle gun, but the *Protection* still lay at anchor out of range. The life savers could only watch and wait. About an hour after their arrival, the wind picked up and shifted to the northwest. Snow began pelting down and at about 9:00 P.M. a series of shrill whistles from the tug filled the air. The *Protection* had begun dragging her anchor and heading for destruction on the beach. The crew, unaware of the life-savers' arrival and convinced that the end had come, shook hands all around and resigned themselves to death.[81]

Stevens, seeing the tug drifting toward the south pier, had his equipment ferried across the harbor. He and his men, aided by a force of excited Saugatuckians, landed the equipment on the pier, which consisted of wooden cribs filled with rough stones. They could not haul the heavy mortar cart over the cribs, so they tore up the lighthouse keeper's plank walk and used it to build an improvised track. By then, night had settled in, but the men hitched drag ropes to the cart and hauled it, plunging and bucking, through the snow and over the driftwood-littered beach. It took them an hour to haul the cart a half-mile down the shore. They set up the Lyle gun, kindled some bonfires of driftwood, and waited as the *Protection* drew nearer and nearer. Out on the tug, crewmen felt the first stirrings of hope as they saw that a life-saving crew had arrived.[82]

The *Protection* came sliding in on the breakers, pitching up and down, riding stern first at a quartering angle to the shore, with the crew gathered on the bow. The *Protection* smashed into a sandbar with a shuddering crash some two hundred yards from the beach. A wave broke over her. The tug rose and fell with the breakers, pounding against the bar. Sea after sea swept over her and tore away the pilothouse. Waves beat in the doors of the engine room and cabin, and water boiled up through the hull. William Grace, a young fireman, ignored his comrade's warnings and stood on the stern, exposed to the full fury of the elements. Suddenly he was gone, swept over the side to his death.[83]

Another sailor had more luck. As astounded rescuers watched from the beach, a young man arose from the pounding surf and walked, dripping and frozen, to warm himself at the beach fire. He had donned a life preserver, plunged overboard, and by a one-in-a-million chance swam through the breakers to safety.[84]

Then the *Protection* went over the bar. The tug grounded with her stern in the lake bottom, then swung around with her bow pointed toward land. Stevens and his men, watching intently from shore, saw their chance. They loaded their Lyle gun and with a resounding bang sent a shell and its attached line arcing toward the tug. Their perfect aim draped the line squarely across the tug, but the line parted from the shot and slipped back into the lake before the sailors could grab it. Another shot, another line amidships, and this time it held. The *Protection's* crew secured it to the tug, and a half-hour later the life savers had a breeches buoy rigged up and began reeling in the first man.[85]

The lines going out and back to the tug worked against each other, so that even though thirty-five or forty men hauled away on them the lines still worked hard. The *Protection* rolled and bucked as the men came across, which slackened the line so that each sailor trailed a wake of foam as the rescuers dragged him waist-deep through the surf. Their clothing froze solid on their bodies the moment they came ashore. William Stevens and two of his men took the most important and dangerous posts, standing out in advance in the frigid water.[86]

By 11:30 that night they had pulled ashore the last of the fifteen survivors. Twelve of them boarded the tug *Graham,* which took them to a Saugatuck hotel for food, shelter, and dry clothing. The *Protection's* cook was in the worst condition of all the crewmen, frozen and exhausted to the point of helplessness. The lighthouse keeper and surfman Charles Lysaght took him and two other sailors to the lighthouse for immediate attention. In the end, all fifteen men recovered.[87]

The United States Life-Saving Service hailed the St. Joseph crew's exploits as "unparalleled in the annals of the service." They had traveled sixty-four miles by boat and train to reach Saugatuck, fought their way over one obstacle after another, and battled against wind, surf, snow, and bitter cold to effect a rescue. In its official report, the Life-Saving Service declared that "but for the gallant aid rendered them it is more than probable the fifteen men on board the *Protection* would have perished."[88]

The *Akeley's* crew was less fortunate. Not until the following day did the *Protection's* men learn that the steamer had foundered and taken five crewmen to the bottom with her. Shortly after she turned the *Protection* loose, the *Akeley* began drifting and dropped anchor. As the *Akeley's* condition deteriorated, Capt. Edward Stretch ordered the remaining lifeboat cleared away. Capt. David Miller of the schooner *Driver* caught sight of the *Akeley* at 12:30 Tuesday afternoon, and his brother Daniel climbed into the rigging for a better view. He called down to the captain that the ship was the *H. C. Akeley.* Then he looked again and cried in horror, "Good God, Dave! She is foundering!" The *Akeley* disappeared stern first beneath the waves, taking Captain Stretch, the first mate, and three sailors with her.[89]

The schooner bore down on the site where the *Akeley* had disappeared and spotted her lifeboat. The *Driver's* crew tried to pick up the survivors, but high seas thwarted their efforts. Daniel Miller then called for a volunteer to help him man the *Driver's* own lifeboat and an Irish sailor named Patrick H. Daly (Miller knew him only as "Paddy") said that he would go. Miller and Daly maneuvered the boat through the waves stern-first toward the *Akeley's* lifeboat. Upon reaching it they transferred three sailors into their own boat to lighten the lifeboat's load, then tossed a line to the remaining survivors and rowed both boats to windward. The *Driver* drew up alongside to place the lifeboats in her lee and pulled the *Akeley's* survivors aboard. At that moment the *Driver's* boat capsized and threw Miller and Daly into the lake, but the two men scrambled up the boat tackle falls to safety. The *Driver* set course for Chicago, arriving on the morning of November 16 with the steamer's surviving crewmen and the first confirmation that the *H. C. Akeley* had gone down.[90]

What began as a simple attempt to salvage a schooner beached at St. Joseph had culminated in a disaster costing seven lives and two ships. The *H. C. Akeley* and the *Arab* still lie at the bottom of Lake Michigan, but the *Protection* survived. Captain R. C. Brittain of Saugatuck bought the salvage rights to her and in the spring of 1884

Steam Barge H. C. Akley of Gr. Haven, Mich.

The final moments of the *H. C. Akeley.*
(Courtesy of the Tri-Cities Historical Museum)

set to work trying to pull her off the bar. Accomplishing that task required the combined efforts of the river steamer *Alice Purdy,* the passenger steamer *A. B. Taylor,* and the fishing tug *Clara Elliott,* but the *Protection* finally came free and went up the river to Saugatuck for repairs. In 1897, sixteen years after grounding on the Saugatuck shore, the old boat remained in service with the Dunham Towing Company of Chicago. The U. S. Life-Saving Service awarded gold life-saving medals to Daniel Miller and Patrick Daly, and a silver medal to David Miller for their daring rescue of the *Akeley's* crewmen.[91]

Regulator, 1883

The same storm that hammered the *Protection* and the *H. C. Akeley* also wrecked the schooner *Regulator.* Built in Buffalo, New York, in 1866, the *Regulator* was rebuilt in 1882, and, according to Chicago newspapers, ranked "among the better class of lumber vessels."[92] The night of Thursday, November 15, 1883, found her bound out of White Lake, Michigan, with a cargo of lumber for her home port of Chicago. That evening gale struck the schooner with full force and drove her ashore just south of Bridgman at about 8:00 P.M.[93]

The *Regulator's* crew took to the rigging, but the mate slipped off the ship and drowned. The surviving crewmen clung to the rigging for hours as they waited in vain for rescue. The schooner's captain later complained bitterly that they watched local residents on the beach as they carted off the wreckage that washed ashore. No one, he declared, made any effort to help the shipwrecked men, nor did they bother to telegraph the St. Joseph Life-Saving Station crew. The life savers remained at the station, unaware of the *Regulator* wreck as they rested after their arduous rescue of the *Protection's* crew. Life-Saving Service Superintendent Nathaniel Robbins pronounced the characters on the beach "the worst kind of pirates" and opined that "they ought to be hanged."[94] Robbins neglected to mention the heroism of Nelson O. Caryl, a Bridgman farmer, who went out before dawn on Friday with ropes and a boat and saved the lives of the remaining crewmen.[95]

A month later the tug *Leviathan,* of Milwaukee, attempted to salvage the *Regulator.* The tug arrived in St. Joseph in early

December, then steamed south to Bridgman and found the schooner still hard aground. The *Leviathan's* crew pumped out the wrecked vessel and freed her, but at the critical moment, the tug's pumps broke down and the schooner again went ashore. The *Leviathan* retreated to St. Joseph for repairs while the *Regulator,* abandoned to the elements, went to pieces on the beach.[96]

1. *St. Joseph Traveler-Herald,* May 1, 1875; Petition for Appointment of an Administrator, April 5, 1880, Berrien County Probate Court, Deceased Files, File No. 1815, Wilhelmina Groenke, Berrien County Historical Association, Berrien Springs, MI.

2. *St. Joseph Traveler-Herald,* May 1, 1875.

3. Ibid.

4. Ibid.

5. Ibid.

6. Ibid.

7. Ibid., May 8, 1875 and March 25, 1876.

8. Ibid. The Returns of Deaths for St. Joseph Township in 1875 recorded only five of the eleven lost fishermen, but four of the five were born in Germany, the other having been born in Connecticut.

9. Petition for Appointment of an Administrator, April 5, 1880, Berrien County Probate Court, Deceased Files, File No. 1815, Wilhelmina Groenke; Marriage Certificates, 1875, Certificate No. 392, Robert Miller to Wilhelmina Groenke, Berrien County Circuit Court, Berrien County Historical Association, Berrien Springs, MI.

10. *St. Joseph Traveler-Herald,* October 9, 1875; Petition for Appointment of an Administrator, April 5, 1880, Berrien County Probate Court Deceased Files, File No. 1815.

11. *Oswego Daily Times,* September 1, 1853. A bark was a three-masted ship with a square-rigged foremast and mainmast, and a fore-and-aft rigged mizzenmast.

12. Peggy Jean Townsend and Charles Walker Townsend III, ed., "Sara Jane Clarke (Grace Greenwood)," *Milo Adams Townsend and Social Movements of the Nineteenth Century,* January 1994, <http://www.bchistory.org/beavercounty/book-lengthdocuments/AMilobook/chapters.html> (February 16, 2002).

13. *St. Joseph Traveler-Herald,* October 7, 1876; Life-Saving Station Logs, Chicago District, St. Joseph Station, October 6, 1876, Record Group (RG) 26, NARA (National Archives and Records Administration)—Great Lakes Region (Chicago); Case Files 422-426, Libel and complaint of Frank Campbell, Charles Clark, Frederick Meares, _____ Dutcher, and Seth Baldwin vs. Schooner *Grace Greenwood,* October 7–8, 1876, Western Division of Michigan, Southern Division at Grand Rapids, Admiralty Records, Admiralty Case Files, RG 21, NARA—Great Lakes Region (Chicago). Case File 425, indexed as Dutcher vs. Schooner *Grace Greenwood,* is missing.

14. *Benton Harbor Palladium,* October 13, 1876.

15. *Chicago Inter Ocean,* October 15, 1877.

16. *South Haven Sentinal,* October 13, 1877.

17. *Chicago Inter Ocean,* October 15, 1877.

18. *South Haven Sentinal,* October 13, 1877.

19. Ibid., October 27, 1877.

20. For biographical information on Hans C. Heg, see Peter Cozzens, *This Terrible Sound* (Urbana: University of Illinois Press, 1992; Illini Books edition, 1996), 41 and 289–90.

21. *Association of Lake Underwriters* (Buffalo, NY: Printing House of Matthews & Warren, 1876), 55; *St. Joseph Traveler-Herald,* November 10, 1877.

22. *Detroit Free Press,* November 5, 1877; *St. Joseph Traveler-Herald,* November 3, 1877; Life-Saving Station Logs, Chicago District, St. Joseph Station, October 30, 1877, RG 26, NARA—Great Lakes Region (Chicago).

23. Ibid.

24. *Detroit Free Press,* November 1 and 3, 1877.

25. *St. Joseph Traveler-Herald,* September 21, 1878.

26. Ibid. I am indebted to an experienced sailor, Rick Seymour of South Lyon, Michigan, for his interpretations of the documentary evidence and his insights into the circumstances surrounding the *Mary's* loss.

27. Ibid.

28. Ibid.

29. *St. Joseph Traveler-Herald,* November 8, 1879; *The Inter Ocean* (Chicago), November 3, 1879.

30. Ibid.; Life-Saving Station Logs, Chicago District, St. Joseph Station, November 2, 1879, RG 26, NARA—Great Lakes Region (Chicago).

31. Ibid.

32. Ibid.

33. *Portrait and Biographical Record of Berrien and Cass Counties, Michigan* (Chicago: Biographical Publishing Company, 1893), 331; *St. Joseph Traveler-Herald,* July 25, 1874.

34. The definitive history of the Goodrich Company is James L. Elliott, *Red Stacks over the Horizon: The Story of the Goodrich Steamboat Line* (Grand Rapids, MI: William B. Eerdmanns Publishing Co., 1967).

35. Frederick Stonehouse, *Went Missing,* vol. 2 (Au Train, MI: Avery Color Studios, 1984), 138.

36. James L. Elliott, 58–59.

37. Dwight Boyer, *Ghost Ships of the Great Lakes* (New York: Dodd, Mead & Company, 1968), 186; *St. Joseph Traveler-Herald,* March 13, 1880.

38. William Ratigan, *Great Lakes Shipwrecks & Survivals* (Grand Rapids, MI: William B. Eerdmanns Publishing Co., 1960; rev. ed., 1977), 70.

39. Ibid.

40. *St. Joseph Traveler-Herald,* October 28, 1880.

41. Ibid.

42. Ibid.

43. Ibid.

44. *Holland City News,* October 23, 1880.

45. *St. Joseph Traveler-Herald,* October 28, 1880.

46. *The Chicago Tribune,* October 21, 1880; *Chicago Daily News,* October 23, 1880. The term "wrecker" applied to people who salvaged the cargo of ships that wrecked.

47. *The Chicago Tribune,* October 21, 1880.

48. Ibid., November 13 and December 4 and 11, 1880.

49. *The St. Joseph Saturday Herald,* November 6, 1880; Life-Saving Station Logs, Chicago District, St. Joseph Station, November 1, 1880, RG 26, NARA— Great Lakes Region (Chicago).

50. Ibid.; United States Life-Saving Service, *Annual Report of the Operations of the United States Life-Saving Service for the Fiscal Year Ending June 30, 1881* (Washington, DC: Government Printing Office, 1882), 125.

51. *Annual Report of the Life-Saving Service for 1881,* 129; *Detroit Free Press,* November 2, 1880; *The Daily Inter Ocean* (Chicago), November 2, 1880; Life-Saving Station Logs, Chicago District, St. Joseph Station, November 1, 1880, NARA—Great Lakes Region (Chicago).

52. *Classification, Association of Lake Underwriters* (Buffalo, NY: Printing House of Matthews & Warren, 1876), 128; Lake Hull Registration of Lake Underwriters (Detroit: Free Press Book and Job Printing House, 1879), 138.

53. *Detroit Free Press,* November 9, 1880.

54. *St. Joseph Saturday Herald,* November 13, 1880; United States Life-Saving Service, *Annual Report of the Operations of the United States Life-Saving Service for the Fiscal Year Ending June 30, 1881* (Washington, DC: Government Printing Office, 1882), 129; Life-Saving Station Logs, Chicago District, St. Joseph Station, November 7, 1880, RG 26, NARA—Great Lakes Region (Chicago).

55. *Annual Report of the Life-Saving Service, 1881,* 129.

56. *St. Joseph Saturday Herald,* November 13, 1880; *Detroit Free Press,* November 9, 1880.

57. Biographical information on John King appeared in his obituary in *The Daily Evening Herald* (St. Joseph, MI), June 10, 1882.

58. An extensive account of the *Industry* wreck appeared in *The Daily Evening Herald,* June 5, 1882.

59. Donahue's account of the disaster is in James Donahue to Capt. Nathaniel Robbins, June 5, 1882, in *The Daily Evening Herald,* June 7, 1882. Robbins was the superintendent of the U. S. Life-Saving Service in St. Joseph.

60. Keeper's Log of the Light House Station at South Haven, 1872–1889, June 3, 1882, A-318, Regional History Collections, Western Michigan University, Kalamazoo, Michigan.

61. *The Daily Evening Herald,* June 7, 1882.

62. Ibid.; Keeper's Log of the Light House Station at South Haven, 1872–1889, June 3, 1882. The *Industry* may also have caught in a fisherman's "pound net," one of many then fastened along the shore. She was found entangled in one when finally beached, and James King blamed the net for its capsizing. *The Daily Evening Herald,* June 8, 1882. A pound net was a net structure used to trap fish and held upright by stakes, usually in shallow water; see Timothy C. Lloyd and Patrick B. Mullen, *Lake Erie Fishermen: Work, Identity, and Tradition* (Urbana: University of Illinois Press, 1990), 7.

63. *The Daily Evening Herald,* June 5 and 7, 1882.

64. Ibid., June 17–27, 1882.

65. *St. Joseph Saturday Traveler-Herald,* December 9, 1882; *The Detroit Free Press,* December 3, 1882.

66. Ibid.

67. *St. Joseph Saturday Herald,* November 3, 1883; Life-Saving Station Logs, Chicago Branch, St. Joseph Station, October 31, 1883, RG 26, NARA—Great Lakes Region (Chicago).

68. *St. Joseph Saturday Herald,* November 10 and 17, 1883.

69. Ibid., November 17, 1883; United States Life-Saving Service, *Annual Report of the Operations of the United States Life-Saving Service for the Fiscal Year Ending June 30, 1884* (Washington, DC: Government Printing Office, 1885), 21.

70. *Annual Report of the United States Lifesaving Service, 1884,* 21.

71. Ibid.

72. Ibid., 22.

73. Ibid.

74. Ibid.

75. Ibid; Richard Gebhart, "The Chaptered Loss of the H. C. Akeley," *Soundings* (Spring 1994): 4.

76. *Annual Report of the United States Lifesaving Service, 1884,* 22.

77. Ibid., 22–23.

78. Ibid., 23.

79. Ibid.; *St. Joseph Saturday Herald,* November 17, 1883.

80. *Annual Report of the United States Lifesaving Service, 1884,* 24.

81. Ibid.

82. Ibid., 24-25.

83. Ibid., 25.

84. Ibid., 25-26.

85. Ibid., 26.

86. Ibid.

87. Ibid, 26-27.

88. Ibid., 27.

89. David Miller's account of the *Akeley* disaster, published in the Inter-Ocean (Chicago) is reprinted in Kit Lane, *Lake Michigan Shipwrecks: South Haven to Grand Haven,* Saugatuck Maritime Series, bk. 4 (Douglas, MI: Pauilion Press, 1997), 77.

90. Ibid.; *St. Joseph Saturday Herald,* November 17, 1883; Wes Oleszewski, *Mysteries and Histories: Shipwrecks of the Great Lakes* (Marquette, MI: Avery Color Studios, 1997), 19.

91. Wes Oleszewski, *Mysteries and Histories,* 20; *Blue Book of American Shipping* (Cleveland: Marine Review, 1897), 45; *South Haven to Grand Haven,* 81–82. Daniel Miller's gold medal is in the collections of the Tri-Cities Historical Museum in Grand Haven, Michigan.

92. *Detroit Free Press,* November 18, 1883.

93. Ibid.; *St. Joseph Traveler-Herald,* November 17, 1883.

94. *Detroit Free Press,* November 29, 1883.

95. *St. Joseph Traveler-Herald,* November 17, 1883.

96. Ibid., December 15, 1883.

Shipwrecks of the Gilded Age

Havana, 1887

Alonzo P. Read had a terrible month. The Kenosha, Wisconsin, ship owner went into the fall of 1887 with four fine vessels: the *Havana, City of Green Bay, D. S. Austin,* and *Myosotis.* By mid-November, three of them lay on the bottom of Lake Michigan, and the *D. S. Austin* had sustained damage to the tune of $12,000.

The ill fortune of the Badger State captain started on Sunday evening, October 3, 1887. At about 7:00 P.M. that evening, a pounding thunderstorm swept through southwest Michigan, driven by a northwest gale that continued through the next two days. Among the ships caught in the storm were the iron-ore schooners *Havana* and *City of Green Bay,* both of which had sailed out of Escanaba for St. Joseph on the preceding Thursday with 551 and 655 tons of iron ore, respectively.[1]

The *Havana* carried a crew of seven: Capt. John Curran; First Mate Samuel McClemant; the cook, John Morse; and seamen Joseph Clint (a cousin of Captain Curran), Charles Hagen, George Hughes, and Robert H. McCormick. All but Morse, a Benton Harbor resident, hailed from Chicago. Curran, a thirty-three-year-old Irishman from Ballyhalbert in County Down, had emigrated to America in 1872 with his father James and brothers James, Thomas, and Robert. The father and all four brothers sailed the Great Lakes. Curran had sailed as mate aboard the schooner *Ada Medora* and in 1886 won command of the *Havana.*[2]

A large crowd had gathered in Oswego, New York, sixteen years earlier, on August 14, 1871, to watch the *Havana's* launch. Spectators occupied every available vantage point and jostled each other for position along the Delaware & Hudson Coal Company trestle at the harbor on Lake Erie. They watched through the hot afternoon as shipyard workers scurried around the foot of East Second Street where they had spent the summer building the schooner. The workmen finally completed their preparations and knocked out the last blocks holding back the *Havana*, and the Great Lakes' newest ship slid gracefully down the ways into the water as the crowd roared its approval. The schooner joined Thomas S. Mott's fleet of four ships: the *Florida, J. H. Gilmore, H. Fitzhugh,* and *J. T. Mott.*[3]

By the fateful fall of 1887, Alonzo Read had purchased the *Havana* and employed her in shipping iron ore. Read decided to risk all four of his ships in late-season runs and paid heavily for his audacity. Savaged by the storm, the *Havana* arrived off St. Joseph about midnight on Sunday, dropped anchor, and hoisted a distress signal. Lake Michigan poured through leaks in her hull as all hands labored mightily at the pumps and bailed with buckets, but the water kept rising in the hold. Early on Sunday morning as the storm still raged, Captain Curran decided to beach the *Havana*. The crew slipped her cable and used the ship's remaining three jibs (the fore and aft sails had been lost during the night) to guide the vessel toward shore about six miles north of the St. Joseph harbor.[4]

They nearly made it. Within a mile of the beach, at 9:00 A.M., the *Havana* struck the bottom, broke in the middle, and sank. As she went under, the schooner's mainmast snapped off and its stump shot twenty-five feet into the air. Captain Curran, John Morse, and Joseph Clint went overboard with the mainmast. One man who fell into the lake never came up again, while the other two clung to some of the fore rigging and disappeared to the northward, adrift in the wreckage. The remaining four crewmen scrambled up the foremast to its cross-trees, which stuck out just above the water.[5] They held tightly to the cross-trees and rigging as the wind whipped around them and the waves tried to lash them from their perch.

The *Havana* escaped the immediate attention of the St. Joseph Life-Saving Service crew. Capt. William L. Stevens had led his men to the rescue of the small schooner *Harvey Ransom,* of South Haven, which had run for the safety of the St. Joseph harbor early on Monday morning. The *Ransom* broke her rudder as she came into port, struck the south pier, and, after rounding the pier, went aground on the beach. The two-man crew escaped to safety and *Ransom* was pulled off the beach a few days later, but the rescue had distracted Stevens and his life savers. Not until they returned from the *Ransom* did the station lookout notice the wrecked *Havana.*[6]

The lookout spotted the *Havana's* distress signal while she still floated at anchor. Stevens eyed the stiff northwest gale and pounding waves, and quickly decided "it was out of the question to row a boat so far to windward in such a wind." He ran into St. Joseph instead and hunted up Capt. Charles Mollhagen who owned the fishing tug *Hannah Sullivan,* which Stevens considered the only tug in the harbor capable of towing his surfboat through the waves. Mollhagen agreed to help as soon as he could fire up the *Sullivan's* boilers and load more coal.[7]

Stevens returned to the life-saving station where the lookout told him that the *Havana* had now slipped her cable and was heading for the shore. The commander ordered out the beach apparatus and sent one crewman ahead with instructions to find a team of horses and rendezvous with the other life savers; in the meantime, Stevens, the other crewmen, and some citizen volunteers pulled the equipment up the beach toward the *Havana.* They lugged the gear four miles up the coast before the team caught up to them. A mile further on they reached the steep bluffs overlooking the lake. There they spotted the wrecked schooner about a mile from shore and sunk in forty feet of water. Stevens saw that the mainmast had disappeared, and the remaining rigging appeared deserted. The life savers dropped the beach apparatus and ran ahead to find out if the crew had made it to shore. When nearly opposite the wreck, they spotted survivors clinging to the foremast.

Stevens had a crew and life-saving gear on hand, but no way to reach across a mile of wild waves to save the stranded sailors. He

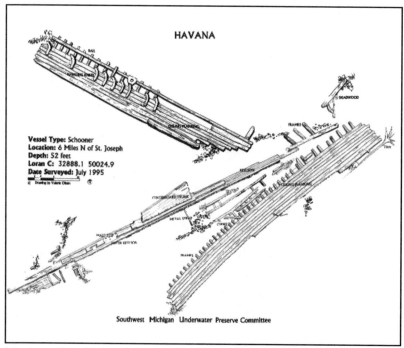

Wreckage of the *Havana* lies scattered across the floor of Lake Michigan near St. Joseph. *(Courtesy of the Southwest Michigan Underwater Preserve Committee)*

hired three rigs, and he and his crew sent their horses galloping back to town to fetch the lifeboat. Twenty minutes before they arrived, Mollhagen and the *Hannah Sullivan* steamed out of the harbor toward the wreck.

Captain Mollhagen and the *Sullivan's* engineer, August Keuhn, had rounded up a scratch crew of volunteer rescuers: Engineer John Carrow of the tug *Artemus Ward*, Capt. John Langley, Louis and Robert Mollhagen, and Alex Crau. With its makeshift crew aboard, the *Hannah Sullivan* set off on a wild, pitching ride through the Lake Michigan storm. They arrived at the wrecked *Havana* in late morning, pulled the four exhausted survivors off the foremast, and steamed triumphantly back into St. Joseph harbor at noon. With the survivors safely off the *Havana*, Captain Stevens sent two of his lifesaving crew to the beach with orders to patrol the shoreline and search for the missing sailors until all the wreckage came ashore.[8]

Captain Curran, John Morse, and Joseph Clint all perished in the disaster, and the *Havana's* survivors bitterly denounced the St. Joseph Life-Saving crew when they returned to Chicago. First Mate Samuel McClemant charged that the lifesavers could have saved the schooner's entire crew had Captain Stevens's men responded promptly to their distress signal. Perhaps unaware of the life savers' response to the *Harvey Ransom*, McClemant complained that Stevens never tried to help the *Havana* until after she went to the bottom.[9] The *St. Joseph Herald*, anxious to preserve hometown pride and reputations, interviewed several local ship captains and came away assured that "Capt. Stevens and his crew acted promptly and did all that it was possible for them to do in this instance."[10]

Meanwhile, A. P. Read's schooner *City of Green Bay* came to grief near South Haven. As the *Havana's* crew fought for their lives at St. Joseph, the *Green Bay* lurched into the bar outside the South Haven harbor just before dawn on October 3, then pounded slowly along the bottom of the lake until she grounded 185 yards from shore. The South Haven Life-Saving-Station crew made a valiant effort to save the crew of seven men, but their exertions went for naught and they could only watch helplessly as the *Green Bay's* crew plunged one by one into the wild surf. In the end, only one crewman lived to tell the story: A. T. Slater of St. Joseph. His six crewmates—Capt. P. W. Costello, First Mate Frank Wood, cook Patrick O'Leary, and seamen Henry Barkett, John Williams, and Thomas Hoitman—all drowned. The Life-Saving Service, in its official report, lauded station captain Barney A. Cross's personal courage, but excoriated his professional judgment in coping with this, the first serious shipwreck that had occurred on his watch at the South Haven station. The report found that, overwhelmed by the responsibility resting on his shoulders, "he completely lost his head and committed a succession of blunders which turned an easy prospective victory into a disastrous defeat and cost the lives of six men."[11]

Rumors circulated after the disaster that the *Havana's* loss was due in part to her being overloaded. McClemant emphatically denied that allegation, pronouncing the schooner "in splendid trim" and stating that she had carried forty tons less cargo than on any other voyage that season. Two weeks prior to the disaster, he said, A. P. Read had written to all his ship captains and instructed them to reduce the cargoes they carried. McClemant learned through inquiries that the captains had obeyed those orders and that the *City of Green Bay* had carried twenty tons less than her usual load.[12]

Two members of John Curran's family arrived in St. Joseph a few days after the storm and began a forlorn and unsuccessful search for the crew's bodies. A. P. Read suffered a financial disaster in the gale. The *Havana* herself, valued at $8,000, was insured for only $4,500, with another $2,250 on her cargo.[13]

The *Hannah Sullivan's* courageous crew all won life-saving medals from the United States government for their efforts on behalf of the *Havana's* sailors. That November, Nathaniel Robbins of South Haven, superintendent of the Eleventh District Life-Saving Service, presented gold medals to Charles Mollhagen and August Keuhn and silver medals to the other seven crewmen. Each medal, appropriately inscribed with the recipient's name and the date and occasion of the award, bore the inscription "In testimony of heroic deeds in saving life from the perils of the sea."[14]

Myosotis, 1887

Alonzo P. Read's run of bad luck that had started with the loss of his ships *Havana* and *City of Green Bay* concluded with the wreck of the schooner *Myosotis*.

The *Myosotis* got her name from the flowering plant *Myosotis scorpioides*, better known as the forget-me-not. She was one of what sailors called a "canaller," a centerboard schooner of the largest class built for the Welland Canal trade, and those who sailed the lakes thought her a "staunch, seaworthy craft…as good as any similar vessel on the lake." Milwaukee Ship Yard launched the *Myosotis* in 1874 and Captain Read bought her for the 1885 shipping season.[15]

The *Myosotis* sailed out of Escanaba bound for St. Joseph in early November 1887 with six hundred tons of iron ore consigned to the Spring Lake Iron Company. Unfavorable winds forced Capt.

John Maloney to put in to Chicago on Tuesday, November 8, but when a pleasant breeze sprang up on Thursday, he started across the lake. It was about 5:00 P.M. when the *Myosotis* headed out of the Windy City into a pretty November afternoon; during the night the weather turned violent, and a stiff northwest wind churned up white-caps on Lake Michigan. The storm caught the *Myosotis* when she had already traveled twenty-five miles, so Captain Maloney elected to continue on to St. Joseph.[16]

The *Myosotis* crew caught the welcome flash of the St. Joseph light late that evening. The waves seemed to settle down as they neared the shore and Captain Maloney breathed a sigh of relief as he steered a course between the two piers. Just outside the harbor at 1:25 A.M., with safe shelter barely five hundred feet away, a huge sea smashed the heavily laden schooner into the outer bar. The impact stopped her way, and before she could regather speed two or three more big seas slammed into her. The *Myosotis* sheered off to the southward and lurched out of control. The waves drove her stern-first toward the shore until she grounded 150 yards from the beach.[17]

Life-saving-station surfman Richard Stines had lookout duty that night and saw the *Myosotis* run aground. His fellow surfmen tumbled out of bed at the sound of the alarm gong and five min-utes later had the station's surfboat in the water. Capt. William Stevens and his men pulled mightily around the south pier to ren-der assistance, only to see the *Myosotis* crew heading for the beach in the schooner's yawl. Captain Maloney and his crew had kept their wits about them and in the pitch-black storm swung out the yawl, climbed aboard, and lowered away. The wild seas gave them a rough ride, but they made the shore in one piece. They reached safety just as the surfboat crunched into the sand beside them. The life savers helped them pull the yawl onto the beach and escorted them to the station, where Stevens's wife, Ella, prepared a hot sup-per.[18] "They left the station at 7A.M.," Captain Stevens reported, "feeling very thankful" for the dry berth and dinner.[19]

The *Myosotis*'s men stayed in St. Joseph for a day to recover their personal effects from the wreck. Captain Stevens and his crew rowed

The three-masted schooner *Myosotis* lies wrecked near St. Joseph, Michigan, on November 11, 1887. *(Courtesy of the Historical Collections of the Great Lakes, Bowling Green State University)*

them out to the *Myosotis* the next day, but they found the ship's hull smashed in and the cabin awash in water and rubbish and could find only a portion of their clothing and gear. An insurance agent came over from Chicago and hired a local contractor, John M. Allmendinger, to salvage the wreck. Allmendinger took advantage of good weather on Sunday, November 13, to pull off the schooner's rigging and everything movable that was of value and packed it away in a Graham & Morton Transportation Company warehouse in Benton Harbor.[20]

The *Myosotis* wreck nearly led to a second disaster. Will Bradford of Benton Harbor sailed out in his sloop *Mamie* on Sunday afternoon to examine the wreck while Allmendinger and his crew labored to salvage the vessel. Rough water at the end of the piers tossed the *Mamie* violently about, thumping her into the north pier and rolling her around until a frightened Captain Bradford hoisted a distress signal. The life-saving-station crew responded and towed the sloop back into calmer water.[21]

Alonzo Read, the *Myosotis's* owner, took a heavy loss on his ship. The thirteen-year-old vessel, valued at $8,000, carried only $4,800 in insurance, although her cargo was fully insured.[22] Like so many Great Lakes vessels that sank only to rise again, Captain Read recovered from the loss of his four ships and went right back into business. He moved from Kenosha to Chicago about 1895, where he expanded his business and had five ships sailing out of the Windy City. He finally retired from the shipping trade and died in 1915 at age seventy-four.[23]

Joseph P. Farnam, 1889

At about two o'clock on Saturday afternoon, July 20, 1889, Capt. Loren G. Vosburgh's wife roused him in their cabin. "What makes it so smoky?" she asked. Captain Vosburgh jumped out of bed and hurried onto the deck only to see flames already bursting through the skylight over the ship's engine room.[24] The steambarge *Joseph P. Farnam* was doomed.

The *Farnam* had discharged her cargo at St. Joseph and steamed out of the harbor at eight o'clock that morning, setting a course for the Death's Door passage and her destination of Escanaba, Michigan. The *Farnam's* course took her directly into a strong north-northwest wind and the wind, heavy seas, and the steambarge's own underpowered engine meant that the *Farnam* made but little progress on her northward track. Captain Vosburgh estimated that by early afternoon she had put only seventeen miles behind her, averaging just under three miles per hour.[25]

William Kibbe, on watch at the South Haven Life-Saving-Station tower, watched the steamer proceeding up the lake. Kibbe noted that the ship appeared to be about twenty miles out but paid no attention to her. Walter Boardman relieved Kibbe in the tower at four o'clock and occasionally had the *Farnam* in sight. About forty-five minutes after his watch began, Boardman was surprised to see that the vessel had altered course and appeared to be heading for the South Haven harbor. A half hour later she changed course again, this time southward, and as she turned broadside to him, Boardman could see that two of her three masts had vanished. With a thrill of horror, he suddenly realized that the smoke he had seen boiling up from the steamer came not from her stack but from the entire ship and that the whole vessel was afire. He instantly raised the alarm and called the life-saving-station commander, John H. McKenzie, who in turn raced down to the dock and summoned Capt. John Boyne of the little steamer *Glenn.* Would Boyne and the *Glenn,* he asked, tow the station's surfboat on a rescue mission?[26]

When Vosburgh ran onto the deck that afternoon, he found the mate already dropping a fire hose onto the main deck, but flames surrounded the hose's donkey pump and rendered the effort useless. Vosburgh next turned to the ship's lifeboat, which he described as in excellent condition and large enough to accommodate the whole crew, but it was slung across the engine room hatch and the fire enveloped it within three minutes of the time the flames first appeared.[27]

Captain Vosburgh had no choice but to abandon ship. His crew quickly set to work improvising rafts from hatch covers and planks and slipped over the side. Miraculously, every man made it safely overboard. By the time they escaped, flames had enveloped the steamer from bow to stern; the last raft, with eight men on it, clung to the *Farnam* until the hawser tethering it to the ship burned off. Captain, wife, and crew watched from their rafts as the *Farnam* burned. The abandoned ship drifted southeast back along the course she had come. Sometime around five o'clock that afternoon, the wind shifted into the northeast and the *Farnam's* funeral pyre, pushed ahead by wind and current, raced down the lake at an astonishing speed.[28]

At the South Haven docks, Captain Boyne explained that any rescue attempt would be delayed, for the *Glenn* had no steam up. Her engineer, Sam Johns, went at his work with a will and by 6:10 P.M. his boat had twenty pounds of steam in her boiler. A few minutes later she was plowing her way out of the harbor, the surfboat plunging along behind, with eighty-five pounds of steam driving her along at a speed approaching fifteen miles per hour. An hour later, the life-saving crew and those aboard the *Glenn* spotted the *Farnam's* burning hull and began scouring the area for survivors.[29]

While the *Glenn* searched, the rafts bearing Captain and Mrs. Vosburgh and the crew followed the *Farnam* southward down the lake. They lost sight of South Haven but drifted along so rapidly that they soon spied St. Joseph. By the light of the setting sun, they made out the pier lighthouse and the massive white form of Plank's Tavern, a huge new hotel closely resembling Mackinac Island's famous Grand Hotel and built by the Grand's owner, John O. Plank.[30]

The survivors were in a desperate situation. They were waist-deep in water on rafts hastily cobbled together from doors, fenders, and hatch covers—rafts that would almost surely fall apart during the night and leave them to drown. Daylight ebbed away, and with it went their chances of rescue. As the sun's last rays painted the early evening sky, the survivors felt a surge of hope. Out of the north came the *Glenn* with the surfboat trailing behind. The survivors waved and screamed frantically, managing to attract the searcher's attention just as darkness set in, and a jubilant and grateful Captain Vosburgh later reported "at 8:30 all my crew were safe aboard the *Glenn.*"[31]

The *Glenn* returned the survivors to South Haven, where they found dry clothing and a place to spend the night. The *Farnam's* burned-out wreckage drifted with the wind until it sank somewhere off Benton Harbor.

Thomas Hume, 1891

Do the remains of the schooner *Thomas Hume* lie off New Buffalo? The vessel disappeared en route from Chicago to Muskegon in 1891 and none of her crew survived to tell her fate. Years later searchers discovered the grave of an unknown schooner, and, although they never identified the wreckage, it may well have been the *Hume.* The big lumber firm of Hackley & Hume owned both the *Thomas Hume* and the schooner *Rouse Simmons.* They left Chicago together on a stormy May evening, bound for Muskegon. Only the *Simmons* arrived in port and the *Hume's* disappearance remained a mystery.[32] Capt. Seth Lee of Muskegon, commanding the tug *Sills,* made a fruitless search for the missing schooner and opined that an outgoing ship from Chicago had accidentally run her down in the storm.[33]

Fourteen years later, in the fall of 1905, fishermen operating out of New Buffalo returned home complaining that underwater obstructions were snagging and ruining their nets. The Michigan

City Life-Saving-Station skipper, Allen A. Kent, decided to investigate and see if he could discover the source of the problem. He organized a diving team and early on Sunday morning, October 8, 1905, set out from port in the life-saving-station launch. The expedition included Kent, his son Ray, diver George E. Culbert, and Culbert's attendant, John Williams.[34]

Kent and his men hoped that their search would locate the fabled wreck of the Graham & Morton Transportation Company steamer *Chicora,* lost with all hands in January 1895. They located the site reported by the fishermen some two and one-half miles northwest of New Buffalo, but when George Culbert went down to examine the wreckage he found not a steamer but the remains of a three-masted schooner. The wreck lay in about fifty-six feet of water. Culbert described it as measuring 175 feet in length, but as its scrollwork was missing, he could not discover its name.[35] No one conclusively identified the wreck, but it seems probable that Kent and his men had found the grave of the *Thomas Hume* and her crew.

Chicora, 1895

When the Graham & Morton Transportation Company's *Chicora* steamed out of Milwaukee into a January 1895 blizzard, she entered a storm of controversy that not even the passage of over a century has quieted. Few Great Lakes shipwrecks have captured the public imagination to the same extent as the *Chicora.*[36]

In 1874, James Stanley Morton of Benton Harbor founded what would become the Graham & Morton Transportation Company when he entered the shipping business with the chartered steamer *Lake Breeze.* A year later, he joined forces with John H. Graham and Andrew Crawford to create the Graham & Morton Company. When Henry W. Williams, owner of the steamer *Skylark,* joined the firm in 1880, Graham & Morton became a stock company named the Graham & Morton Transportation Company. Graham & Morton prospered with the freight and passenger trade between Chicago and the twin cities of St. Joseph/Benton Harbor, and by 1890 the company owned two fine vessels, the *Puritan* and the *City of Chicago.*[37]

Graham & Morton opened negotiations with the Detroit Dry Dock Company of Detroit, Michigan, in 1891 to build a replacement for the *Puritan.* Late that December, company president John H. Graham returned triumphantly to Benton Harbor with a $110,000 contract for a propeller steamer that would be the *Chicora.*[38] Famed marine architect Frank E. Kirby designed the ship, which Detroit Dry Dock built at its Ocean Street yard. Graham & Morton named her for a Civil War ironclad ram, also named *Chicora,* that had fought in an epic battle against blockading Union ships in 1863. The ram had, in turn, received her name from the Chicora Indians, the aboriginal people of South Carolina. Graham & Morton sold the *Puritan* soon after contracting for the *Chicora,* assuming that their new ship would be finished by the spring shipping season, but construction delays forced Graham & Morton to charter the steamer *Arundel* for much of the 1892 season.[39]

At 3:00 P.M. on June 25, 1892, the *Chicora* slid down the ways into the Detroit River. Shipyard workers took another six weeks to install her boilers and machinery and finish the cabins. Shortly after midnight on August 13 the *Chicora* sailed out of Detroit and headed up Lake Huron. Capt. Levi Mann took her through the Straits of Mackinac and down Lake Michigan; at about six o'clock on Monday morning, August 15, she steamed into the St. Joseph harbor, greeted by a shrill chorus of tugboat and factory whistles. Only a few early risers had turned out to welcome her, but twin cities residents soon flocked to the Graham & Morton docks as news of her arrival spread.[40]

The new ship delighted her visitors. The *Chicora* featured a double wooden hull, the outer hull protected by steel guards that flared out just above the waterline to fend off the heavy slush ice that ships often encountered during the winter. Two massive steel boilers, twelve feet long and fourteen feet in diameter, supplied steam to a triple-expansion engine that boasted cylinders of 20, 33, and 54 inches in diameter and a 42-inch stroke. The engine turned a single screw that could propel the *Chicora* to a top speed of eighteen or nineteen miles per hour and a normal speed of fourteen miles per hour.[41]

The steamer *Chicora* shortly before her launch at the Detroit Dry Dock Company, 1892. *(Courtesy of the Steffke Memorial Maritime Collection—Keith M. Steffke)*

But the crowd admired more than the *Chicora's* great size. Mahogany-panelled walls and ceilings with fancy wood inlays graced the passenger staterooms, and plush carpeting covered the floors. Stateroom furnishings included beds, dressers, chairs, and writing tables, while the ship's dining room featured mahogany paneling and oak tables, chairs, and sideboards. The *Chicora's* staterooms accommodated two hundred passengers, and she carried an excursion license for fifteen hundred people. A magnificent one-hundred-foot-long arched ceiling covered the ship's main cabin and gangway. Passengers enjoyed such luxuries as a grand piano, leather upholstered chairs, and persian carpets. The *Chicora* gleamed throughout with electric lights.[42] In short, everyone proclaimed the *Chicora* the last word in comfort and speed, giving lie to the old adage that a shipboard voyage amounted to going to prison with a chance of being drowned.

The *Chicora* left St. Joseph on her maiden voyage at 4:30 P.M. on August 16, and arrived in Chicago exactly three hours and forty-nine minutes later. The officers were Capt. Edward Stines, First Mate William J. Russell, Second Mate George E. Leggett, First Engineer Robert McClure, Clerk William J. Hancock, and Steward

The Chicora's passenger salon, 1892. *(Courtesy of the Plee Family)*

Charles Springsteen. An additional fifteen or sixteen other crewmen served the ship's passengers or ran her boilers and engine.[43]

During the next two years, the *Chicora* steamed back and forth across Lake Michigan to Chicago, Ludington, and Milwaukee. A passenger from Niles reported weathering a storm on the ship in the spring of 1893 and had only praise for the vessel and her crew. "The waves in huge masses flung themselves against the boat to be dashed away in sheets of foam," he marveled, "and to the whole onslaught the graceful craft would grant only a stately roll and salutation. The *Chicora* is a splendid boat."[44]

Besides passengers, the *Chicora* carried untold thousands of tons of freight back and forth across the lake. During 1893, her first full year of service, she ran from April 3 to Christmas Eve and crossed Lake Michigan 214 times. The following year she made 196 trips to Chicago and 40 trips to Milwaukee.[45]

On January 12, 1895, Graham & Morton idled the *Chicora* at her St. Joseph dock due to lagging freight business and the slim winter passenger trade, and workmen placed the ship's furniture, carpets, and grand piano in storage. Early on the morning of January 19,

The *Chicora* entering the harbor at St. Joseph.
(Courtesy of the Fort Miami Heritage Society)

1895, John H. Graham received a telegram from the Big Four (Cleveland, Cincinnati, Chicago, and St. Louis) & Vandalia Railroad, notifying him that some thirty-eight carloads of flour and other miscellaneous freight, totaling 640 tons, awaited shipment in Milwaukee. Railroad officials asked him to put the *Chicora* back in service for one more run.[46]

Graham immediately contacted the *Chicora's* crew and told them to be ready to sail by noon the next day. Robert McClure, the chief engineer, arrived from Detroit by train that afternoon and set to work restarting the ship's boilers and engine. Second Mate William Russell had fallen ill, so Captain Stines's son Benjamin took his place. William Hancock, the clerk, missed his train from South Haven and a substitute, former Berrien County Sheriff James R. Clarke, went in his stead. A full crew of twenty-two officers and men took their stations by sailing time; Benton Harbor druggist Joseph F. Pearl elected to go along as the ship's sole passenger.[47]

Only one incident marred an otherwise uneventful trip to Milwaukee: Pearl, an avid sportsman, shot a duck while the *Chicora* lay off the Wisconsin port. The incident bothered Captain Stines, who perhaps remembered the Curse of the Ancient Mariner, and his dark mood communicated itself to the other crew members.[48]

That night the *Chicora* took on her cargo of flour and early the next morning made ready to sail. A light rain swept through and the wind began to pick up, but Captain Stines saw no reason to delay sailing. At 5:45 A.M. (Wisconsin time) the *Chicora* headed out into Lake Michigan. Soon afterward, the light southeasterly winds shifted to the south-southwest. The barometer readings plunged, as did the temperature. At the St. Joseph Life-Saving Station, Keeper William L. Stevens watched the conditions change from "Fresh SE wind, foggy weather, barometer 29.15, smooth surf, 40 degrees" at midnight to "strong SSW gale, cloudy weather, barometer 28.88, high surf, 32 degrees" at noon. The mid-morning's light breeze had become a howling blizzard with winds up to sixty miles per hour. Out on Lake Michigan, Captain Stines and his crew fought a bitter battle against the storm.[49]

The *Chicora's* schedule called for her to arrive in St. Joseph at 1:30 P.M. Michigan time. The hour came and went with no sign of the ship, and twin cities residents began to fear for her safety. Afternoon drifted into evening and still the *Chicora* failed to appear. Ice built up in huge layers and closed the harbor. While much of the city drifted off to sleep, John H. Graham kept a dark and lonely vigil in his house overlooking the lake, peering into the darkness in the forlorn hope of spotting his missing ship. On Tuesday morning, a thirty-five-mile-per-hour wind still shrieked through St. Joseph. Throughout Benton Harbor and St. Joseph, residents awaited word of the *Chicora*. Hopes rose and fell as unconfirmed reports came in from people along the shoreline, all claiming to have seen the vessel or heard her whistle.[50]

On late Wednesday afternoon, searchers found the first conclusive evidence of the ship's fate as debris began to wash up on the beaches. Graham received a message from Capt. Edward Napier, son of Nelson Napier of *Alpena* fame, who had been scouring the shoreline near South Haven: "We have just found some of the *Chicora's* upper works in the ice off this place. There is no doubt she has foundered."[51]

Searchers discovered more wreckage during the succeeding days: part of the pilot house, a passenger gangway frame, the clerk's office door, and other bits of flotsam. They did not, however, locate the *Chicora's* hull or the bodies of her crew. Then on Sunday, February 3, came electrifying news that people had sighted the *Chicora's* hull stuck in the ice a few miles off South Chicago, Illinois, and that they could see nineteen men moving about on it. William Hancock, the ship's regular clerk, rushed to the scene while John H. Graham made emergency preparations for the crew's rescue. Disappointment crushed Hancock when he trained his binoculars on the supposed wreck, for vivid imaginations had turned dark windrows of ice into a hull and a flock of seagulls into surviving crewmen.[52]

Despite intense efforts, searchers never found the *Chicora*, nor did they ever recover the bodies of any of her crew. What happened in the *Chicora's* final hours as she battled the storm may never be known.

Jesse Davis, an African-American porter, sailed with the *Chicora* on her final voyage. *(Courtesy of the Morton House)*

Captain Stines may have reached St. Joseph, found the harbor iced in, and tried without success to make South Haven. Or he may have apprehended the danger and turned his ship about for Milwaukee, only to be caught in the storm's full fury before reaching safety.

In many respects, the *Chicora's* loss left little room for romantic speculation. Marine experts debated the specific circumstances of her sinking, but the important facts remained obvious to all: the *Chicora* had fallen victim to a vicious January storm and sank somewhere on Lake Michigan. Even so, the *Chicora's* sinking took her to both the depths of Lake Michigan and the realm of folklore. Like other famous shipwrecks, popular culture kept the *Chicora* in the public eye long after the tragedy itself ceased to be a news story.

In *The Titanic: End of a Dream*, Wyn Craig Wade documented the songs, poems, motion pictures, and other popularized chronicles of the White Star liner's sinking in 1912. Musician Gordon Lightfoot enjoyed a hit in 1976 with his ballad "The Wreck of the *Edmund Fitzgerald*" which told of that ore freighter's loss on Lake Superior the previous year.[53]

In like manner, popular culture immortalized the *Chicora*. Nixon Waterman penned a syrupy poetic tribute to the ship and her crew. Entitled *Song and Sigh*, it began "Here's a song for the *Chicora*, for the beautiful *Chicora!*"[54] Other memorial poems included *The Lost Chicora*, by Frances Browning Owen; *The Chicora's*

Crew, by J. C. Shuler; and *The Brave Dead,* by J. L. Anderson of Battle Creek, which appeared in *The Daily Palladium.*[55] "Babe," a young Grand Haven poet, offered *The Wreck of the Chicora* for the *Grand Haven Evening News.*[56] W. C. Robey and Frank D. Smith composed an 1895 song, *The Ill-Fated Chicora,* that sang of the ship's final voyage in sentimental lyrics. "When the dreadful moment came," Robey and Smith assured their listeners, the *Chicora's* crew "stood with calm despair" and "Shoulder to shoulder, they calmly met their fate." The song attached no blame to John Graham for risking vessel and crew on a January run, for "Fate decreed they should not live in such an awful gale"; the chorus told that "Men so true and brave, within the ship *Chicora* met a sailor's honor'd grave."[57]

Businessmen also found ways to capitalize on the disaster. The *Benton Harbor Palladium* printed ten thousand copies of a special *Chicora* memorial edition and sold them faster than they could come off the presses. The Benton Harbor publishing firm of Chaddock & Smith offered 14" x 18" prints of the lost steamer, complete with images of the crew and passenger ("suitable for framing"), for twenty-five cents each. A local photographer, Harry Hughson, sold prints of the *Chicora* produced from his own negatives. Even Joseph Pearl's place of employment, Howard & Pearl's drugstore, displayed an original crayon picture of the *Chicora* to entice passers-by.[58]

Innumerable bottles containing purported messages from the *Chicora's* crew washed up on Lake Michigan beaches. Most were dismissed as hoaxes, but one message, found on April 14, 1895, seemed genuine. The scrawled note read: "All is lost. Could see land if not snowed and Blowed. engine give out. drifting to shore. In ice." The note bore Robert McClure's signature, under which appeared an apparent postscript: "Captain & Clerk are swept off and we have a hard time of it. 10:15 o'clock Good by."[59]

McClure's terse note could only hint at the terror and despair that must have run through the ship's crew, Robey and Smith's lyrics notwithstanding. If the message was genuine, the engineer must have spent his last hours in the engine room frantically working to keep his vessel alive. The rising storm annoyed him at first as the *Chicora* rolled in the gathering waves, but his concern changed to worry and then alarm. What happened to the engine can only be conjecture. Did it break down suddenly, or did McClure fight desperately to keep a faltering engine turning over, in the end watching helplessly as the pistons shuddered to a halt and the propeller stopped, leaving the *Chicora* adrift in the night at the storm's mercy? How long afterward did he work to restart the engine before giving up in despair?

At some point after he realized that the engine would never run again, McClure found an empty bottle, a scrap of paper, and a pencil and braced himself against a bulkhead to jot a message to whoever might find it. His despair comes through in his first words: "All is lost." He and the other crewmen stared into the night as they tried to see land through the swirling snow, perhaps hoping that the *Chicora* might run aground and be sighted in time for a life-saving service crew to rescue them. Then Captain Stines and Clerk James Clarke went overboard to their deaths in the freezing water. Shortly afterward, McClure scrawled the final words to his message, stuffed it into the bottle, jammed a stopper in the bottle's neck, and pitched it overboard into the storm.

Scores of people regaled friends and family with tales of how only a last-minute change of plans had saved them from taking passage on the *Chicora*. In early 1896, residents of Allegan County's Cheshire Township founded a little hamlet that they named Chicora in honor of the lost ship, and a small avenue in Chicago also bears the *Chicora's* name.[60]

The most bizarre episode related to the lost ship took place in the fall of 1896 when James Gustin, a Benton Harbor clairvoyant, presented John H. Graham with a most unusual document. Gustin claimed to have established communication with the *Chicora's* dead crew, who had agreed to divulge the wreck's location in exchange for Graham's payment of reward money to their heirs. Graham had offered a $10,000 reward to the finder of the *Chicora's* hull. According to Gustin's document, the crewmen had agreed to divide the reward money, with the largest share going to Captain Stines and each crewman taking a lesser amount. The crew, Gustin assured the

Graham & Morton president, had agreed to the division on their own accord, without his prompting, and had specified that the clairvoyant himself should receive $1,000 of the reward money for his efforts. Gustin claimed to have negotiated the business with Clerk James R. Clarke, whose spirit had visited him for the first time at two o'clock one morning. The agreement, dated August 31, 1896, bore the purported signatures of both Clarke and Captain Stines. A separate document revealed that the *Chicora* lay in one hundred and eighty feet of water a little over ten and one-half miles from the St. Joseph lighthouse. Whatever the true nature of Gustin's vision, the clairvoyant received no money and searchers never found the wreck.[61]

For Graham & Morton, the *Chicora's* loss made 1895 "the most disastrous in the history of this company."[62] The company lost the pride of its fleet and the crewmen aboard her, many of them long-time employees. Insurance companies usually refused to cover vessels that sailed after the regular shipping season because of the inherent risk of bad weather, so Graham & Morton had carried no insurance on their nearly new ship.[63] Moreover, the company felt itself obligated to pay the shippers $15,000 for the loss of their cargo of flour. Although Graham & Morton officials did not consider the company legally responsible for the cargo, they felt a moral obligation and paid the claim.[64]

The *Chicora's* sinking stunned people in southwest Michigan partly because of the heavy loss of life, but also because it occurred at a time when Americans felt that technological progress had conquered Nature. Scarcely a year earlier, twenty-seven million people had toured the Colombian Exposition in Chicago, an 1893 world's fair that showcased human progress on the eve of a new century. The Exposition, staged in the fabulous White City built on the shores of Lake Michigan, valorized technology and its ability to overcome all natural obstacles. Indeed, the introduction of such marvels as electric lights, telephones, and phonographs into American households provided tangible proof of the triumph of technology. Societal problems, many people believed, would disappear with the application of scientific wonders. The *Chicora* herself, upon whose decks many fairgoers had traveled to the Exposition, served as a floating example of technological and maritime progress. Her loss doubly shocked residents of the Great Lakes states, for it revealed the frailty of man-made technology in the face of nature's adversity.[65]

The *Chicora* still lies at the bottom of Lake Michigan, her officers and men most likely resting with her. While she survives in the legends and folklore that grew out of her last day of life on the Great Lakes, the mystery of her loss remains as great as on that fateful night of January 21, 1895.

City of Duluth, 1898

The sandbars off St. Joseph harbor wrecked many ships, and both crew and passengers often lost their lives. Although the harbor frequently became the scene of tragedy, it also witnessed great heroism when the St. Joseph Life-Saving-Station crew came to the rescue. Life-Saving Service men possessed enormous dedication, for they often gambled—or gave—their lives for their meager government pay. Sometimes they risked everything for no monetary compensation at all, as occurred when they saved the passengers and crew of the *City of Duluth*.

At 2:30 P.M. on Wednesday, January 26, the 1,310-ton propeller steamer *City of Duluth* sailed out of Chicago for St. Joseph with a cargo of 28,000 bushels of corn, ten carloads of flour, and four carloads of general merchandise. Twenty-four crewmen manned the vessel and seventeen passengers elected to make the mid-winter voyage.[66]

Philander Lester had built the *City of Duluth* in 1874 at Marine City, Michigan, for Eber B. Ward of Detroit. Ward's business failed before he finished the steamer, but Sam Gardner and C. C. Blodgett, both of Detroit, bought and completed the ship. They later sold her to John Pridgeon, Sr., who had her rebuilt in Buffalo, New York, in 1887, putting nearly $50,000 into her hull.[67] Pridgeon then sold her to Albert T. Spencer of Waukegan, Illinois, and Capt. Lyman Hunt of Buffalo. Spencer and Hunt, together with Samuel F. Leopold of Chicago and Joseph Austrian of Hancock, Michigan, formed the Lake Michigan and Lake Superior Transportation Company, which owned her in 1898. That fall the Graham & Morton Transportation Company leased the *City of Duluth* from Lake Michigan and Lake Superior Transportation Company to help carry cargo from Chicago to St. Joseph/Benton Harbor.[68]

John H. Graham, president of Graham & Morton, telegraphed the *Duluth's* skipper, Capt. Donald MacLean of Chicago, on the morning of January 26 and advised him not to leave Chicago later than noon or else wait until 11:30 that evening so as to arrive at St. Joseph during daylight. Undoubtedly the Graham & Morton president recalled that his steamer *Chicora* had vanished almost three years to the day before the *Duluth's* intended voyage, and under strikingly similar circumstances: a January run across Lake Michigan into deteriorating weather. Graham, however, left the decision to sail up to MacLean, and Joseph Austrian pressured the captain to sail that afternoon. Graham may have leased the *Duluth,* but Austrian, her owner, outranked him; the *City of Duluth* departed Chicago at 2:15 P.M.[69]

MacLean must have questioned the wisdom of making a midwinter run that would end in an attempt to enter the harbor at night. The *Duluth* had run aground only three weeks before at the St. Joseph harbor mouth, stuck fast on a sandbar and in the ice just off the north pier. The tug *Andy* had labored fruitlessly all day to pull her off. Graham & Morton finally sent out the steamer *City of Louisville,* which took off enough of the *Duluth's* cargo to lighten her and allow her to struggle over the bar.[70]

Nevertheless, the *City of Duluth* made an uneventful trip across the lake and arrived outside the St. Joseph harbor at about 8:15 P.M., well after dark. The steamer *City of Traverse* had already come to grief trying to enter the harbor that same morning, tearing her rudder off on a new sandbar that had formed in front of the harbor entrance. A strong southwest wind had blown up and formed moderately heavy seas, but Captain MacLean felt confident that he could bring his ship into port without assistance. Passengers watched the lights of St. Joseph with a feeling of security as MacLean slowly eased the *Duluth* into the harbor mouth. Then a sickening jar shook the ship and her crew realized that the *Duluth* had struck bottom on the same bar that had snagged the *City of Traverse*. Captain MacLean ordered the *Duluth's* engines at full speed ahead in hopes that the next swell would lift the steamer up over the bar and into deeper water. Black smoke poured from the funnel and she trembled with the pounding of her engines as the propeller thrashed the water. Instead of lifting with the waves, the steamer grounded firmly on the bottom. The *Duluth* lay stranded for over an hour, then broke free at about 11:00 P.M. Wind and waves swept her northward several hundred feet until she grounded on a newly formed bar.[71]

The steamer slowly swung around, pivoting on her bow until her stern pointed at the St. Joseph pier, and there she stayed as the wind and waves pounded against her. Frightened passengers heard windows breaking as ominous creaks and groans rose up from the depths of the ship's hull. The *City of Duluth* was dying, and her death grieved Henry Chalk. Chalk, a Chicagoan and the chief engineer, had tended the ship for eighteen years, coming aboard for the first time in 1880 when she was young. To him the steamer was an old friend. For much of his adult life Chalk had kept the *Duluth's* engines in good running order, but now she lay stranded and slowly dying and neither he nor any one of the crew could save her. As all aboard waited for the inevitable, the ship slowly settled deeper. The starboard arch gave way, her steam pipes split, and then with a great rending groan the vessel broke amidships and filled with water over her main decks. The rising water extinguished the boiler fires and snuffed out her life, rendering the *City of Duluth* entirely helpless. Although in grave danger, the ship's passengers refused to panic. Ship's steward Edward Nolan passed around hot coffee and everyone awaited assistance.[72]

The first rescuers on the scene were the crew of the Graham & Morton Company tug *Andy*. The *Andy's* skipper maneuvered alongside the *City of Duluth* and made several attempts to get a line out to the stricken steamer, but the wind and waves overwhelmed them. At last the tug fled to safety, leaving the passengers and crew still aboard the steamer.

In the meantime, William L. Stevens of the life-saving station and Capt. Lloyd Clark of the lighthouse supply station kept close

The broken *City of Duluth* lies in the ice off St. Joseph's north pier on January 27, 1898.
(Courtesy of the Morton House)

One of the photographs of the wrecked *City of Duluth* offered for sale to tourists.
(Courtesy of the Plee Family)

watch on the grounded steamer. At last, seeing that the *City of Duluth's* plight had grown desperate, Stevens called out the station crew. The life-saving station had closed down for the winter but the off-duty crewmen "responded just as promptly and cheerfully and bravely as though under government pay."[73]

With the help of twenty-five to thirty volunteers, composed of citizens of St. Joseph and Benton Harbor and the crews of the *City of Traverse* and the *City of Louisville,* the life-saving crew hauled their equipment a half mile through the snow to the lighthouse pier. Ice coated the north pier and had built up in a huge mound near its end, forcing the men to scale the slippery mountain with lines, mortar, and breeches buoy as the wind howled around them. A careless misstep would plunge a man down into the frigid water and probable death, yet one by one the life-saving crewmen climbed up and over in the darkness until they got their equipment assembled at the end of the wind- and water-swept pier. They loaded the Lyle gun and fired a line to the *Duluth,* but high winds carried the shot away into the darkness. The men reloaded and their second shot landed squarely across the *Duluth.* Crewmen aboard the wrecked steamer quickly fastened the line to the ship's rudderpost at the stern, and the life-saving crew rigged up the breeches buoy and sent it across through the dark. A passenger, August Kernwein of St. Joseph, made the first trip from the *Duluth,* alighting safely on the pier at 1:30 A.M.[74]

One by one, passengers rode the breeches buoy to safety. The line's slack let each person drop waist deep into the freezing water, with the added danger of being smashed by floating ice cakes. One cake carried the line away as Robert Tripp of South Haven came across on the buoy and for a terrifying moment the life savers thought they had lost him, but with a frantic effort they reeled him in.[75]

As the passengers landed on the pier and climbed stiffly out of the breeches buoy, willing hands helped them into the foghorn station at the pier's end where they thawed out before a hot fire. Captain Stevens's wife greeted them with food and hot drinks, and Dr. Alexander H. Scott, Jr., tended those who needed medical attention. August Kernwein had brought word that one passenger, seventy-one-year-old Mary E. Tryon of Berrien County's Royalton Township, was an invalid returning from Chicago where she had undergone medical treatment. Mrs. Tryon, he said, "wanted one of the Life Saving Boys to come out and take her ashore."[76] Surfman Charles Roberts rode the breeches buoy out to the wreck to assist her. Captain MacLean, seeing that she could not walk, hoisted her in his arms, carried her up a ladder and deposited her in the breeches buoy, and with Roberts's help whisked her to safety. As she warmed herself at the foghorn fire, Mrs. Tryon declared "Considering everything I am very thankful. There is no kinder men than those in charge of the city of Duluth last night."[77]

Her fellow passenger, seventy-five-year-old Mrs. Marie Clark, agreed. A newspaper reporter found the elderly woman cheerfully drying her wet shoes at the foghorn boiler. She proudly said, "At no time was I badly frightened and my experience of last night would not keep me from making a lake voyage today were it necessary."[78]

After the passengers reached safety, the crewmen took their turn with the breeches buoy, until at last Captain MacLean, setting a splendid example, stood alone on the wreck. As he jumped into the buoy he swung his lantern and yelled "Let's go!" and as he landed, the life-saving crew sent up a chorus of cheers.[79]

While the rescue was underway, John H. Graham, president of Graham & Morton, remained at the E. A. Graham docks at the foot of the south pier, where he kept in communication by telephone to the life-saving station and Chicago. When the ship's crew had dried out and warmed up, he sent them up the bluff into town, where those from Chicago boarded at the Lake View Hotel—at Graham & Morton expense—until they could leave for home.[80]

The *City of Duluth* settled into the sand, and as the days passed the ice built up around the grounded vessel until she resembled a giant ice sculpture. St. Joseph enjoyed a tourism boom in the days immediately after the disaster as thousands of people braved the bleak weather to walk down to the piers to gaze upon the wrecked steamer. Owners of the St. Joseph and Benton Harbor streetcar line happily counted extra profits from fares paid by hundreds of curious patrons eager to see the *Duluth*. An enterprising *Chicago Tribune* agent arrived in St. Joseph armed with extra edition papers describing the wreck, and with him came a reporter and an artist, S. T. Collins, Jr., who made sketches of the scenes that appeared in the paper's Saturday editions. The day after the disaster, *The Evening News* of Benton Harbor carried an advertisement, "Photographs of the wrecked *City of Duluth* 25 cents each at A. D. Lacy's photo car."[81]

Salvage efforts began almost immediately. The Lake Michigan and Lake Superior Transportation Company valued the *City of Duluth* at $30,000 and had insured her for exactly half that amount. The cargo, with a total value of $25,000, carried a blanket policy for $10,000. On the Thursday after the wreck, the McDonald Insurance Company dispatched the tug *T. T. Murford* from Chicago with heavy steam pumps on board to pump out the cargo of corn.[82]

Some salvers examined the *Duluth* in an official capacity to recover the ship herself or at least her cargo and furnishings; others,

A view from the pilothouse of the *City of Duluth* during salvage operations.
(Courtesy of the Morton House)

the general public, arrived to see what they could wrest from the wreck by way of souvenirs. An insurance company representative boarded the *Duluth* with a crew of men a few days after the wreck to strip the vessel of everything of value. They removed the piano, carpets, chairs, lifeboats, and furniture, loaded them onto scows, towed them to the E. A. Graham docks, and packed them into warehouses. Relic hunters contested the insurance men for every item, for not all who came to see the wrecked ship could content themselves with a mere look. The ice that built up around the *Duluth* formed a bridge to the ship, and photographers and souvenir hunters descended like jackals. Looters swarmed over the ship and carried off everything moveable. The *Duluth's* china service and silverware vanished, and some ax-wielding looters even smashed the marble slabs of toiletry tables into portable chunks. One dismayed insurance official declared, "If you only give the people a little time there won't be enough left of the boat to go to pieces. This is the worst place I ever struck for relic hunters and I will be surprised if some one don't try to get the boat's engines and boiler for a souvenir."[83]

Shortly before midnight on Thursday, the *Andy* towed a scow out alongside the *City of Duluth* and took off the local freight (which was stored atop the flour barrels) and the baggage (which had been transferred to the cabin before the crew abandoned ship) and brought it into port on Friday morning. Some of the freight escaped damage due to its storage location, but the cold water ruined much of it.

The Graham & Morton Company towed in the steamer *City of Louisville* as a salvage ship, and contractor John M. Allmendinger fired up a big centrifugal pump to salvage the corn. Allmendinger gave up almost immediately when he discovered that the corn was water soaked and full of sand.[84] Much of the flour, however, was still good, and Graham & Morton recovered almost 1,600 sacks of it, amounting to nearly half the total.[85] St. Joseph residents hated to see the remaining sacks of flour go to waste, so they climbed aboard as soon as the Graham & Morton crew departed and helped themselves. Some people hauled home as many as twenty sacks of fine quality flour. They discovered that water penetrated only part way through the flour and left that in the center of the bag untouched, and at a value of three dollars per hundred pounds they declared the flour well worth the risk of salvaging.[86]

Although Lake Michigan and Lake Superior Transportation contemplated salvaging the *Duluth* as well, the company soon gave up the idea, deciding that the ship was too old to

The steamer *City of Louisville* tied up along-side the wrecked *City of Duluth* during salvage operations. *(Courtesy of the Morton House)*

warrant the expense of refloating and repairing. The *Duluth's* engines were then nearly twenty-five years old and the boilers could not safely carry more than thirty-five to thirty-seven pounds of steam.[87]

At last the salvers finished their work, the souvenir hunters went home, and the picked-over carcass of the *City of Duluth* lay an abandoned hulk near the end of the north pier. It remained there all through the spring and summer of 1898, a hazard to ships trying to enter the harbor. The United States government finally declared the derelict a hazard to navigation, and that August posted notice that it would accept bids to have it removed. In late September, a Toledo, Ohio, firm won the contract to remove the wreckage with a bid of $1,994.75. During November, a schooner maneuvered back and forth alongside the wreck and dynamited the *Duluth* to pieces.[88]

Tourist, 1898

Logan J. Drake gained fame in St. Joseph not for his riverboat, the *Tourist*, but for a much grander attraction: the Silver Beach Amusement Park. In 1891, Drake and his partner, Louis D. Wallace, bought the Silver Beach property and began to develop an amusement park on the sparkling stretch of sandy beach below the city of St. Joseph. Local concessionaires sold novelties to draw tourists, and in 1902 Drake and Wallace built a bathhouse, roller-skating rink, and dance pavilion. On April 19, 1915, they incorporated the

Silver Beach Amusement Company to operate a "Bathing pavilion, Restaurant and lunch stands, Dancing pavilion, Bowling alleys, Pool room and other Amusement Devices." Thousands of Chicago tourists and vacationers took steamships to St. Joseph to enjoy warm summer days on the beach. Between 1910 and 1930, Drake and Wallace added more and more attractions, including a carousel, the "Chase Through the Clouds" roller coaster, and the Shadowland Ballroom dance hall. Other amusements included a fun house, the Mirror Maze, a penny arcade, bumper cars, and a miniature railroad. At its peak, the Silver Beach park stretched over a half mile along the sand.[89]

Drake had met Louis Wallace in 1885 when Wallace began working for him at his boat livery in St. Joseph. The two became friends, then business partners, and (when they married sisters Maude and Laura Slanker) brothers-in-law. In the fall of 1896, Drake and Wallace decided to build a riverboat to sail the St. Joseph River. They launched their new sternwheeler on Thursday, April 1, 1897, and christened her *Tourist,* no doubt hoping to capitalize on the lucrative sightseeing passenger trade.[90] During the next two summers, the *Tourist* carried passengers and freight up and down the scenic St. Joseph River, running in competition with St. Joseph businessman Edmon A. Graham's larger and more famous sidewheeler *May Graham.*[91]

Tuesday evening, September 6, 1898, found the *Tourist* tied up at her St. Joseph dock after a day's run on the river. At about 10:30 that evening fire somehow escaped from the boiler's firebox and, fanned by a strong westerly wind, crept across the deck and set the upper superstructure ablaze. A Chicago & West Michigan Railroad train happened to pass over the swing bridge at the harbor entrance just as the fire took hold; the locomotive's engineer saw the flames devouring the *Tourist* and began yanking frantically on the whistle. The shrieking whistle alerted the town and soon the fire-hall bell summoned the St. Joseph Fire Department. Firefighters raced to the docks and quickly had the blaze under control. The tug *Andy* drew up alongside, too, and her crew played a stream of water onto the burning woodwork until they extinguished the fire. Despite the firefighters' quick work, the flames had destroyed the *Tourist's* superstructure. The

The sternwheel riverboat *Tourist* in the St. Joseph harbor in 1898.
(Courtesy of Daryl Schlender)

fire had also spread to the adjacent John Wallace & Sons lumberyard (belonging to Louis's father) and destroyed a quantity of shingles, slabwood, and lumber.[92]

Fortunately the *Tourist* carried insurance for the typical amount of half her value. Wallace Preston rebuilt her at his lumberyard on the tip of present-day Industrial Island in St. Joseph during the winter of 1898–1899. The St. Joseph newspaper reported the rebuild nearing completion in April, and noted that "she will be a better boat than she was originally." The resurrected *Tourist* took to the river again the following month, in time for an excursion chartered by the St. Joseph Military Band.[93]

Drake and Wallace sold the *Tourist* to the Benton Harbor-St. Joe Railway & Light Company in April 1907. The latter firm had no interest in running a steamboat in addition to its successful electric streetcar business, but the *Tourist* had made a nuisance of herself by forcing the railway to raise its drawbridge between St. Joseph and Benton Harbor to allow her to pass up and down the river. Raising the bridge delayed the streetcars and annoyed their passengers, so the railway bought the *Tourist* to eliminate that inconvenience. William W. Preston, a Benton Harbor businessman, purchased the *Tourist* from the railway in June 1907, and docked her just upstream from the bridge. From that point he ran her up the St. Joseph River to the little riverboat landings at Somerleyton and King's Landing.[94]

The sternwheeler eventually wound up under the ownership of the South Shore Steamship Company of Chicago. On August 18, 1911, she again caught fire and burned on the Calumet River at Riverdale, Illinois. This time its owners did not choose to rebuild her.[95]

Lena M. Neilson, 1898

The wrecked *City of Duluth* obstructed the St. Joseph harbor entrance throughout 1898. Although the government had the steamer dynamited to oblivion in November, the contractor carried out the work a few weeks too late to help the schooner *Lena M. Neilson.* The *Neilson* became one of the harbor's last victims, and her crew owed their lives to the skill of the local life-saving-station men.[96]

Thursday morning, November 10, 1898, dawned cold and snowy, with a fierce Lake Michigan gale shrieking through the port of St. Joseph. Out on the lake, the 86-ton *Lena M. Neilson* was bound from Manistee to St. Joseph with a cargo of lumber for the Peter Brothers Lumber Company of Benton Harbor.[97] Her captain and owner, thirty-two-year-old Evan Neilson of Ludington, Michigan, was a Norwegian who had emigrated to the United States in 1885; like so many of his countrymen, Neilson plied the sailor's trade he knew so well from the old country. Running his schooner in November was a risky proposition, but Evan Neilson had a good reason for taking chances. He had an extended family back in Ludington to support: his wife, Lena, their eight-year-old son Neil, and his mother-in-law and her two young children all lived in his home and depended on him for a living. The skipper could not afford to put up for the season prematurely.[98]

As the ship neared the harbor's safety, Captain Neilson had to sweep her around the wrecked *City of Duluth,* still lying at the end of the north pier where she had come to grief nearly a year before.[99] The federal government had fixed a white light to a mast mounted atop some pilings to mark the wreck, but even with this precaution the wind and waves overpowered ship and crew, and the *Neilson* risked being swept onto the shore.[100] Neilson dropped anchor and saved the vessel from going aground, but the waves lashed angrily at the ship as they tried to beat her to pieces.

Capt. William L. Stevens led his life-saving-station crew out into the lake in their little surfboat, assisted by the harbor tugs *Andy* and *McClellan.* The *Andy's* skipper asked Stevens's men to run a line from the schooner to the tug; but although the life savers succeeded in fastening the line to the *Neilson,* they found the current too strong to pull against and could not reach the tug. Waves tossed Captain Stevens into the lake and smashed several of the boat's oars. The life savers themselves nearly drowned when their surfboat filled with water, but they managed to bail it out and made another attempt. Finally, they had the lines all set, but the *Andy* refused to steam in close to pick them up. "We had to drop the lines," an exasperated Stevens reported, "and pull for shore." The exhausted life-saving crew eventually landed about a mile south of the harbor.[101]

In the meantime, the *Lena M. Neilson* lost both of her anchors and broke her rudder. Captain Neilson made a desperate attempt to beach her but finally let the schooner ride with the wind. The storm swept her into the snowstorm and out of sight, carrying her south along the Lake Michigan shoreline. Captain Stevens dispatched a surfman with orders to trail the schooner from the shore, but the man returned to the life-saving station to report that he had lost track of her in the storm.[102] The mayor of St. Joseph, John Starr, dispatched a wagon filled with food, medicine, and dry clothing along the beach to be ready for the schooner's crew when she came ashore.[103]

The *Neilson* rode with the waves until she went aground that afternoon off Lakeside, some twenty-two miles south of St. Joseph. Lakeside residents spotted the *Neilson,* and two men, Jirah A. Kitchell and Orin Glidden, set off for help. They flagged down the evening Chicago & West Michigan Railroad passenger train and rode into St. Joseph, where they notified Captain Stevens of the *Neilson's* plight.[104]

Undaunted by the morning's experience, Stevens and his crew immediately gathered their equipment together, secured a special train, and set off for Lakeside. They arrived at the scene at midnight and immediately set up their equipment on the beach, loaded their

Lyle gun, and fired a line out to the schooner. The sailors failed to fasten it properly, so Amil Risto, whom Captain Stevens had hired to go along on the rescue, bravely volunteered to go out on a breeches buoy. Risto failed, but a surfman, Frank Fowler, made a successful attempt.[105]

Fowler brought off one crewman and others followed until by four o'clock in the morning the captain and all four crew members—Neilson, John Olsen, James Fay, and Henry Peterson—were safe ashore. A roaring bonfire on the beach soon thawed out the frozen men. Residents of Lakeside took them to the nearby home of James A. Wilkinson, who filled them with hot food and coffee. Lakeside residents even provided them with a change of dry clothing.[106]

Out on the lake, the wind and waves pounded the *Lena M. Neilson* until she went to pieces. The two-year-old ship and most of her cargo were a total loss, but the life-saving-station men had saved all her crew.

Experiment, 1902

Nearly fifty years before a second disaster struck her, the little schooner *Experiment* had capsized off St. Joseph. Henrietta Napier had lost her infant son in the accident, but with a crewman and another of her sons she miraculously survived in an air pocket in the overturned cabin. The *Experiment,* righted and repaired, went back to sailing Lake Michigan. On the night of September 12, 1902, she approached St. Joseph harbor with a cargo of winter firewood.[107]

The *Experiment* and her crew had a hard time of it that night. The night was darker than a stack of black cats as the schooner ran southbound along the lake before a heavy northwest gale. Her crew had met the weather's challenge and felt confident that they could bring the *Experiment* safely into port.

Workmen for the Lydon & Drew Company had built cribs out from the shore a mile or so north of the harbor entrance. As the *Experiment* swept in from the north, her master and owner, Capt. John Withey of Benton Harbor, made out a light that he believed marked the end of the crib. Withey ordered his crew to man the lines and prepare to tack the ship around the north pier and into the harbor. Suddenly an obstruction loomed out of the darkness. Horrified, Withey realized that the unlighted crib lay directly in the schooner's course. He had mistaken the north pier light at St. Joseph for the light at the end of the crib, and the *Experiment* was seconds away from smashing into the crib.[108]

Withey cried to his crew to swing the *Experiment* around the crib. They tried, but the wild turn swung the ship off course and the crew lost control of her sails. The schooner skidded helplessly before the wind until she grounded on the beach three-quarters of a mile north of the harbor.

Someone called out the St. Joseph Life-Saving-Station crew, who put out in their surfboat. They drew up alongside the *Experiment* but no one answered their repeated hails. A surfman finally boarded her and found the schooner deserted. The crew of six, soaked through and through and half perished from the cold, had waded ashore and trekked down the beach to the life-saving station. Capt. William Stevens found them there in his wife's care; Ella Stevens had already thawed them out at the fire and given them dry clothing and warm beds for the night.[109]

The *Experiment* had come to grief for the last time. Waves smashed the old schooner to pieces and spread her cargo of firewood up and down the beach for a distance of two miles. In St. Joseph, newspaper reporters sought out an elderly Henrietta Napier and sat back to listen to her reminisce about her own night of terror aboard the *Experiment* a half-century before.[110]

1. *St. Joseph Traveler-Herald,* October 8, 1887.

2. Background information on the Curran family appears on the World Wide Web at www.geocities.com/Heartland/Meadows/1725/curran.htm; *Detroit Free Press,* October 4, 1887.

3. *Oswego Advertiser & Times,* August 15, 1871.

4. *St. Joseph Traveler-Herald,* October 8, 1887; James L. Donahue, *Schooners in Peril* (Cass City, MI: Anchor Publications, 1995; reprint, Holt, MI: Thunder Bay Press, n.d.), 114–15.

5. Ibid., *Detroit Free Press,* October 7, 1887.

6. Capt. William L. Stevens's official report of the incident appeared in the *St. Joseph Traveler-Herald,* October 8, 1887.

7. Ibid.

8. Ibid.

9. *Detroit Free Press,* October 7, 1887.

10. *St. Joseph Traveler-Herald,* October 8, 1887.

11. United States Life-Saving Service, *Annual Report of the Operations of the United States Life-Saving Service for the Fiscal Year Ending June 30, 1888* (Washington, DC: Government Printing Office, 1889), 20–25.

A full account of the *City of Green Bay* disaster appears in Wes Oleszewski, *Keepers of Valor, Lakes of Vengeance: Lakeboats, Lifesavers & Lighthouses* (Gwinn, MI: Avery Color Studios, 2000), 91–109. A Life-Saving-Service investigation after the disaster revealed that Captain Cross had almost certainly overcharged the Lyle gun; as a consequence, three lines snapped in succession with the loss of all the available projectiles. Cross then attempted a rescue with the station surfboat which proved fruitless and nearly caused his own death.

12. *Detroit Free Press,* October 7, 1887.

13. *St. Joseph Traveler-Herald,* October 8, 1887.

14. *Detroit Free Press,* November 27, 1887.

15. *The Palladium* (Benton Harbor, MI), November 18, 1887; *St. Joseph Traveler-Herald,* November 12, 1887.

16. Ibid.; *Detroit Free Press,* November 12, 1887; *St. Joseph Traveler-Herald,* November 12, 1887.

17. Ibid.

18. *The Palladium,* November 18, 1887; *Detroit Free Press,* November 12, 1887; Life-Saving Station Logs, Chicago District, St. Joseph Station, November 11, 1887, RG 26, NARA, Great Lakes Region (Chicago).

19. Life-Saving Station Logs, Chicago District, St. Joseph Station, November 11, 1887. RG 26, NARA, Great Lakes Region (Chicago).

20. *The Palladium,* November 18, 1887.

21. Ibid.

22. *Detroit Free Press,* November 12, 1887.

23. *Kenosha* (Wisconsin) *Evening News,* October 23, 1915.

24. Lane, *South Haven to Grand Haven,* 95–96.

25. Ibid.

26. *South Haven Sentinel,* July 27, 1889.

27. Lane, *South Haven to Grand Haven,* 96.

28. Ibid.

29. *South Haven Sentinel,* July 27, 1889.

30. Lane, *South Haven to Grand Haven,* 96–97; Robert C. Myers, "The Grand Hotel," in *Historical Sketches of Berrien County, Vol. 2* (Berrien Springs, MI: Berrien County Historical Association, 1989), 31–32.

31. Lane, *South Haven to Grand Haven,* 96–97; *South Haven Sentinel,* July 27, 1889.

32. *Detroit Free Press,* June 3, 1891 and October 10, 1905.

33. Ibid., June 3, 1891.

34. *The Michigan City News,* October 11, 1905.

35. Ibid.; *Detroit Free Press,* October 10, 1895. The *Thomas Hume's* sister ship, the *Rouse Simmons,* gained melancholy fame many years later as the "Christmas Tree Ship." After Charles Hackley sold her, the *Rouse Simmons* passed through a number of hands until Herman Schuenemann (and co-owners Charles C. Nelson and Mannes J. Bonner) bought her in 1910. Her nickname came from Schuenemann's practice of bringing a cargo of Christmas trees to Chicago on the last voyage of the season. In November 1912, the *Simmons* sailed out of Manistique, Michigan, for Chicago with a load of Christmas trees and ran into a vicious storm. She disappeared near Kewaunee, Wisconsin, taking with her Capt. Herman Schuenemann and fifteen crewmen and passengers. Christmas trees from the deck cargo washed back and forth in the waves to mark her passing, but an intensive search by the Two Rivers Life-Saving-Station crew failed to locate the wreck. In 1971, Milwaukee diver Kent Bellrichard found the *Rouse Simmons's* grave six miles from shore between Two Rivers and Kewaunee in 180 feet of water. See Herbert Pitz, *Lake Michigan Disasters* (Manitowoc, WI: n. p., 1925; reprint, Manitowoc, Manitowoc Maritime Museum, n.d.), 61–62; *"Rouse Simmons,"* in the Central Humanities Marine Collections, Ship File Reference, Milwaukee Public Library.

36. The best history of the *Chicora* is Kit Lane, *The Chicora: Lost on Lake Michigan* (Douglas, MI: Pavilion Press, 1996); also worthwhile is Pete Caesar, *Chicora* (Green Bay, WI: Great Lakes Maritime Research, 1982).

37. James Stanley Morton, *Reminiscences of the Lower St. Joseph River Valley* (Benton Harbor, MI: The Federation of Women's Clubs, n. d.), 84–85.

38. *St. Joseph Saturday Herald,* January 2, 1892.

39. Ibid., July 2, 1892; Morton, 85; John Orville Greenwood, *Namesakes, 1930-1955* (Cleveland, OH: Freshwater Press, 1978), 122.

40. *St. Joseph Saturday Herald,* August 20, 1892.

41. Ibid., July 2, 1892; *The Daily Palladium* (Benton Harbor, MI), February 11, 1895; *"Around the Lakes"* (Cleveland, OH: Marine Review Print, 1894), 142. The speed of ships on inland waterways is measured in miles per hour, not knots.

42. *The Daily Palladium,* February 11, 1895. The cost of her furnishings raised the *Chicora's* total price to $140,000.

43. *St. Joseph Saturday Herald,* August 20, 1892.

44. Ibid., April 29, 1893.

45. Minutes of the Annual Meetings of the Graham & Morton Transportation Company, January 13, 1894 and April 19, 1895; Records of the Graham-Morton Steamship Co.; and Family Papers of the Morton Family, 1872–1936, A-1641, Regional History Collections, Western Michigan University, Kalamazoo, Michigan.

46. Lane, *Chicora*, 24–25. Lane notes that the railroads (important Graham & Morton customers) frequently threatened to find alternative shippers if the steamship line failed to meet their demands—hence the pressure on Graham & Morton for a post-season run.

47. Ibid., 121–34; *The Daily Palladium*, February 11, 1895. Because no official list of people on board existed, weeks passed before the identities of all those on the *Chicora* were firmly established. Several men thought lost showed up in the days and weeks after the disaster. As Kit Lane points out, *The Daily Palladium's* memorial edition of February 11, 1895 still listed deckhand Archibald Bentley among the dead when in fact he was never aboard; he later turned up alive on a farm at Hersey, Michigan. The possibility remains, however, that some anonymous and unrecorded laborer may have vanished with the ship.

48. So went the story in the *Milwaukee Sentinal* of January 24, 1895. The tale may be true, but it smacks of the journalistic embellishments common to newspapers of the time.

49. Lane, *Chicora*, 31–32; Life-Saving Station Logs, Chicago District, St. Joseph Station, January 21, 1895, RG 26, NARA, Great Lakes Region (Chicago). Although some sources reported the barometric pressure falling as low as 28.00, the St. Joseph Life-Saving Station weather log, recorded four times each day, shows that it never dropped anywhere near that point.

50. Lane, *Chicora*, 35–36.

51. *St. Joseph Saturday Herald*, January 26, 1895.

52. *The Daily Palladium*, February 3 and 4, 1895.

53. Wyn Craig Wade, *The Titanic: End of a Dream* (Rawson, Wade Publishers, 1979; reprint, New York: Penguin Books, 1980), 430–42; Phil Hood, ed., *Artists of American Folk Music* (New York: William Morrow, 1986), 111–12.

54. *The Daily Palladium*, February 11, 1895.

55. Ibid., January 29, 1895.

56. *The Grand Haven Evening News*, January 28, 1895. The full text of all these poems can be found in Lane, *Chicora*, 136–42.

57. Lane, *Chicora*, 106–10; *St. Joseph Saturday Herald*, February 2, 1895.

58. *St. Joseph Saturday Herald*, February 9, 16, and 23; March 2,1895.

59. Caesar, *Chicora*, 77–80. Caesar dismisses the note as a hoax, but historian Kit Lane argues that it may have been authentic.

60. Walter Romig, *Michigan Place Names* (Detroit: Wayne State University Press, 1986), 114; Lane, *Chicora*, 146.

61. Lane, *Chicora*, 149.

62. Minutes of the Annual Meetings of the Graham & Morton Transportation Company, January 14, 1896, Records of the Graham-Morton Steamship Co. and Family Papers of the Morton Family.

63. *St. Joseph Saturday Herald,* January 26, 1895.

64. Minutes of the Annual Meetings of the Graham & Morton Transportation Company, January 14, 1896, Records of the Graham-Morton Steamship Co. and Family Papers of the Morton Family.

65. For descriptions and analyses of the Columbian Exposition, see Reid Badger, *The Great American Fair: The World's Columbian Exposition and American Culture* (Chicago: N. Hall, 1979); H. W. Brands, *The Reckless Decade: America in the 1890s* (New York: St. Martin's Press, 1995); and Rossiter Johnson, *A History of the World's Columbian Exposition Held in Chicago in 1893,* 4 vols. (New York: D. Appleton and Company, 1897–1898).

66. Extensive accounts of the *City of Duluth* wreck appeared in the *St. Joseph* (Michigan) *Saturday Herald,* January 29, 1898, and *The Evening News* (Benton Harbor, Michigan), January 27, 1898. Some disagreement exists regarding the exact number of people aboard the *Duluth* on her final voyage. St. Joseph Life-Saving Station Keeper William L. Stevens reported rescuing forty people from the wreck, but the newspaper accounts list, by name, forty-one passengers and crew. Life-Saving Station Logs, Chicago District, St. Joseph Station, January 26, 1898, RG 26, NARA, Great Lakes Region (Chicago).

67. John Pridgeon, Sr., numbered among Detroit's largest owners of tugs, steamers, and sailing ships. Mansfield, 2:421–22.

68. *St. Joseph Saturday Herald,* January 29, 1898.

69. *The Evening News,* January 27, 1898.

70. *St. Joseph Saturday Herald,* January 8, 1898.

71. Ibid., January 29, 1898; *The Evening News,* January 27, 1898. The *Saturday Herald* described the weather as a gale with heavy seas, although *The Evening News* claimed that the seas were not thought high or dangerous.

72. *St. Joseph Saturday Herald,* January 29, 1898.

73. *The Evening News,* January 27, 1898.

74. Ibid.; *St. Joseph Saturday Herald,* January 29, 1898; United States Life-Saving Service, *Annual Report of the Operations of the United States Life-Saving Service for the Fiscal Year Ending June 30, 1898* (Washington, DC: Government Printing Office, 1899), 138–39. The *Evening News* claimed that Kernwein, "a Hebrew gentleman," shoved his way in front of the women passengers and demanded to be first off the ship. Captain MacLean pushed Kernwein back twice, but finally let him go ahead. While the *Evening News* account might be accurate, it is suspiciously anti-Semitic. Newspapers often attributed despicable behavior by shipwrecked passengers to racial or ethnic minorities; see, for example, Wyn Craig Wade's *Titanic: End of a Dream,* which notes that newspapers covering the *Titanic* sinking almost always identified cowardly passengers as Italian immigrants. At any rate, the *St. Joseph Saturday Herald* of February 5, 1898, refuted the charges against Kernwein, declaring that he had volunteered to make the first trip when Captain MacLean could find no other passenger brave enough to make the attempt.

75. *St. Joseph Saturday Herald,* January 29, 1898; Ellis, 309.

76. Life-Saving Station Logs, Chicago District, St. Joseph Station, January 26, 1898, RG 26, NARA—Great Lakes Region (Chicago).

77. *The Evening News,* January 27, 1898; *Annual Lifesaving Service Report for 1898,* 138.

78. *The Evening News,* January 27, 1898.

79. *St. Joseph Saturday Herald,* January 29, 1898; *The Evening News,* January 27, 1898.

80. *St. Joseph Saturday Herald,* January 29, 1898.

81. Ibid.; *The Evening News,* January 27, 1898.

82. Ibid.

83. *The Evening News,* January 27 and 31, 1898.

84. Ibid., January 31, 1898.

85. Ibid., February 4, 1898.

86. *St. Joseph Saturday Herald,* February 5, 1898.

87. Ibid., January 31, 1898.

88. *The Daily Palladium* (Benton Harbor, MI), September 7, 1898; *St. Joseph Saturday Herald,* October 1 and 29, November 19, 1898.

89. Alan Schultz, "Silver Beach: A Scrapbook of Summers Past," *Michigan History* 63 (July/August 1979): 8–19; Annual Report of the Silver Beach Amusement Co., Inc., for 1915, Berrien County Historical Association, Berrien Springs, Michigan.

90. Ibid., 9; Berrien County Marriage Certificates, February 2, 1901, certificate no. 40, Logan J. Drake to Maude Slanker, and December 8, 1907, certificate no. 1594, Louis D. Wallace to Laura Slanker; *St. Joseph Saturday Herald,* November 28, 1896 and April 3, 1897.

91. For a history of the *May Graham,* see Robert C. Myers, "The May Graham: Steamboat Travel on the St. Joseph River," *Michigan History* 70 (March/April 1986): 24–29.

92. *St. Joseph Saturday Herald,* 10 September 1898; *Benton Harbor Palladium,* September 7, 1898.

93. Ibid.; *St. Joseph Saturday Herald,* April 22 and May 20, 1899.

94. *St. Joseph Evening Herald,* April 22, June 21 and 28, 1907; *St. Joseph Daily Press,* June 20, 1907.

95. The *Tourist,* in Vessel Listings, Historical Collections of the Great Lakes, Bowling Green State University, Bowling Green, OH; *Merchant Vessels of the United States* (Washington, DC: Government Printing Office, 1912), 420.

96. The account of the *Lena M. Neilson's* loss appears in the *St. Joseph Saturday Herald,* November 12, 1898.

97. Ibid.

98. Bureau of the Census, Twelfth census of the United States (1900), village of Ludington, Mason County, Michigan.

99. *St. Joseph Saturday Herald,* November 18, 1898; *The Michigan City News,* November 16, 1898. Captain Neilson threatened to sue the federal government for failing to remove the wrecked *City of Duluth,* claiming negligence in leaving the *Duluth* there for so long. Neilson declared that he could have easily brought his ship into port despite the storm, but having to skirt the *Duluth's* wreckage allowed the wind and waves to beat the *Lena M. Neilson* south of the pier, where she could not enter the harbor.

100. *St. Joseph Saturday Herald,* March 12, 1898.

101. Ibid., November 12, 1898; Life-Saving Station Logs, Chicago District, St. Joseph Station, November 10, 1898, RG 26, NARA, Great Lakes Region (Chicago).

102. Ibid.

103. *The Michigan City News,* November 16, 1898.

104. *St. Joseph Saturday Herald,* November 12, 1898; Life-Saving Station Logs, Chicago District, St. Joseph Station, Box 7, November 11, 1898, RG 26, NARA, Great Lakes Region (Chicago).

105. Ibid.

106. *St. Joseph Saturday Herald,* November 12, 1898; *Pentwater* (Michigan) *News,* November 18, 1898.

107. The account of the *Experiment's* second and final wreck appears in the *St. Joseph Evening Herald,* September 13, 1902.

108. Ibid.

109. Ibid.; Life-Saving Station Logs, Chicago District, St. Joseph Station, September 13, 1902, RG 26, NARA, Great Lakes Region (Chicago).

110. *St. Joseph Evening Herald,* September 13, 1902.

The *Eastland* Disaster
and the House of David's Ill Fortune

Emily and Eliza, 1910

They wore long hair and beards; abstained from alcohol, meat, tobacco, and sexual relations; and created one of America's most successful communal religious societies. At its peak, the Israelite House of David boasted nearly one thousand members at its Benton Harbor colony. Besides a unique religious faith that promised believers salvation of the body as well as the soul, the House of David established many profitable businesses, including its own shipping company. Its Great Lakes ships, however, met with more than one catastrophe.[1]

The House of David grew out of a unique millennialist religious movement that traced its origins back to eighteenth-century England. In 1895, Benjamin Franklin Purnell, a Kentucky-born itinerant preacher, declared himself the seventh in a series of messengers foretold in the book of Revelation. He and his wife, Mary, spread their message throughout the Midwest for the next seven years until they finally settled in Benton Harbor, Michigan.

In 1903, the Israelite House of David membership totaled seven people, including Mary and Benjamin. Four years later, membership topped seven hundred. Converts arrived from all over the world, faster than they could be accommodated. The House of David needed land, housing, and money. Benjamin and Mary Purnell, experienced only as itinerant preachers, found themselves in charge of a growing communal society whose members looked to them for clothing, food, and shelter. Nothing in the Purnells' background prepared them to manage a large group of men, women, and children and secure the necessities of life for them. The responsibility appeared overwhelming. It soon developed that regardless of whatever people thought about the Purnells' religious message, no one could doubt their genius at organization and management.

The Seventh Messenger proved himself a natural businessman in the secular world. Benjamin had an uncanny sense of people's

Benjamin Purnell, founder of the Israelite House of David. *(Courtesy of Mary's City of David)*

abilities and steered Israelites toward money-making projects for which they had an aptitude. Benjamin's wide-ranging interests let him appreciate and encourage his flock's efforts, and he had a natural knack for smoothing over interpersonal conflicts. The colony flourished under his leadership.

Soon after he founded the colony, Benjamin decided to go into the logging business. The House of David bought the timber rights to five hundred acres of land at the hamlet of Aral in Benzie County, on the northern shores of Lake Michigan, in 1908. The little logging village had been founded in the 1870s on Platte Bay at the mouth of Otter Creek and boasted a boarding house, grocery store, bakery, and blacksmith shop. The House of David bought Aral's sawmill from one Zeke Walters, who had run it for the Mann Brothers of Three Rivers, Wisconsin. The Israelites impressed the locals with both their skills and their religious faith, enough so that a few Aralites became Israelites. Several Israelites dropped out of the sect, however, so as far as membership numbers went, it ended up a fairly even swap. The House of David resurrected Aral's decaying sawmill and also ran the town's general store. Like the Shakers, with whom they shared many religious beliefs, the Israelites possessed a strong work ethic, and within a short time they logged off two large cedar swamps.[2]

The Aral lumber camp required ships to transport finished lumber to market, so on April 6, 1909, the House of David incorporated the Great Waters Transportation Company. The company issued twelve shares of stock, divided evenly between company president Benjamin Purnell, vice-president and secretary Thomas Rowe, and treasurer Charles Schutz. The company's stated business was "hauling lumber," and its assets amounted to $274 in tangible property and $26 in cash.[3] Great Waters purchased the small two-masted scow schooner *Emily and Eliza* to carry lumber from Aral. On September 9, 1910, the Israelites loaded her with cedar posts for the last voyage of the 1910 shipping season and, anxious to transport as much cargo as possible on this last trip, greatly overloaded the schooner. The *Emily and Eliza* began taking on water as soon as she set sail and sank only two hundred feet out from the Otter Creek dock. Cedar posts drifted for weeks all along the Benzie County shore.[4] Fortunately, all four crewmen survived.[5]

The Israelite House of David's logging camp at Aral, Michigan, ca. 1910.
(Courtesy of Mary's City of David)

The Israelite House of David's scow schooner *Emily and Eliza* sank in Platte Bay under a heavy load of fence posts. *(Courtesy of the Historical Collections of the Great Lakes, Bowling Green State University)*

The House of David continued its seafaring enterprises with other vessels after the loss of *Emily and Eliza*. In 1911, the House of David launched a ship of its own design and construction, the sixty-four-foot-long propeller *Morning Star,* designed by colony member Quinto Rosetta and built by the Israelites at their Benton Harbor headquarters. She was employed on the Benton Harbor to Aral run.

The Israelites intended that Benjamin Purnell would use the ship to retrace an epic evangelizing mission carried out by four Israelites in 1910. Forest Lanier, Charles Dissen, George Nelson, and Gale Dart had set out in a twenty-six-foot, gasoline-powered launch called *House of David Messenger Boat.* They sailed the tiny craft across Lake Michigan to Chicago, where they ascended the Chicago Canal and took the Illinois River into the Mississippi. They descended the Mississippi to the Gulf of Mexico, rounded the tip of Florida, followed the Atlantic coast to New York City, sailed up the Hudson River to the Erie Canal, and headed home through the Great Lakes. Brother Benjamin never did retrace their voyage, but its completion by the four Israelites helped spread the colony's fame.[6]

The House of David Aral enterprise did not long survive the *Emily and Eliza*. When the logging business at Aral played out, Benjamin Purnell turned his attention to High Island, one of the Beaver Island group in northern Lake Michigan, and in 1912 bought lumber rights there. Aral died after the Israelites left, and its few remaining residents finally tore down the mill for its lumber.[7] Platte Bay, which became the *Emily and Eliza's* grave, is now part of Sleeping Bear Dunes National Shoreline.

Evening Star, 1911

Charles Carland of the Chicago Life-Saving Station hailed Capt. Oscar Osmondson of the fishing tug *Evening Star* as she steamed out of Chicago on Saturday morning, November 11, 1911. A storm was on its way, he told the tug's skipper. Osmondson, who had pulled out from the Wells Street Bridge at 9:00 A.M., looked up into a clear sky. Temperatures had reached an unseasonably warm seventy-five degrees. It was a beautiful day for Lake Michigan fishing.

Osmondson called back to Carland and assured him that when he saw the storm coming he would put in to Waukegan, Illinois. In the meantime, he and his crew of six—Joseph and John Litz, Frank G. Harmste, Fred Pankow, John Boreise, and John Cook—would head for the fishing grounds off Waukegan.[8]

The *Evening Star* reached its destination and put down her nets. She stayed off Waukegan until after dark that evening, when Osmondson's men lifted their nets and the boat set course back to Chicago. From that moment on, nothing went right.

Ten minutes into the return trip the *Evening Star* lost her rudder. Then the boat's cook stove broke down and the crew, fearful of fire, pitched it into the lake. Sunday arrived with the predicted change in the weather; thunderstorms swept through, drenching the crew and dropping the temperature to fifty-six degrees with strong winds. Without the stove, the crew had no heat or hot food and suffered from cold, wet, and exposure.[9]

The *Evening Star* was due back in Chicago at 9:00 P.M. on Saturday. The crew's families began to worry as the night wore on without word from the ship, and early on Sunday morning John Litz's wife, Mary, went to a local police station to report the *Evening Star* missing.[10] William L. Stevens at the St. Joseph Life-Saving Station got word from Chicago later that day to keep a lookout for the missing fishing tug. At about one o'clock the next morning, a local resident, John E. Brookins, telephoned him that the *Evening Star* had come ashore about four and one-half miles north of St. Joseph on the Stephen Cook farm in Hagar Township. Most of the crew, Brookins reported, had waded ashore and scrambled up the eighty-foot-high bluff to a farmhouse, but one man remained aboard the boat. Brookins had no clothing for the men—could the life-saving station supply some?[11]

Stevens hired rigs and set off up the beach, leaving one man on watch in St. Joseph. The life savers found the tug aground and near-ly on the shore. John Cook, however, still refused to leave the boat, so the life savers waded out to the boat, threw him a line, and pulled him off to safety. All seven men were cold, wet, and miserable, but otherwise uninjured. The life-saving-station crew had brought dry clothing with them, and J. J. Brookings, the Cook farm manager, gave them food and a place to sleep.[12]

Hattie Wells, 1912

The *Hattie Wells* began life as a three-masted schooner, but by 1912 she was forty-five years old and coming to an ignominious end as a tow barge. She had already died and come back to life twice before. She was wrecked and declared lost, and her document surrendered, after she ran ashore with a load of lumber at Point Pelee, Ontario, on November 18, 1892. In October 1907 her owners surrendered her document again after she burned at Marysville, Michigan. Rising like a phoenix, she was redocumented at Marquette, Michigan, in 1909, and returned to service.[13] In early November 1912, the tug *James H. Martin* towed her out of Marinette, Wisconsin, with a cargo of lumber for Waukegan, Illinois, and Muskegon, Michigan. Aboard were the masters and owners of both vessels, D. L. MacKinnon and William Scott; the former served as engineer and master on the *Hattie Wells,* while the latter skippered the *Martin.*[14]

The *Hattie Wells* unloaded her first consignment at Waukegan on Tuesday. The following morning the *Martin* towed her and her five-man crew out of Wisconsin for Muskegon to deliver her lumber to the Brunswick-Balke-Callendar Company. A northwest gale blew in while they were en route, churning Lake Michigan into mountainous waves. The *Hattie Wells's* pumps struggled to keep ahead of the water that poured in as the waves washed over her deck. At ten o'clock in the morning, when the *Martin* had pulled the *Hattie Wells* to about fifty miles northwest of St. Joseph, the constant shifting of the lumber in her hold put the donkey engine out of commission. With no power source, the pumps quit working, and the water rose in its hold. By late afternoon the barge crew knew they faced real trouble. MacKinnon and Scott conferred and decided to head for the safety of South Haven harbor. Their crews worked valiantly, but the wind and waves carried them off course and nightfall found them in a hopeless situation, halfway between St. Joseph and South Haven with the *Wells* fast taking on water.[15]

The tug dropped its towline and began the dangerous, difficult work of rescuing the barge's crew. Time after time MacKinnon tried to maneuver the *James H. Martin* alongside the sinking barge, but the sea ran so high that he had to back off, fearful that the two vessels would collide and both go to the bottom. So close did the *Martin* come to the *Wells* that seaman Ernest Vance judged the plunging up-and-down motion of the two vessels and leaped from the barge to land on the tug's deck. Jumping from deck to deck invited death, so the two skippers abandoned the attempt to bring the tug alongside, and instead threw a lifeline from the *Martin* to the *Wells*. One by one the sailors tied the line around their waists and plunged into the lake as their comrades pulled frantically on the line, reeling them aboard the tug like hooked fish.[16]

Two teenaged stewardesses aboard the *Martin,* Margaret LaJoyce and Elizabeth DeBeck, shamed the sailors with their determination and courage. An admiring Captain MacKinnon declared later that "The girls were the bravest of us all." LaJoyce and DeBeck stood on the deck through the worst part of the rescue, braving the icy waves spraying over them as they cheered on the crew. Some of the *Martin's* sailors had argued against bringing the tug up alongside the barge, but the girls berated them for cowardice and begged MacKinnon to do everything possible to save those on the *Hattie Wells*. "In a tight pinch, give me a woman for courage," MacKinnon declared.

The *James H. Martin* steamed safely into St. Joseph about midnight with an exhausted crew suffering from cold and exposure. The two captains took the tug back out on Thursday afternoon in faint hope that they would find the *Wells* still afloat. As they expected, the barge and her cargo had gone to the bottom of the lake.[17]

City of Chicago, 1914

The Graham & Morton Company of Benton Harbor had the splendid steamer *City of Chicago* built for its St. Joseph to Chicago route. In 1914, she ran a race against death across Lake Michigan.

F. W. Wheeler & Company of West Bay City, Michigan, built the *Chicago,* a sidewheel steamer whose massive engines could produce up to 1,200 horsepower, for Graham & Morton in 1890. The *City of Chicago* slid down the ways on March 18, 1890. Shipyard owner Frank W. Wheeler was then serving a term as a U. S. congressman, and the *City of Chicago* had already gained some notoriety in West Bay City as the first steel-hulled ship produced there. Delighted residents feted Congressman Wheeler at a big banquet in honor of this grand achievement.[18] Graham & Morton's new ship required another two months of finishing work at Wheeler's shipyard, but by the end of May, the craftsmen had completed the final touches. Frank Wheeler and his wife hosted a celebratory reception on board the new ship, and the following day treated some fifteen hundred citizens of West Bay City to a complimentary excursion on Lake Huron.[19]

The *City of Chicago* steamed out of West Bay City for St. Joseph at 3:00 A.M. on Sunday, June 1. John H. Graham, president of Graham & Morton, sailed with her, as did Frank Wheeler, his wife, and a select group of seventeen guests. St. Joseph went wild with enthusiasm when she pulled into the harbor at 3:30 Monday afternoon. Throngs of people lined the harbor docks or jostled for position along the bluff at Lake Front Park. Tugboat and factory whistles erupted in a shrill chorus, cannons boomed salutes, bands struck up lively airs, and hundreds of people cheered themselves hoarse.[20]

That evening the Graham and Wheeler party basked in the warm glow of a reception held in their honor by St. Joseph residents at the Whitcomb Hotel. Congratulatory toasts flowed back and forth across the tables, and the honorees accepted floral presentations that must have emptied every greenhouse in the area. Those without the influence or status to attend the reception could at least stroll down to the harbor just below the Whitcomb to gaze on the grand *City of Chicago.* On Thursday morning the new marvel steamed up the ship canal to Benton Harbor to bask in further adulation, then returned to St. Joseph to embark at 11:00 P.M. on her maiden voyage to Chicago.[21]

For twenty-four years the *City of Chicago* helped Graham & Morton maintain a highly successful freight and passenger trade between Chicago and the twin cities. Thousands of Chicagoans knew the vessel on sight and took passage aboard her every summer to enjoy the beaches and other amusements that southwest Michigan offered. A complete rebuild of the vessel in 1905 increased her length to 254 feet and her gross tonnage to 1,439 tons.

The *City of Chicago* represented the best that the Gilded Age had to offer. Passengers slept in spacious, comfortable staterooms. During the day they enjoyed the ship's magnificent grand salon with its fine wood paneling, brass fittings, and fixtures, and skylight with imported stained-glass windows. Walnut and mahogany furniture reposed on red velvet wall-to-wall carpeting.[22] The ship even featured an elegant honeymoon suite to accommodate the thousands of Chicagoans who took advantage of Michigan's lenient marriage laws and sailed to Berrien County to get married.[23]

The *City of Chicago's* grand staircase exemplified the splendor of the Gilded Age.
(Courtesy of the Morton House)

At eleven o'clock on the evening of Monday, August 31, 1914, the *City of Chicago* cleared St. Joseph harbor on what promised to be yet another uneventful voyage across Lake Michigan. She carried some two hundred passengers, forty crewmen, and an enormous cargo of fruit—grapes, cantaloupes, and peaches—bound for Chicago markets. Early the next morning, fire suddenly erupted from the coal bunkers.[24]

Capt. Oscar C. Bjork, a thirty-one-year-old Swede, commanded the ship. Bjork glanced astern as his ship came abreast of the Carter Harrison crib about three miles from the pier and noticed "a puff of smoke, shaped like a balloon." The smoke rose from behind the walking beam. Bjork knew that it could not have come from the smokestacks, and that left only one possibility: an on-board fire. At that moment he shared the bridge with Second Mate Peter Fisher and Lookout George Bruce. Captain Bjork instantly ordered Fisher to call out the crew for a fire drill, then turned to Bruce and told him to have the chief steward awaken the passengers and herd them to the forward end of the promenade deck. Fisher and the fire crew turned

Passenger salon of the *City of Chicago*, 1892. *(Courtesy of the Morton House)*

fire hoses on the blaze, but the flames continued to spread and threatened to turn the ship into a gigantic furnace.[25]

Among the passengers were Mr. and Mrs. John Bruley of Benton Harbor and their three-year-old son. The Bruleys, asleep in their cabin, awoke when a porter came racing down the corridor, hammering and kicking on cabin doors and shouting "fire!" Bruley woke his wife and child and hurried them onto the deck. Although they noticed little smoke, fire was consuming the *City of Chicago's* interior.[26]

With firefighting efforts underway and passengers heading forward, Captain Bjork considered his options. He first thought of abandoning ship but quickly rejected the notion. Putting two hundred terrified passengers off in lifeboats far out in the lake, even with the ship's crew to help row, would almost certainly have cost several lives. The *Titanic* disaster of just two years earlier with its great loss of life remained fresh in everyone's mind, and Bjork knew that passengers watching the lifeboats lower away would panic. He therefore decided on an alternative course of action: run for Chicago. Engineers and firemen held steadfast to their posts, and Bjork had all the power he wanted. He ordered Engineer William Johnson to put the ship at full speed ahead, and Johnson opened up the engines and sent the burning vessel toward Chicago under a double head of steam. Captain Bjork told wireless operator Arthur Hedlund to radio ahead to the Chicago station to send firefighting and life-saving equipment. Hedlund sat down at the wireless but found to his dismay that the apparatus was dead—flames had already destroyed the generator.[27]

By then all of the passengers had come up on deck. Like the Bruley family, who stood helplessly at the vessel's stern, they waited in terrified silence as the burning ship sped on toward Chicago. The crew kept pouring water on the flames, but the fire spread relentlessly through the ship. As the vessel neared Chicago, smoke started boiling up through the staterooms.[28]

But Captain Bjork had won his race. The *Chicago* covered the three miles from the Carter Harrison crib to the Chicago Life-Saving Station pier in ten minutes, an eighteen-mile-per-hour sprint and faster than any speed she had posted in many years. As the pier

Fire reduced the *City of Chicago's* elegant passenger salon to charred wreckage. *(Courtesy of the Morton House)*

loomed up ahead, Bjork decided against taking time to bring the ship alongside and tie up, opting instead to "ram her right in. I had a solid hull beneath me and I trusted it."[29]

The giant *City of Chicago,* burning furiously, tore into the Chicago Life-Saving Station pier with a thunderous crash and wedged herself in the wooden timbers. The Life-Saving Service crew saw the smoke billowing out of her as she sped across the lake and had rescue ladders ready. The tug *Gary* drew alongside. Passengers leaped aboard the tug or scrambled down ladders onto the pier. John Bruley handed his little boy to someone on the tug, then helped his wife jump to the deck. In true captain's tradition, Oscar Bjork remained aboard until everyone else had gone, then escaped himself.[30]

Firefighting tugs played endless streams of water onto her, but the *City of Chicago* burned to the waterline. Thanks to the heroic efforts of her captain and crew and the Chicago Life-Saving Station crew, no loss of life or serious injury resulted from the disaster.[31]

The burned-out *City of Chicago* rests against the pier in Chicago.
(Courtesy of the Morton House)

The *City of Chicago* fared worse than the passengers. The fire completely destroyed most of her superstructure and cabins, but her steel hull escaped virtually undamaged, so Graham & Morton had her towed to the shipyard at South Chicago and completely rebuilt. Workmen replaced the original twin funnels with a single stack. The boat deck was redesigned and additional lifeboat capacity added—a retrofit stemming from the *Titanic* "lifeboats for all" legislation adopted by the International Conference for the Safety of Life at Sea in January 1914. Besides these structural and mechanical necessities, Graham & Morton also restored her original luxurious interior. After completing the restoration, Graham & Morton renamed her the *City of St. Joseph* and put her back on her old route.[32]

Years later, John Roen of Sturgeon Bay, Wisconsin, bought the *City of St. Joseph* as well as the steamers *City of Benton Harbor, City of Holland,* and *City of Saugatuck* at a federal-court sale held to pay the debts of the bankrupt Goodrich Transportation Company. Roen

Graham & Morton rebuilt the *City of Chicago* and renamed her the *City of St. Joseph.*
(Courtesy of the Morton House)

elected to convert the *City of St. Joseph* to a barge.[33] On April 14, 1936, fire again swept the *St. Joseph* as the wrecking crew of Price and Brown worked to remove its engines and superstructure. The fire at the Benton Harbor ship canal work site sent up a column of smoke visible for miles, attracted hundreds of curious spectators, and razed the *St. Joseph's* pilothouse and superstructure.[34] The vessel's burned-out hull was towed to Sturgeon Bay and converted into a pulpwood barge.

Later, even the hull of the *City of St. Joseph* met a tragic fate. It and another barge, the *Transport,* were in the tow of the tug *John Roen* on Lake Superior, bound from Green Bay, Wisconsin, to Grand Marias, Minnesota, when a storm hit them on September 21, 1942. The *Roen* cut them loose and both barges wrecked on the Lake Superior shore near Eagle Harbor, Michigan. The barge captain's wife died in the wreck, her body later washing ashore with the pulpwood logs. The *St. Joseph's* wrecked steel hull was cut up for scrap the following winter—a sad end for the great ship that twin-cities residents had greeted so enthusiastically a half-century before.[35]

Eastland, 1915

She was sleek and beautiful, but the crowd of 2,500 people crammed aboard the *Eastland* knew nothing of her deadly nature. As passengers cavorted on the decks and listened to a band play lively tunes, they could never have guessed that over eight hundred of their number would soon be dead. That morning the *Eastland* would become one of the worst maritime disasters in history.

The Jenks Shipbuilding Company of Port Huron, Michigan, built the *Eastland* in 1903 for the Michigan Steamship Company. John C. Pereue, a veteran Great Lakes skipper, had founded Michigan Steamship in 1902 to compete with the Dunkley-Williams Company, which ran the South Haven-Chicago route, and the Graham & Morton Transportation Company, which had the St. Joseph/Benton Harbor-Chicago run. Besides Pereue, the principal partners in Michigan Steamship were Robert R. Blacker and Patrick Noud, both of Manistee, and Capt. J. J. McKean of Chicago. Michigan Steamship placed a contract for a new passenger steamer with Jenks on October 7, 1902—the first and, as it turned out, only—passenger ship that Jenks would ever build. Mrs. David Reid of South Haven won a company-sponsored public competition to name the new vessel with her entry of the name "Eastland," which met the contest's requirement for an eight-letter name.[36]

Sidney G. Jenks designed the *Eastland.* Jenks Shipbuilding launched it on May 6, 1903, and spent the next two months fitting her out. On July 13, the fitting-out process completed, Jenks showed off the *Eastland* at a public reception. She steamed out of Port Huron for South Haven three days later under command of Capt. Pereue and arrived at her destination early in the morning of July 18. She took on coal and hosted area residents anxious to inspect her, then set out on her first regular run to Chicago at ten o'clock that evening.[37]

The *Eastland* failed to meet her guaranteed speed of twenty miles per hour across Lake Michigan, which led to the first of several modifications that eventually contributed to her undoing. The *Eastland* returned to Port Huron, and during the winter of 1903–1904, Jenks installed the Ellis and Eaves system of induced draft, which used heat exchangers to warm the air being fed into the boiler. In addition, Jenks put in an early air-conditioning system to relieve the ship's rather stuffy interior. Both of these modifications increased the ship's weight and made her disconcertingly top-heavy, but the induced draft system also increased her top speed so that during the 1904 season, she exceeded twenty-two miles per hour on her Lake Michigan crossing.[38]

Despite her improved speed, the *Eastland* soon earned an unsavory reputation as an unsafe ship. Disaster nearly struck when she pulled out of South Haven on July 17, 1904, with over 2,300 passengers on board, many of whom, because of the hot day, climbed up to the hurricane deck. Shortly after her departure, she listed to port by about twelve to fifteen degrees. The chief engineer, William P. Eeles, tried to counter the list by shifting water in the ballast tanks, but she straightened out only to list to starboard. The skipper, Frank Dority, called on the passengers to move down to the main deck, by which time her list had reached an alarming twenty to twenty-five degrees. Water surged through the two aft starboard gangways, which only cleared the waterline by a few feet even when the *Eastland* was on an even keel. Some of the passengers panicked, but Dority and his crew kept their heads and finally regained control and continued on to Chicago.[39]

The Lake Shore Navigation Company bought the *Eastland* in 1907 for a Lake Erie route that ran from Cleveland to the Cedar Point amusement park. Two years later, a group of businessmen headed by Cleveland politician Peter Witt bought her and organized the Eastland Navigation Company, keeping her on Lake Erie. The ship again narrowly escaped disaster on July 1, 1912, when, according to a passenger, she listed twenty-five degrees to port and then thirty degrees to starboard soon after departing Cleveland on a trip to Cedar Point. Again, the crew regained control and the *Eastland* completed her voyage safely.[40]

The *Eastland* returned to Lake Michigan in 1914 when a new St. Joseph firm bought her to run from St. Joseph to Chicago. The Graham & Morton Transportation Company had shifted its operations to Benton Harbor a year earlier, which left St. Joseph without

The steamer *Eastland* entering the harbor at South Haven.
(Courtesy of the Michigan Maritime Museum)

direct ship service to Chicago. In response, a group of businesspeople organized the St. Joseph-Chicago Steamship Company to compete with Graham & Morton. Ironically, the principles in the firm were Edwina C. Graham (widow of Edmon A. Graham, and sister-in-law to John H. Graham of Graham & Morton), her son-in-law, William H. Hull, and Walter C. Steele. The new firm's first steamer, the *Eugene C. Hart*, proved too small for the trade, so St. Joseph-Chicago Steamship bought the larger *Eastland* on June 1, 1914, for $150,000.[41] The *Eastland* went on the St. Joseph to Chicago run on June 14. Two weeks later, her owners hired Harry Pederson of Millburg, a town a few miles east of Benton Harbor, as captain. She operated without incident as a passenger vessel for the next year, running in competition with Graham & Morton's newest steamer, the *City of Grand Rapids*.

An event occurred in April 1912 that would have a profound impact on the *Eastland's* future. Hundreds of miles away, out on the North Atlantic, the White Star liner RMS *Titanic* sank with the loss of over 1,500 lives after striking an iceberg. Politicians and the public alike were dumbstruck when official inquiries revealed that there had not been enough lifeboats to save all the passengers and crew, even though the new passenger liner carried more than enough boats to meet all existing legal requirements. The *Titanic* disaster and the hearing that followed established, at least in the public mind, the need for government regulations to improve maritime safety. This ultimately resulted in the La Follette Seamen's Act, which President Woodrow Wilson signed into law on March 4, 1915. The law included numerous provisions relative to seamen and, most importantly for the *Eastland*, required that ships carry enough lifeboats or life rafts for all passengers and crewmen aboard.

Prior to the start of the 1915 shipping season, the *Eastland's* owners had sought to repair a rotted area of the decking below the linoleum on the main and 'tween decks by pouring a bed of concrete over it and laying down new linoleum. This added between thirty and fifty-seven tons of weight to the already top-heavy ship. Then, in the wake of the "boats for all" legislation, the St. Joseph-Chicago

Company added three lifeboats and six life rafts to the hurricane deck to provide for the desired capacity of 2,500 passengers. The ship designed for six lifeboats now carried eleven lifeboats, thirty-seven life rafts, and a workboat, allowing space for 776 passengers. Life jackets were provided for all passengers and crew. The work of adding the extra lifeboats and rafts was completed on July 2, 1915.[42]

The Hawthorne Club, a social organization of the Western Electric Company Hawthorne factory in Cicero, Illinois, on Chicago's west side, had sponsored an annual employees' picnic in Michigan City, Indiana, since 1911. The *Eastland* had taken part of the group to the picnic in 1914 in cooperation with the Indiana Transportation Company's steamer *Theodore Roosevelt.* The event had gone well, so the Hawthorne Club made the same arrangements for the 1915 picnic.[43] For their part, Michigan City residents eagerly awaited the arrival of the *Eastland* and her passengers and, especially, the spending money they would bring with them. The town had made big plans for the arrival of the *Eastland* and *Theodore Roosevelt* and other smaller ships chartered for the excursion, and hotels and restaurants had stocked up in anticipation of all the extra business. Red, white, and blue bunting and balloons flew everywhere, accompanied by prominent displays of "Welcome" signs.[44]

Early on the morning of the picnic, Saturday, July 24, 1915, the *Eastland* lay at her dock in Chicago. Passengers began boarding for the excursion at 6:40 A.M., and as they swarmed aboard, the ship began to list to starboard. Engineer Joseph M. Erickson and his men observed the list and admitted water into the ballast tanks to counteract it. Like the *Hippocampus* nearly a half-century before, the *Eastland* had a negative metacentric height or reached it as passengers boarded and climbed to the upper decks and added their weight to the ship.[45] Whereas an overload of peaches had doomed the *Hippocampus,* the *Eastland* suffered from the additional weight of equipment, concrete, and, ironically, lifeboats.

Shortly after 7:00 A.M., the *Eastland* had boarded her licensed maximum of 2,500 passengers and had taken on a slight list to port. As the list grew worse, Erickson attempted to compensate by admitting water to the ballast tanks, but with a negative metacentric height there was nothing he could have done to save the ship. The list increased, and at about 7:20 Erickson noticed water flowing in through a port side scupper. He ordered the engines stopped, thinking that vibration was contributing to the instability. The ship tilted still more. Erickson had one of his assistants ask the passengers to move to the starboard side, which they did, but water began flowing onto the deck through the port gangway. Captain Pederson remained unconcerned. He rang up "Stand by" on the engine room telegraph and ordered the stern line cast off. The *Eastland's* stern swung out into the river, her bow lines still attached to the wharf.[46]

With agonizing slowness, the topheavy *Eastland* rolled over to port. Dishes poured from their racks, the ship's piano rolled across the promenade deck and crashed into the port wall, and the refrigerator behind the bar toppled over with a resounding crash. The *Eastland* continued to roll until at last she came to rest on her port side, half submerged in the Chicago River.[47] To her first officer, Delwin Fisher of St. Joseph, the *Eastland* went over "not with a sudden jerk but with the ease and deliberation of a horse lying down upon the grass."[48]

Hundreds of passengers were trapped below decks or on the port side, jammed together with little possibility of escape. Tugboats on the river swarmed to the rescue, taking survivors off the hull and pulling others from the river, but for many passengers they arrived too late. Officials set up a makeshift morgue in the Second Regiment Armory in Chicago, where friends and relatives came to identify bodies of those drowned in the disaster, and where the ghoulishly curious thronged to gape at the victims' bodies.

A young Benton Harbor man, Martin Collins, ran a refreshment stand aboard the *Eastland*. His boyhood chum, Harry Brown, ran a stand on the competing *City of Benton Harbor*. As the *City of Benton Harbor* pulled into her dock, Brown was horrified to see his friend's ship lying on her side, surrounded by riverboats, police, and rescue squads. He ran to the disaster site, got a fireman's pass, and went looking for Collins. He finally found him working with a rescue party,

The *Eastland* lying on its side in the Chicago River.
(Courtesy of the Michigan Maritime Museum)

helping to pull survivors to safety. Collins had fortunately been on the dock when the *Eastland* rolled over.

Other passengers were not as lucky as Collins. By the time rescuers finished their grim work, they had pulled over eight hundred bodies from the *Eastland;* more would die later in hospitals. The death toll reached about 844—no one would ever know with certainty how many people died. It was by far the worst disaster in Great Lakes history, and among the worst maritime catastrophes of all time.

Gwalter C. Calvert, then an eleven-year-old newspaper delivery boy, recalled many years later the sad morning that he delivered the newspaper from house to house through Michigan City. At nearly every stop, the home's occupants would ask him if he planned to see the Western Electric Picnic. Calvert stunned his customers when he told them that there would be no picnic, that the *Eastland* had capsized in Chicago, and that many of those picnickers now lay dead. Workmen quietly gathered up all the festive bunting, he remembered, piled it up, and burned it.[49]

The *Eastland* was pulled from the harbor and later sold to the federal government. The U. S. Navy had her cut down and rebuilt as a training vessel; renamed the USS *Wilmette,* she served as a naval

The USS *Wilmette*, formerly the *Eastland*. *(Courtesy of the Michigan Maritime Museum)*

training gunboat in two world wars. She was decommissioned in 1946 and scrapped in Chicago two years later.[50]

Martin Collins, who had escaped death on the *Eastland*, became the first twin-cities man to die in World War I. The 3,819-ton steamer *Florence H.*, on which he served as a reserve engineer, blew up in Quiberon Bay, France, on April 17, 1918. A few days later, Collins died of burns in a hospital in Brest.[51]

Rising Sun, 1917

The Israelite House of David, whose Great Waters Transportation Company had lost the schooner *Emily and Eliza* in 1910, continued its shipping business—and run of bad luck—with the propeller steamer *Rising Sun*.

After its logging enterprise at Aral petered out, the House of David bought the lumber rights to about 3,500 acres of High Island in 1912. Lumberman George Heimforth had started a logging camp on that northern Lake Michigan island, gone bankrupt, and sold his buildings to the House of David. An island lumber camp required a ship to haul in supplies and carry out finished lumber, so the House of David bought the *Minnie M.* and renamed her *Rising Sun.*[52]

Built in Detroit in 1884 for a group of St. Clair, Michigan, investors headed by Ira Owen, the passenger and freight steamer *Minnie M.* had enjoyed a long and colorful career. She sailed between Cheboygan and Sault Ste. Marie from 1884 until 1892, when the Milwaukee & Eastern Transit Company put her on a St. Joseph-to-Chicago route. In later years, the Arnold Line of Mackinac Island ran her between Cheboygan, Mackinac Island, and Sault Ste. Marie, and the Algoma Central & Hudson Bay Railway sailed her from Sault Ste. Marie and Michipicoten, Ontario, to supply the Helen Mine near Wawa.[53]

The House of David bought the *Minnie M.* on May 1, 1913, and a month later renamed her *Rising Sun.* The name *Rising Sun* had important connotations for the Israelites. Colony founders Benjamin and Mary Purnell had worked as itinerant preachers from 1895 until 1902, when Dan and Clara Pelton took them in at their farm in the Fostoria, Ohio, area near the village of Rising Sun. The *Rising Sun* thus signified the place where the sect's founders had come to rest after seven years of travel.[54]

The *Rising Sun* as the *Minnie M.*, ca. 1915. *(Courtesy of Mary's City of David)*

During the three years after the House of David bought her, the *Rising Sun* steamed faithfully back and forth between St. Joseph and High Island carrying colonists, supplies, and lumber. She prepared to sail out of High Island for St. Joseph on the afternoon of October 29, 1917, under the command of Capt. Charles D. Morrison of St. Joseph, a non-Israelite and veteran skipper of the Great Lakes. She carried a cargo of three thousand bushels of potatoes and some turnips from the colony's farm and over forty thousand board feet of lumber—some sixty tons in all. Eighteen crewmen manned the ship, including First Mate William Schaeffer and Chief Engineer John Smith (both Israelites); fourteen passengers took passage as well.[55]

Forty-nine years and a few days earlier Morrison, then a teenaged wheelsman, had plunged into the cold waters of Lake Michigan when his ship, the steamer *Hippocampus,* capsized. He and fourteen other passengers and crewmen survived the ordeal. During the intervening years, he had built a career on the lakes, winning respect as skipper of the Benton Transit Line steamer *Frank Woods.* When he steered the *Rising Sun* out of High Island, he was a sixty-seven-year-old veteran who had survived just about everything Lake Michigan could throw at him.[56]

The *Rising Sun* at the House of David's dock on High Island.
(Courtesy of Mary's City of David)

A storm blew up shortly before the *Rising Sun's* scheduled departure time and created a strong undertow that began to hammer the ship against the dock. Captain Morrison, afraid that the pounding would damage his vessel, decided to cast off and head southward down the lake and seek shelter in a safe harbor. The wind picked up shortly after the ship left port and soon Morrison and the *Rising Sun* were fighting one of the heaviest fall storms in memory, with churning waves and blinding snow. The mate complained that the ship's compass was acting up and that he could not see ten feet ahead for the snow, but Captain Morrison relied on dead reckoning to traverse the Manitou Passage between the Manitou Islands and Michigan's mainland coast.[57]

At about 9:40 that night, the *Rising Sun* suddenly lurched to one side as she smashed onto rocks off Pyramid Point, some seven miles south of Sleeping Bear Point. Morrison cried to Schaeffer to hold her

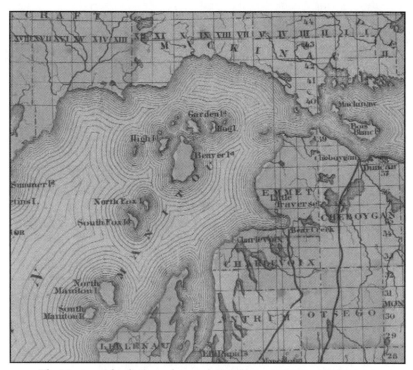

The Manitou Islands in northern Lake Michigan, including High Island.
(Courtesy of the Berrien County Historical Association)

steady, but the mate answered that the ship was swinging in a circle. The impact had torn away her propeller and rudder shoe, allowing the rudder to drop free and catch on the bottom. Helpless, she swung broadside to the waves. A few more seas struck her and carried her over on her beam ends. Within minutes the *Rising Sun* lay wrecked two hundred feet from shore. The passengers and crew first elected to stay with the ship, but then she began to break up. A steam pipe split and put out her engine and electrical system, plunging the ship into darkness.[58]

Captain Morrison weighed the hazards of wind, waves, and darkness and decided to abandon ship. The *Rising Sun* carried five lifeboats. He ordered the first one lowered away with a crew of young men, hoping that after they reached the beach they could help the second boat ashore with the women and children. The lifeboat dropped safely into the water on the ship's lee side and the waves instantly swept it onto the beach. The second lifeboat, loaded with several schoolgirls returning to Benton Harbor, capsized when a heavy sea struck it. Screams from the terrified girls pierced the storm. The men on shore worked frantically to pull them out of the freezing water and somehow, despite the wind, darkness, cold, and snow, managed to rescue them all.[59]

All five lifeboats reached shore safely and some men from the first boat went off to seek help. They soon found the home of Fred Baker near the top of the bluff at Point Oneida, pounded on the door, and woke him up.[60] At 12:40 A.M., the Sleeping Bear Point Coast Guard station at Glen Haven received a telephone call from Baker that the *Rising Sun* was stranded and needed assistance. The Coast Guardsmen, led by Capt. Sigzal B. Johnson, hired two local farmers and their teams of horses, hitched up their surfboat wagon, and set off for Pyramid Point.[61]

In the meantime, Baker hitched up a team and wagon and headed down the road to the beach. The Israelites loaded the children and a sick woman into the wagon and Baker took them up to his house for the night. The Coast Guard crew arrived on the wreck scene at 10:15 that morning, and with the help of local residents lent what

Male survivors of the *Rising Sun* shipwreck. The Israelites did not shave or cut their hair. *(Courtesy of Mary's City of David)*

The Israelite women who survived the wreck of the *Rising Sun*.
(Courtesy of Mary's City of David)

assistance they could to the ship's passengers and crew. As the *Rising Sun* gradually settled into the lake, a wave swept away the pilot house and smokestack. Suddenly someone called out and pointed to a figure still standing on the ship. One of the crew, an elderly man named Ben Putnam, remained on board the doomed vessel having—incredibly—slept through the whole ordeal. Everyone else had overlooked him in the general confusion of abandoning ship. The Coast Guard crew hauled their Lyle gun to the beach and two hours later fired a line across the ship and pulled Putnam to safety. Pyramid Point residents sheltered the women and children in a local home, while the men dried out at a beach bonfire.[62]

The *Rising Sun* went to pieces on the rocks, scattering lumber and potatoes up and down the coast. Her remains still lie in seven to twelve feet of water in the Manitou Passage, easily visible from the shore and a popular attraction for beachcombers, protected from looters by the 282-square-mile sanctuary of the Manitou Passage State Underwater Preserve.

The ship's loss dealt a financial blow to the Israelite community, for the colony carried no insurance on it. Although local newspapers estimated the vessel's worth at $80,000, an enormous sum in 1917, the Israelites themselves reported a value of only $5,000.[63] To replace the *Rising Sun*, Great Waters bought an aged schooner named the *Rosa Belle*. The *Rosa Belle* proved unluckier than either the *Emily and Eliza* or the *Rising Sun* and met with an even more tragic fate.

The steamer *Rising Sun* lies broken a short distance offshore.
(Courtesy of Mary's City of David)

Capt. Charles Morrison, who had survived the wrecks of both the *Hippocampus* and *Rising Sun,* soon returned to the Great Lakes. He retired to his home in St. Joseph in 1924 at age seventy-three, but strolled down to the beach every day to gaze out at the lake waters on which he had spent so much of his life. He died on January 12, 1935, having been the last living survivor of the *Hippocampus* disaster some sixty-seven years before.[64]

Rosa Belle, 1921

Storm, collision, explosion—what tore off the *Rosa Belle's* stern and killed her Israelite passengers and crew? To this day no one knows, and the reason for the schooner's loss will remain forever a mystery.

The House of David Great Waters Transportation Co. bought the old schooner *Rosa Belle* after the *Rising Sun* disaster in 1917. Replacing the relatively modern steamer *Rising Sun* with a fifty-four-year-old sailing ship suggests a diminishing profitability of the High Island logging operation. Great Waters placed a value of only $1,776 on the old schooner, whereas they had valued the *Rising Sun* at $5,000.[65] The *Rosa Belle* had no passenger staterooms, unlike the comparatively luxurious *Rising Sun*, so passengers slept in the cargo hold in spaces partitioned off by worn-out sails. The crew and passengers ate meals at tables in the deck house, but the cramped room could only accommodate a few people at a time. The *Rosa Belle* also depended on the wind instead of steam power, so a light or contrary breeze could extend the passage time for a trip to Benton Harbor by hours or even days.[66]

The *Rosa Belle* was built in Milwaukee, Wisconsin, in 1863 for her owner and master, John Miller. She changed hands several times until 1898, when Nels Petersen, John Kane, John Dillon, and Martin Madson of Sheboygan, Wisconsin, bought her. They spent $3,000 having her completely overhauled in Manitowoc, then sailed her for years, later recalling proudly that she was the last schooner operating out of Sheboygan. John Kane remembered that they usually sailed between Sheboygan and Charlevoix, Michigan, hauling lumber from the Michigan mills to Wisconsin furniture factories and carrying the finished furniture back to Michigan. On occasion, they sailed as far north as Lake Superior. Sometimes, instead of the scent of freshly sawn lumber, the yeasty aroma of Gutsch or Schreier beer drifted up from her hold when the *Rosa Belle* took on a cargo for the saloons of Charlevoix. The crew's spirits always picked up whenever the frothy beverage came aboard, for the cargo manifest invariably came up a little short by the time they made port.[67]

Despite John Kane's fond recollections, the *Rosa Belle* came to the House of David with a checkered past. She had capsized near Grand Haven during a squall in August 1875 while bound for Chicago from Muskegon with a load of lumber, drowning the steward and seriously injuring her captain, Peter Johnson. Captain Johnson and his crew had clung to the rigging for hours until people on shore saved them. The firm of Heber Squier and T. Stewart White rebuilt the *Rosa Belle* at Grand Haven that winter at a cost of $2,500.[68] Years later, in September 1918, the local Coast Guard had to tow her in after a bad storm caught her and her Israelite crew and tore away part of her rigging.[69] The *Rosa Belle* performed adequately for the House of David despite her limitations, carrying supplies from the main colony to the island and hauling finished lumber to Benton Harbor, Mackinaw City, and Cheboygan.

The *Rosa Belle* set sail for High Island in October 1921 with enough provisions from the main colony in Benton Harbor to see the lumber camp through the winter. She reached her destination without incident, took on a full cargo of lumber, and on Monday evening, October 26, headed back to Benton Harbor on what was intended to be her last trip of the 1921 shipping season. Capt. Erhart Gleise of Benton Harbor, a veteran seaman and non-Israelite, commanded the vessel and her crew of eleven Israelite sailors and two passengers.[70]

No one received further word about the *Rosa Belle* until the morning of October 31, when a frightening telegram arrived at the House of David from Capt. Charles Frederickson of the Grand Trunk Railroad car ferry *Ann Arbor No. 4*:

> Steamer Ann Arbor No. 4 at 10:30 Sunday morning sighted sailing vessel Rosa Belle, of Benton Harbor, 42 miles east of Milwaukee. Vessel bottom side up. Apparently vessel had been in

a collision. Stern broken off and all her rigging floating around her side. There was no member of the crew to be seen aboard or in any lifeboat around the wreck as we hung around 30 minutes before proceeding to Grand Haven. Notified Milwaukee Coast Guard which started at once for the wreck.[71]

Frederickson's telegram arrived almost four years to the day after the *Rising Sun* wreck.

The *Ann Arbor No. 4* scanned the derelict for a half hour but found no sign of life. The motor launch usually carried near *Rosa Belle's* stern was missing and presumed carried away in the collision. Few ships then carried wireless sets, and the House of David hoped that whatever vessel collided with her had rescued her crew and simply remained out of communication with shore. Even then the rescued crew might be en route to a safe port. To make the uncertainty even more unbearable, no one at the House of David knew the identities of the *Rosa Belle* crew or even how many Israelites had been aboard. People at the House of David feared that, in addition to her crew, several members of the High Island colony might have boarded her as passengers. With no telegraph or telephone on the island, the Israelite community could only wait and pray.[72]

On High Island, Israelites set off in small boats to scour the shorelines of every nearby island in hopes that the *Rosa Belle* crew had taken to the lifeboat and were either adrift or marooned.[73] The Milwaukee Coast Guard Station sent out the revenue cutter USS *Tuscarora* on a fruitless fourteen-hour search for survivors. Fog set in the following day, but the *Tuscarora* returned to the search on November 2 and spent the entire day cruising the area with no more luck than before.[74] The *Ann Arbor No. 4* had found the *Rosa Belle* far off course; searchers speculated that a strong east wind had blown her into the shipping lanes on the west side of Lake Michigan where some unknown freighter had run her down in the dark. Some Israelites feared foul play. Altercations had occurred between the crews of the car ferries and the *Rosa Belle* during the preceding year, and the Israelites suspected that a ferry had intentionally rammed the schooner.[75]

The crew of the schooner *Rosa Belle*. *(Courtesy of Mary's City of David)*

The *Tuscarora's* quest on November 2 ended thirteen miles from Kenosha, Wisconsin, where she met the USS *Cumberland,* an Engineering Corps ship, towing the *Rosa Belle's* wrecked hull into the harbor at Racine. The *Cumberland* left her on the beach behind the U. S. Life-Saving Station. Early the following morning a wrecking team righted the schooner and divers descended into the submerged hull to look for the remains of her crew. Members of the House of David had given up the possibility of finding survivors, but hoped that at least they might recover the victims' bodies. Upon righting the vessel, workmen discovered that her cabin, most of the stern, and her rigging and both masts were gone. Divers who examined the *Rosa Belle* opined that another ship had rammed her. Only a catastrophic collision, they declared, could have inflicted the kind of damage that the *Rosa Belle* had sustained.[76]

The divers found the *Rosa Belle's* hold empty. A thorough search of the wreck turned up nothing but a few articles of clothing, although what little remained of the cargo blocked the entrance to the forecastle. Israelites hoped that opening the forecastle where most of the crew slept would reveal the bodies, but later investigation found the forecastle vacant as well. Although the Coast Guard and general public kept watch on the beaches, none of the crew's bodies ever washed ashore.[77]

Not until nearly two weeks had passed did Israelites from High Island arrive at the House of David's Benton Harbor colony to report the identities of those who had boarded the *Rosa Belle* for her fateful last voyage. Besides Capt. Erhart Gleise, the dead included First Mate Charles Anderson; Second Mate Waldermer Fredrickson; deck hands Alvin Winder, Robert Daily, Edwin Marshall, Erwin Winge, Jake Von Moulken, and Ulysses Daily; cooks Otis Vaughn and Cecil Caudle; cabin boy Edwin Wilson; and passengers George Hinman and Lauren Nye. All except Gleise were Israelites.[78]

The precise fate of the *Rosa Belle's* crew remains a mystery to this day. Did the capsizing schooner throw them into the lake to drown, or did they launch the lifeboat only to die before reaching safety? What events transpired to wreck the schooner? No bodies were ever recovered, nor did any ship ever admit to colliding with the *Rosa Belle*. The schooner and her lost crew took the secrets of the disaster with them to their watery graves.

The House of David's schooner *Rosa Belle* met a mysterious fate on Lake Michigan.
(Courtesy of Mary's City of David)

The House of David sent a colony member, Edmond Bulley, to Racine to tend to the *Rosa Belle's* wreckage. After helping conduct the unsuccessful search for bodies, Bulley sold the schooner's wreckage and the remainder of its cargo for $125.[79]

The House of David never replaced the *Rosa Belle,* but the High Islanders did build a small motorboat, the *High Island,* in 1925 to make local runs off the island. The Israelites built the *High Island* of wood felled and sawn on the island and planed by hand. The *Rosa Belle,* forgotten and abandoned, was left to rot on the shore at Racine.

Forelle, 1923

The storm must have struck the *Forelle* just as the little packet neared Milwaukee and safety. Other packets like her survived the blow, but the *Forelle's* five crewmen became victims of Lake Michigan.

Julius Meyer and Cornelius Tamms had become commercial fishing partners in Milwaukee by 1890, then became brothers-in-law when Julius married Cornelius' sister Ida in 1894. When their first fishing tug, the *Arthur,* became unseaworthy, they bought a new steel-hulled vessel. Ida Meyer christened her the *Forelle*—the German word for "trout"—and the two partners treated their new investment with tender care. They divided responsibilities so that Cornelius was captain, Julius the engineer, and Cornelius's brother Henry handled the nets.[80]

The *Forelle* arrived in Benton Harbor in the late fall of 1923 as one of a small fleet of packet boats hauling fruit across Lake Michigan to Chicago and Milwaukee. The fishing season had ended, but Tamms and Meyer earned extra money by engaging temporarily in the fruit-hauling business. On September 19, the *Forelle* took on a cargo of 5,800 baskets of grapes at the Robinson Dock on the Benton Harbor Ship Canal. At 7:20 that evening, she chugged down the canal and out of the St. Joseph harbor with Tamms at the helm and Meyer tending the engine. William Lahmann, Jr., had gone along to take care of some business in Michigan and two other passengers, brothers Carl and Walter Rosenstock, offered to help the crew as needed. The *Forelle* had an easy sail nearly halfway across the lake. Then the storm hit.[81]

Capt. Harry Searfoss, skipper of the Benton Harbor-bound fruit packet *American Girl,* passed the *Forelle* at about midnight as he fought a heavy sea churned up by a northeast gale. He saw the *Forelle* laboring against the storm, but she seemed in no real trouble and Searfoss had his own hands full battling the gale. He had loaded up his own boat with grapes at the Israelite House of David docks on the ship canal, unloaded in Milwaukee, and pulled out for the return trip at four o'clock in the afternoon, anticipating an arrival in Benton Harbor at five o'clock the following morning. When the *American Girl* failed to dock on schedule, many mariners feared for her safety; observers thought her top-heavy when she left port and, perhaps recalling the loss of the *Hippocampus* in similar circumstances almost exactly fifty-five years earlier, wondered if history might not repeat itself. Fears deepened when word came that a third fruit packet from Benton Harbor, the wooden-hulled *Golden Girl,* captained by Clarence Graham of Milwaukee and carrying 2,500 packages of fruit, was overdue in Chicago.[82]

Capt. Samuel J. Carlson, commanding the St. Joseph Coast Guard Station, had had a peculiar feeling about the *Forelle,* a sort of uneasy sense of foreboding. His concern led him to follow the fruit packet out onto the glassy smooth lake in a power boat. He noticed an odd light on her, but as he drew nearer he realized that one of the *Forelle's* crewmen was walking around on the deck carrying a hand-held light. He decided that the boat was secure. The following afternoon found Carlson back on the lake hunting for the missing packet.[83]

Some good news about the missing boats arrived on Friday. The *Golden Girl* made port in Chicago some seven hours overdue, and although the violent storm drove the *American Girl* far off course to the north, she finally limped into Muskegon harbor hours late. Still no word came from the *Forelle.* Cornelius Tamms's wife put up a brave front. When Byron C. Bury, manager of the Michigan Fruit & Produce Company which had shipped the grapes aboard the *Forelle,*

The fish tug *Forelle*, lost with all hands in 1923.
(Courtesy of the Historical Collections of the Great Lakes, Bowling Green State University)

contacted her in Milwaukee by telephone, Mrs. Tamms assured him "they are all right and will come to port in time, I am certain."[84]

Coast guard crews from St. Joseph, Milwaukee, and Michigan City, aided by a government tug from Chicago, scoured the region, concentrating their search in the waters of southwest Lake Michigan. Despite their best efforts, another fruit packet discovered the *Forelle's* fate. Three miles off Milwaukee, the *Helen B.* found an oil slick, grape baskets and basket covers, and running lights from the missing boat. The *Forelle* was gone, and with her all five of her crew.[85]

Isabell K., 1937

The *Isabell K.* fell victim to an unprovoked assault.

The thirty-eight-foot fishing tug, owned by John Mollhagen, lay quietly at her dock in the St. Joseph harbor early on Sunday morning, June 27, 1937. She shared the harbor with the big tanker *Comet,* out of East Chicago, Indiana, which had steamed into St. Joseph the previous day with 819,000 gallons of gasoline for the Thiesen-Clemens Company. Heavy fog prevented the 250-foot *Comet,* owned by Marine Tankers, Incorporated, from entering the harbor at her scheduled arrival time on Saturday morning, so she lay off St. Joseph for several hours until the fog lifted. She finally made port at about one o'clock on Saturday afternoon.[86]

After discharging her volatile cargo, the *Comet* swung around in the harbor turning basin. Someone at the helm misjudged distances. The tanker struck the *Isabell K.*, crushing the fishing tug and smashing the dock and some of the local fisherman's gear. The *Comet* soon headed into Lake Michigan without further incident, but the *Isabell K.* lay a sunken wreck at her dock.[87]

City of Cleveland III, 1950

Newspaper editors in Benton Harbor and St. Joseph hardly knew which story to headline. On some days little of note occurred either locally or in the outside world, and they had to fumble about to find something truly newsworthy. On June 25, 1950, however, big stories poured into the newsrooms. An airliner crashed in Lake Michigan near South Haven, killing all aboard, while halfway around the world the Korean War broke out. Across the state on Lake Huron, a collision involving the cruise ship the *City of Cleveland III* killed and

The *City of Cleveland* in about 1908, shortly after she began service with the Detroit & Cleveland Steam Navigation Company and before the Roman numeral III was added to her name. *(Courtesy of the Berrien County Historical Association)*

injured several members of the local Chamber of Commerce. The screaming headlines jostled each other for space on page one. The *City of Cleveland III* disaster, however, made the greatest personal impact on most southwest Michigan residents.

The Detroit Shipbuilding Company launched the *City of Cleveland* on January 5, 1907, at its Wyandotte, Michigan, yard. Frank E. Kirby, architect of the *Chicora,* designed it for the Detroit & Cleveland Steam Navigation Company. Detroit & Cleveland intended to put her into service that spring, but on May 13 her superstructure burned before she left the builder's Orleans slip. Her rebuild cost $1,250,000 and delayed her entry into service until 1908. In 1912 the owners added the Roman numeral III to her name.[88]

On Thursday evening, June 22, 1950, eighty members (all men) of the St. Joseph-Benton Harbor Chamber of Commerce boarded the *City of Cleveland III* at Grand Haven, Michigan, for the chamber's fourth annual Great Lakes cruise. The group had chartered the

The *City of Cleveland III* taking on passengers for what would be her final voyage, 1950. *(Courtesy of the Berrien County Historical Association)*

ship for a week, and chamber members looked forward to a Great Lakes cruise capped off by watching the Detroit Tigers play a doubleheader baseball game on Sunday. The weather refused to cooperate. A storm rocked the ship on Thursday night, then the *Cleveland* spent much of Friday fogbound off Grand Traverse Bay. The *Cleveland* put in at Harbor Springs, on Little Traverse Bay, on Saturday morning due to the fog and stayed in port until 2:30 that afternoon. The fog delay forced cancellation of scheduled stops at Mackinac Island and Sault Ste. Marie, so when the *Cleveland* steamed out of Harbor Springs on Sunday, she headed directly through the Straits of Mackinac and down Lake Huron for Detroit.[89]

That same morning, June 25, found the Norwegian freighter *Ravnefjell* northbound up the lake. The 1,338.74-ton steamer, owned and operated by Olsen & Uglestad of Oslo, had pulled out of Sarnia, Ontario, at 1:15 A.M. that morning bound for Milwaukee.[90] Her course took her almost straight up Lake Huron and nearer to the *Cleveland*, still miles away, with every passing minute.

The *Cleveland's* master, Capt. Rudolph J. Kiessling, maintained his ship's full cruising speed of eighteen miles per hour. As she steamed down Lake Huron in the pre-dawn hours, he put her on a course between the upbound and downbound lanes established for ships on the lake so that he could avoid weaving in and out as he overhauled slower downbound vessels. It never occurred to the captain that another master on an upbound ship might decide to do the same thing. The lake was calm, with no sea or swell. At 5:40 A.M. the passenger liner's crew noted that the light at Harbor Beach, Michigan, just off the tip of Michigan's thumb, lay directly off the *Cleveland's* starboard beam some 6.7 miles away. Thirteen minutes later she entered fog. The mate on watch immediately began making the Great Lakes' fog signal: three blasts on the horn at one-minute intervals. He did not, however, order a reduction in speed. A few minutes later the first mate, who was then being relieved at the helm by the twenty-five-year-old third mate, Carl P. Luttenbacher, ordered his replacement to summon Captain Kiessling to the bridge.[91]

The *City of Cleveland III* at dock during her final cruise.
(Courtesy of the Berrien County Historical Association)

Rudolph Kiessling reached the *Cleveland's* pilot house a few minutes before 6:00 A.M. His ship carried radar, a military surplus Raytheon SC-1 set left over from World War II, but it was not working: Detroit & Cleveland's general superintendent had ordered it rendered inoperable the previous September.[92] The fog and dead radar set left Kiessling as blind as the first sailors on the Lakes. As Kiessling strained to see through the enveloping mist, he heard another ship's foghorn. *Cleveland* replied with her own horn. Kiessling listened intently as the heavy tones carried across the water. He decided that the other ship, invisible in the fog, was also southbound and ahead of the *Cleveland.*[93]

The *Ravnefjell* had set a course up Lake Huron that morning that put her at least 3,500 feet west of the normal upbound lane. The Norwegian entered areas of patchy fog shortly after 3:30 A.M. and, like the *Cleveland,* immediately started sounding a fog signal. Unlike the American liner she slackened speed slightly, dropping from seven to six and one-half knots.[94] The *Ravnefjell* carried an English-made radar set, but hers, unlike the *Cleveland's,* was working. At 5:44 A.M. the Norwegian's first mate picked up a radar contact bearing five degrees on the starboard bow at a distance of eight miles and rang up stand-by on the engine room telegraph. The activity brought the captain to the pilot house to investigate.[95]

During the next few minutes, the freighter and passenger liner called back and forth to each other through the dense fog. Passenger H. Thomas Dewhirst, head of the Israelite House of David, listened from his cabin as the other foghorn drew nearer and nearer to the *Cleveland.* He looked out through his cabin's porthole, but saw only thick, swirling fog. Carl Luttenbacher, too, stared out into the fog from his lookout perch on C deck in the bow, trying to see the other ship. Still Kiessling gave no order to slacken speed, no order to sound a danger signal.[96]

Across the narrowing gap, the *Ravnefjell* plowed through the fog on a collision course with the liner. The distance between the two ships closed rapidly. The Norwegian's thirty-seven-year-old skipper, Rolf W. Thorsen, watched with mounting alarm as the *Cleveland's* radar blip slid across the screen from starboard, drawing ever closer to his vessel. Thorsen altered course to port and sounded a two-blast whistle to signal the other ship of the change.[97]

Captain Kiessling tried to make sense of what he was hearing and decided that he was overtaking another downbound ship, just as he had anticipated. From the sound of the foghorn, she was so far away that he would not need to sound a passing signal. To be on the safe side, he turned ten degrees to starboard. He intended to give the other ship a wider berth, but the turn put the *Cleveland* on a collision course with the freighter.[98]

At 6:11 A.M. the *Cleveland's* blip disappeared inside the minimum limits of the *Ravnefjell's* radar. Two minutes later, the liner emerged from the fog directly off the Norwegian's port side and Thorsen yelled a command to turn.[99]

Luttenbacher gaped in horror as the dark form loomed out of the mist. The *Ravnefjell* "had a bone in her mouth"—a term sailors used to describe the white foam a ship's bow kicked up when moving at speed—and was headed directly for the *Cleveland's* port side. A bare quarter mile separated the vessels.[100] Kiessling instantly ordered right full rudder. A few seconds later, as the relative positions of the two ships and their closing angles and speeds became apparent, he reversed his order and called for left full rudder.[101]

On the *Ravnefjell's* bridge, Thorsen spotted the *Cleveland* racing across his ship's bow at her full sixteen miles per hour. He rang up full speed astern on the engine room telegraph in a desperate attempt to swing the freighter's bow to starboard. The fog blotted out all outside reference points, which meant that Thorsen was turning in a gray void with little sense of relative motion. He had trouble determining whether his own bow was swinging around, especially since the *Cleveland* was turning at the same time. A minute after his first call to the engine room, Thorsen ordered right full rudder and full speed ahead to accelerate the freighter's turn. The hard right rudder swung the bow to starboard, but the *Cleveland* seemed drawn to the *Ravnefjell.* Thorsen ordered full speed astern once more, then finally all stop.[102]

The *Ravnefjell* needed at least a quarter mile to stop, even with the engine full astern. She had nowhere near that distance.

A final blast sounded from the Norwegian's foghorn, followed by a rending crash as her bow sliced into the *Cleveland* just aft of the port paddlewheel. The bow drove through the liner's sponson until it reached the hull, then tore aft through the superstructure for about one hundred feet until it swung clear. The freighter stopped dead in the water behind the injured liner.[103]

The impact smashed staterooms to kindling. Passengers in cabins far from the spot hardly noticed the crash, but others felt the full force of the blow. The freighter's bow had plunged directly into Tom Dewhirst's cabin. He and Louis Patitucci, a South Bend frozen-food dealer who had occupied the adjacent cabin, lay trapped and severely injured in the wreckage.

"Tell Dorothy, Michele, and Susan goodbye for me," Patitucci said, thinking of his family.

Dewhirst replied that he did not know whether he himself would survive, but Patitucci assured him that he would live.

"If I make it you will make it, too," Dewhirst said resolutely. Patitucci answered only, "Well, maybe."

A moment later their cabins crumbled, the decks gave way under them, and the two men plummeted into the lake amid a crushing cloud of debris.[104]

Dewhirst swam out from under the wreckage. He at first found nothing large enough to hold onto to keep his head above water, but soon discovered that he could "dog paddle" with his hands and thus stay afloat. His legs seemed useless and he would learn later that they were both broken. Patitucci had disappeared, but Dewhirst at last found a piece of wreckage and crawled onto it to stay afloat.[105]

Many passengers in cabins located farther from the impact site remained unaware of the collision. Nelson Foulkes, a reporter for St. Joseph's *Herald-Press* newspaper, shared a cabin with George Culverhouse, a reporter for the competing *Benton Harbor News-Palladium.* To the two newspapermen, the collision seemed only "a jar that shook the two beds in our stateroom." The impact woke them from a sound sleep and a moment later the ship's alarm bell began ringing.

"What the hell is that?" Culverhouse asked.

"That is the alarm for a fire or distress signal," Foulkes replied. "It is probably a fire drill."

As the reporters finished dressing, they heard the ship's maids calling "Get into the life preservers." They hurried on deck and joined a general rush for the lifeboats. Crewmen and passengers set to work with the davits to lower the lifeboats, but ship's officers soon stopped them. Many passengers, still unaware of the gravity of the situation, stood on deck looking out into the fog, joking about all the activity and listening to the two foghorns still blowing. A moment later someone exclaimed, "We have been hit. Look at the mess back there." The jokes stopped. The fog began to lift and the cruise members could distinguish the *Ravnefjell* lying about two hundred yards off the port side. A couple of lifeboats were picking their way through the wreckage.[106]

Both lifeboats belonged to the *Ravnefjell.* One drew up to Tom Dewhirst and the crew pulled the 310-pound Israelite from the water and eased him into the bow of the boat. A sailor gave Dewhirst a heavy knitted wool sweater to keep him warm. The crew also found Mervyn Stouck and Talma "Tom" Spooner and pulled them aboard. Spooner was alive but badly injured. Stouck was dead. The former mayor of Benton Harbor had taken an early morning walk on deck and bad luck had put him at the impact site when the freighter struck the *City of Cleveland.*

The Norwegian freighter *Ravnefjell* lies dead in the water as her crew searches for survivors. *(Courtesy of the Berrien County Historical Association)*

As the sailors in the lifeboats pulled for the cruise ship, the deeply religious Dewhirst looked back at the place where they had pulled him from the water. There he saw "a beautiful array of fog or mist in the shape of a half sun at sunrise on the water about 50 to 75 feet across, and shooting white rays into the air like an aurora borealis, and in the background two large pillars, one on each side. It seemed to me the Lord himself was there."[107]

Confusion abounded over the identities of the crash victims or who remained unaccounted for. The freighter's crew had heard survivors calling from the water and immediately lowered both their lifeboats and began a search. In the meantime, Captain Thorsen got on his ship's radiotelephone and inquired as to the severity of damage to the liner and whether she had anyone missing. The *Cleveland* replied that all her passengers and crew were aboard and that she anticipated getting underway for Detroit, a surprising statement in view of the fact that the crew could hardly have accounted for all her passengers by that time. Thorsen recalled his lifeboats, then learned that his starboard boat contained three survivors. He personally rode over to the *Cleveland* with the three injured passengers, climbed up

Anxious passengers watch recovery operations from the deck of the crippled *City of Cleveland III. (Courtesy of the Berrien County Historical Association)*

to the pilothouse to meet with Captain Kiessling, and used the *Cleveland's* radiotelephone to order his lifeboats to continue the search for survivors. The other lifeboat recovered the body of former Benton Harbor Police Chief Alvin Boyd, who had died instantly in the crash. Louis Patitucci and Fred Skelley, a Benton Harbor automobile dealer, were missing. Crewmen hoisted the dead and injured up to the *Cleveland,* where the ship's doctor, assisted by Dr. Charles J. Ozeran of Benton Harbor, gave the injured medical attention. Father Revas O'Neil of Notre Dame performed the last rites over Boyd's body.[108]

No one at first missed Richard Lybrook, a sales manager for the Twin City Chevrolet Agency, until passenger Robert Cannell noticed his hand protruding from the wreckage. Only after consultation with the ship's purser, who had the stateroom assignments, did cruise members determine that Patitucci and Skelley were missing.[109] Rescuers pulled Lybrook from the debris, injured but expected to live, and found Patitucci's body in the water several hours later. Skelley's body was never recovered. Two crewmen, one on the *Cleveland* and one on the *Ravnefjell,* suffered minor injuries.[110]

As with so many maritime disasters, chance determined who would live or die. Mervyn Stouck had simply walked into the wrong place at the wrong time. Others had better luck. Thomas O'Hara of Watervliet, disgusted with the bad weather that had plagued the cruise, left the ship at Harbor Springs; the crash destroyed his stateroom. Richard Cronin, also of Watervliet, narrowly escaped death when the impact drove a plank through his window and past his head while he was shaving.[111]

The Harbor Beach Coast Guard Station officer-in-charge, Kenneth Call, arrived on the scene shortly after the wreck in one of the station's boats and carried the injured to the Harbor Beach hospital. Captain Kiessling found that the *Cleveland* could still move under her own power, so he continued to Detroit, where the cruise ship finally docked late Sunday night. The *Ravnefjell* survived the collision with minimal damage and proceeded to Milwaukee, then had temporary repairs made in Chicago in preparation for her return to Norway. A sober-faced Chamber of Commerce group boarded a special train

Damage to the *City of Cleveland III* from the collision.
(Courtesy of the Berrien County Historical Association)

at Detroit and returned to St. Joseph-Benton Harbor that evening.[112]

A Marine Board of Investigation conducted an inquiry into the disaster at the Federal Building in Detroit from July 6 to 8, 1950. The inquiry concluded with Captain Kiessling charged with misconduct, particularly with regard to navigating between the upbound and downbound lanes through dense fog at eighteen miles per hour and without reducing speed even when he heard another ship's fog signal ahead. The Board fixed less blame on Captain Thorsen, but noted that he had continued to steam ahead at six and one-half knots despite his inability to determine the course of the vessel on his radar and had failed to blow a danger signal.[113]

H. T. Dewhirst and Tom Spooner returned home from the hospital to recuperate, but Richard Lybrook remained in the hospital, drifting in and out of consciousness. Then came word that Lybrook was worse—Lybrook was dead. His passing brought to five the number of fatalities in the cruise-ship collision.[114]

The Chamber of Commerce cruise turned out to be the *City of Cleveland III*'s final voyage. The vessel sustained damage estimated at nearly $600,000, but the collision had only injured the *Cleveland's* superstructure, not her hull, and Detroit & Cleveland officials decided to repair her. After the steamer completed its voyage to Detroit, Detroit & Cleveland took her to the Great Lakes Engineering Works at River Rouge for repairs. Later, however, Detroit & Cleveland decided to cut the old liner down for use as a crane barge. In October 1954, she caught fire and burned at Windsor, Ontario, while that work was underway. From Windsor she was towed to Cleveland, Ohio, where vandals opened the seacocks and sank her. She eventually went to the scrapyard at Buffalo, New York, in 1956.[115]

---

1. The definitive history of the Israelite House of David is Clare E. Adkin, Jr., *Brother Benjamin: A History of the Israelite House of David* (Berrien Springs, MI: Andrews University Press, 1990); also good is Robert S. Fogarty, *The Righteous Remnant: The House of David* (Kent, OH: The Kent State University Press, 1981). For a brief overview of the colony's history see Robert C. Myers, *Millennial Visions and Earthly Pursuits: The Israelite House of David* (Berrien Springs, MI: Berrien County Historical Association, 1999).

2. John Haswell, "History of Aral" (Frankfurt, MI: Benzie Shores District Library, n.d.); Adkin, Jr., *Brother Benjamin,* 87.

3. Annual Corporation Report of the Great Waters Transportation Company, 1910, Berrien County Historical Association, Berrien Springs, MI.

4. Clare E. Adkin, Jr., "Island Israelites," in Florence C. Frank, ed., *The Journal of Beaver Island History,* vol. 4 (Beaver Island, MI: Beaver Island Historical Society, 1998), 59.

5. *Merchant Vessels of the United States* (Washington, DC: Government Printing Office, 1911), 410.

6. Adkin, Jr., 87–89.

7. Ibid., 88; John Haswell, "History of Aral."

8. The *Evening Star's* loss was reported in the *St. Joseph Saturday Herald,* November 18, 1911.

9. Ibid.

10. *The Chicago Daily Tribune,* November 13, 1911.

11. *St. Joseph Saturday Herald,* November 18, 1911; Life-Saving Station Logs, Chicago District, St. Joseph Station, November 13, 1911, RG 26, NARA, Great Lakes Region (Chicago).

12. Ibid.

13. The *Hattie Wells,* in Vessel Listings, Historical Collections of the Great Lakes, Bowling Green State University, Bowling Green, OH.

14. The account of the *Hattie Wells* wreck appears in the *St. Joseph Saturday Herald,* November 9, 1912.

15. Ibid.

16. Ibid.

17. Ibid.

18. *St. Joseph Saturday Herald,* March 22, 1890.

19. Ibid., June 7, 1890.

20. Ibid.

21. Ibid.

22. James L. Elliott, *Red Stacks over the Horizon: The Story of the Goodrich Steamboat Line* (Grand Rapids, MI: William B. Eerdmanns Publishing Company, 1967), 263.

23. Indiana and Illinois laws required couples to apply for a marriage certificate and then wait several days before marrying, while Michigan had no waiting period. Impatient brides and grooms often hurried to Michigan to get married, so that during the early twentieth century about two-thirds of marriages performed in Berrien County were for out-of-state couples.

24. *St. Joseph Saturday Herald,* September 5, 1914; *Chicago Tribune,* September 2, 1914.

25. Ibid.

26. *Chicago Tribune,* September 2, 1914.

27. Ibid.

28. Ibid.

29. Ibid.

30. *St. Joseph Saturday Herald,* September 5, 1914.

31. Ibid.

32. Elliott, 264; Wade, 419.

33. *The Herald-Press* (St. Joseph, MI), March 7, 1936.

34. Ibid., April 15, 1936.

35. Elliott, 264; Greenwood, 362.

36. George W. Hilton, *Eastland: Legacy of the Titanic* (Stanford, CA: Stanford University Press, 1995), 15–25.

37. Ibid., 29–36.

38. Ibid., 39–43.

39. Ibid., 46–47.

40. Ibid., 55–61.

41. Ibid., 64–65; Annual Corporation Report of the St. Joseph-Chicago Steamship Company, 1914, Berrien County Historical Association, Berrien Springs, MI.

42. Hilton, 70–78.

43. Ibid., 69–71.

44. *The Michigan City News,* July 28, 1915.

45. Hilton, 94–97.

46. Ibid., 87–108.

47. Ibid., 109–11.

48. *St. Joseph Daily Press,* July 24, 1916.

49. Gwalter C. Calvert to Capt. Merwin S. Thompson, February 13, 1967, in the "Ships and Shipwrecks" file, Michigan City Public Library, Michigan City, Indiana.

50. Peter J. Van der Linden, *Great Lakes Ships We Remember* (Cleveland, OH: Freshwater Press, 1979; rev. ed. 1986), 169.

51. *St. Joseph Herald-Press,* April 26 and May 1, 1918.

52. Ramon Nelson, *The House of David on High Island* (Ann Arbor, MI: Sarah Jennings Press, 1990), 11; Adkin, Jr., *Brother Benjamin,* 88–89.

53. Peter J. Van der Linden, *Great Lakes Ships We Remember II* (Cleveland, OH: Freshwater Press, 1984), 226; Steve Harold, *Shipwrecks of the Sleeping Bear* (Traverse City, MI: Pioneer Study Center, 1984), 25.

54. Ibid.; Clare E. Adkin, Jr., *Brother Benjamin,* 13.

55. *St. Joseph Herald-Press,* October 30, 1917; *The News-Palladium* (Benton Harbor, MI), October 30, 1917; U. S. Coast Guard Casualty and Wreck Reports, 1913–1939, National Archives Microfilm Publication T 925, Roll 3, File No. 275, RG 26, NARA—Great Lakes Region (Chicago). Newspaper reports stated that the *Rising Sun* carried twenty crew and six passengers; the complement in the text is taken from Capt. Charles Morrison's accounting in the Coast Guard's Casualty and Wreck Report.

56. *The News Palladium,* January 13, 1935.

57. *Traverse City* (Michigan) *Record-Eagle,* October 31, 1917; *St. Joseph Herald-Press,* October 30, 1917; *The News-Palladium,* October 30, 1917.

58. Ibid.

59. Ibid.

60. Harold, 28.

61. Chicago District, Log of the No. 261 Coast Guard Station, October 30, 1917, RG 26, NARA—Great Lakes Region (Chicago); *Traverse City Record-Eagle,* October 31, 1917.

62. Ibid., *St. Joseph Herald-Press,* October 30, 1917; Harold, 28; The News-Palladium, October 30, 1917.

63. U. S. Coast Guard Casualty and Wreck Reports, 1913–1939, National Archives Microfilm Publication T 925, Roll 3, Rile No. 275, RG 26, NARA—Great Lakes Region (Chicago); Annual Corporation Report of the Great Waters Transportation Company, 1918, Berrien County Historical Association, Berrien Springs, MI. The *Rising Sun's* boiler is still visible at this date (2002) at the wreck site.

64. *The News Palladium,* January 13, 1935.

65. Annual Reports of the Great Waters Transportation Company, 1918–1921, Berrien County Historical Association, Berrien Springs, Michigan.

66. Ramon Nelson, *Island Life, Island Toil: The House of David on High Island* (Ann Arbor, MI: Sarah Jennings Press, 1990), 128.

67. Undated newspaper clipping, David D. Swayze collection, Weidman, Michigan.

68. *The Grand Rapids Daily Morning Times,* August 7, 1875; *The News-Palladium* (Benton Harbor, MI), November 1, 1921; Mansfield, 1:731; *Detroit Tribune,* April 15, 1876; Libel of Heber Squier and T. Stewart White against the Schooner *Rosabelle,* April 6, 1876, Admiralty Records, Admiralty Case Files, Western Division of Michigan, Southern Division at Grand Rapids, RG 21, NARA—Great Lakes Region (Chicago).

69. *The News-Palladium,* October 31, 1921.

70. Ibid., November 11, 1921.

71. Ibid., October 31, 1921.

72. *St. Joseph Herald-Press,* October 31, 1921.

73. Ibid., November 1, 1921.

74. Ibid., November 3, 1921.

75. Ibid., October 31, 1921; Adkin, Jr., 100.

76. *St. Joseph Herald-Press,* November 3, 1921. Capt. William Kincaid of the U. S. Coast Guard initially attributed the ship's loss to a leak in her hull that waterlogged her cargo and swamped her. A later report declared that a gasoline tank used to power a pump had exploded. Unidentified newspaper clippings, David D. Swayze collection, Weidman, Michigan.

77. Ibid.

78. *The News-Palladium,* November 11, 1921; U. S. Coast Guard Casualty and Wreck Reports, 1913–1939, National Archives Microfilm Publication T 295, Roll 6, File No. 259, RG 26, NARA—Great Lakes Region (Chicago).

79. U. S. Coast Guard Casualty and Wreck Reports, 1913–1939, National Archives Microfilm Publication T 295, Roll 6, File No. 259, RG 26, NARA—Great Lakes Region (Chicago).

80. Ruth Kriehn, "The Meyer-Tamms Families," unpublished manuscript, *Forelle* folder, The Herman G. Runge Collection, Milwaukee Public Library, Milwaukee, WI, n.d.

81. Ibid.; *St. Joseph Herald-Press,* September 21, 1923.

82. Ibid.

83. Ibid., September 22, 1923.

84. Ibid., September 21, 1923.

85. Ibid., September 23 and 24, 1923.

86. *The Herald-Press,* June 28, 1937; The *Comet,* in Vessel Listings, Historical Collections of the Great Lakes.

87. *The Herald-Press,* June 28, 1937.

88. Peter Van Der Linden, *Great Lakes Ships We Remember II* (Cleveland, OH: Freshwater Press, Inc., 1984), 66.

89. *The Herald-Press* (St. Joseph, MI), extra edition, June 26, 1950.

90. United States Coast Guard, "Report of the Marine Board of Investigation on the collision involving the SS *City of Cleveland III* and SS *Ravnefjell* on June 25, 1950," September 21, 1950, United States Coast Guard Headquarters, Washington, DC. Hereafter "Report of the Marine Board of Investigation."

91. Ibid.

92. Ibid. The Coast Guard's report did not explain the Detroit & Cleveland official's reason for disconnecting the *Cleveland's* radar set.

93. Ibid.; *The Herald-Press,* June 28, 1950.

94. "Report of the Marine Board of Investigation." As a sea-going vessel, the *Ravnefjell* calculated its speed in knots, not miles per hour as a Great Lakes ship would do.

95. Ibid.

96. *The Herald-Press,* July 7 and 11, 1950.

97. "Report of the Marine Board of Investigation"; *The News-Palladium* (Benton Harbor, MI), June 29, 1950.

98. "Report of the Marine Board of Investigation."

99. *The News-Palladium,* June 29, 1950.

100. *The Herald Press,* July 7, 1950.

101. "Report of the Marine Board of Investigation."

102. Ibid.

103. Ibid.; *The Herald Press,* July 7, 1950.

104. Ibid., July 11, 1950.

105. Ibid.

106. Ibid., extra edition, June 26, 1950.

107. *The Herald Press,* July 11, 1950.

108. "Report of the Marine Board of Investigation"; *The News-Palladium,* June 25, 1950.

109. *The News-Palladium,* June 25, 1950.

110. "Report of the Marine Board of Investigation"; *The Herald Press,* June 26, 1950.

111. *The Herald Press,* June 26, 1950.

112. Ibid; "Report of the Marine Board of Investigation." Dr. Charles J. Ozeran reportedly stated that falling debris killed a lookout on the *Ravnefjell,* but he was mistaken.

113. "Report of the Marine Board of Investigation."

114. *The Herald-Press,* June 27, 1950.

115. "Report of the Marine Board of Investigation"; Van Der Linden, *Great Lakes Ships We Remember II,* 66.

Epilogue

T he port of St. Joseph/Benton Harbor remains an important commercial harbor. Freighters that call there no longer carry the fruit and lumber that comprised much of the nineteenth-century cargoes; instead, they haul limestone, foundry sand, blast furnace-slag, cement, and salt. Eighty-seven ships arrived at St. Joseph in 2001, bearing 1,118,964 tons of cargo. Sixty-two of the arrivals were destined for Consumers Asphalt Company, the port's most active shipper, which imported 785,591 tons of limestone, sand, and slag for its facility on Industrial Island. Ships arriving for Consumers included the American Steamship Company's *Buffalo* and *Sam Laud,* and the Lower Lakes Towing Company's *Maumee, Calumet,* and *Cuyahoga.*[1] McCoy Docking brought in smaller quantities of limestone and salt, accounting for thirteen of the arriving ships and 120,853 tons of cargo.[2]

Lafarge North America, a French-owned company, imports cement in its own ships, including the *Alpena, J. A. W. Inglehart,* and *Paul H. Townsend,* and the barge *Integrity* and its tug, the *Jacklyn M.* In 2001, thirty-two arrivals brought in 212,520 tons of cement, which the company offloaded into its big elevators near the harbor entrance.[3]

Passenger vessels, however, no longer visit St. Joseph/Benton Harbor. The Graham & Morton Transportation Company, which had dominated the local shipping scene for a half century, suffered declining revenues as automobiles and trucks driving on improved roads cut into the company's trade. When Graham & Morton merged with its arch rival the Goodrich Transportation Company in 1924, the proud Graham & Morton name passed from existence. Graham & Morton's five remaining ships—the *City of Benton Harbor, City of Grand Rapids, City of St. Joseph, City of Holland,* and *City of Saugatuck*—became part of the Goodrich fleet. The *City of St. Joseph's* fate has already been noted; the rest of the grand old Graham & Morton vessels eventually went to the scrapyards.[4] Goodrich later fell victim to the same changes in transportation that destroyed Graham & Morton, and the Great Depression of the 1930s destroyed any hopes that the company might survive. The line went bankrupt in 1933 and its assets were liquidated over the succeeding two years.[5]

The United States Coast Guard still maintains a station at St. Joseph whose crew serve with the same courage and resolve of their predecessors in the old Life-Saving Service. The nature of the service has changed, however, for the great passenger steamers have disappeared from the Great Lakes, and the small wooden schooners have given way to a much smaller number of steel-hulled freighters. By the mid-twentieth century, shipwrecks had become a rare occurrence, a far cry from the situation of only a few years before when dozens of schooners annually came to grief. Big freighters can still fall victim to storm, as witness the fate of the *Edmund Fitzgerald* on Lake Superior, but in the past century the wrecks have usually taken place far from shore, not immediately outside a harbor. Improved technology and the changed nature of the mission have replaced the old lifeboats and surfboats with aircraft and powerful engine-driven rescue vessels. Likewise, modern navigation aids have reduced the importance of lighthouses for Great Lakes sailors.

William L. Stevens, keeper of the St. Joseph Life-Saving Station from 1879 onward, stayed with the service after the Life-Saving Service merged with the Revenue Marine to become the United States Coast Guard in 1915. He retired two years later. Captain Stevens had saved the lives of scores of sailors and passengers on Great Lakes ships, but the gratitude those people felt never found expression in monetary compensation from the federal government. A few years later, the elderly captain found himself a childless widower, living in poverty in a little second-floor, rented room on Empire Avenue in Benton Harbor. For several years he spent the winter with friends in Orlando, Florida, where he died on January 26, 1932.[6]

Captain Stevens's entire estate at the time of his death amounted to less than forty dollars. He owed seventy-three dollars in back rent and his landlord confiscated his household goods to pay it. His meager Coast Guard pension at least provided for burial expenses, and his body was returned to his native Michigan for the funeral. When he was laid to rest in Benton Harbor's Crystal Springs Cemetery, his pallbearers included three members of his old Coast Guard crew—John Karsten, Charles Burkhard, and Charles Roberts—and an active Guardsman, Michael Muszynski.[7]

The old St. Joseph lighthouse on Lake Street remained standing for many years after it ceased to serve its original purpose. In 1936, the government gave the building to the city of St. Joseph. The lighthouse stood until 1955, when—over the bitter protests of many citizens—St. Joseph demolished it to make way for a parking lot. The lights at the end of the north pier remain, however, and still use the original fourth-order Fresnel lens to mark the harbor entrance. In the fall of 1983, the U. S. Coast Guard announced that it would demolish the steel catwalks leading out to the lighthouses at St. Joseph, South Haven, Manistee, Grand Haven, and Michigan City, citing their poor condition and expense of maintenance. The catwalks had been built to allow lighthouse keepers to reach the lights during bad weather when waves might have swept them off the piers and to provide a walkway easier to traverse than the rough rock piers that led out to many of the lights. Although long obsolete for any practical purpose, the catwalk retained an undeniable aesthetic appeal. In response to the threatened demolition, St. Joseph residents formed a "Citizens to Save the Catwalk" Committee, chaired by Judy Butzbaugh. Their work culminated in the city of St. Joseph obtaining ownership of the catwalk in the summer of 1988 and an allocation of funds to repair and repaint it.[8] The lighthouse with its intact catwalk is probably the most photographed landmark in St. Joseph; in 1995 the U. S. Postal Service featured it on a commemorative postage stamp.

Of all the ships wrecked along the Berrien County coast, the remains of only one vessel—the *Havana*—are known to survive at the present time. The wreckage lies in fifty-five feet of water some six miles north of St. Joseph where the ship sank in 1887. It still attracts sport divers who desire a personal contact with Great Lakes maritime history. As previously noted, tourists can view the grave of the *Rising Sun* in Northern Lake Michigan in the Manitou Passage. Wooden parts of the ship have long since vanished, but metal pieces of wreckage remain. The *Rising Sun's* single-piston, steeple-tower engine, bilge framing, and heavy machinery can still be seen at the vessel's gravesite.[9]

The greatest prize, at least for divers intent on the romance of shipwrecks, is the *Chicora,* whose grave remains one of Lake Michigan's darkest secrets. In many respects, the propeller steamer lost in 1895 has little to offer maritime historians: the vessel's design and manner of operation are well known, she carried no cargo of note, and no great mystery exists about the reasons for her loss. Despite this, the *Chicora* continues to fascinate divers and maritime historians. Something about the nearly new steamer, lost with all aboard at the height of America's Guilded Age, stirs an unquenchable desire to learn what happened to her and her crew in their final hours of life.

The mysterious fate of the Graham & Morton steamer caught the imagination of several members of the Southwest Michigan Underwater Preserve (SWMUP) board of the directors, who in the late 1990s set out to locate and document the wreck. Funding the search with volunteer time as well as money contributed by interested members of the public, Bernie Harris, Craig Rich, Jack van Heest, Valerie van Heest, and noted side-scan sonar expert David Trotter mounted a ten-day hunt for the *Chicora* in the spring of 1998. Using the side-scan sonar to examine the lake bottom, they searched a forty-square-mile area between Saugatuck and Ganges, hoping to find the wreck and gain insights into the ship's disappearance over a century earlier. Trotter's side-scan sonar system used sound waves to create a visual image of the lake floor and, they hoped, any wreckage lying there. The system had the advantage of covering relatively large areas of the lake bottom much faster—and with much less expense and physical risk—than divers conducting visual searches of the dark water. Despite the use of modern technology, the *Chicora* remained as elusive as ever: the search turned up nothing.[10]

After several expeditions met with no more success than had any others over the past decades, a new member of the team, Jan Miller, contacted Arthur Allen of the National Oceanic and Atmospheric Administration (NOAA) in Connecticut to seek his assistance in finding the wreck. Allen specializes in drift theory to aid the U. S. Coast Guard in search-and-rescue operations, essentially using known weather conditions to extrapolate the distance and direction from which debris have drifted after a disaster. Would Allen's search methodology, developed for present-day disasters, help locate a wreck that occurred over one hundred years ago? The concept intrigued Allen and he expressed a willingness to help but explained that he could do nothing without weather data.[11]

Could the search team members discover the precise wind and wave conditions on southwest Lake Michigan on the night of January 21, 1895? To answer that question, Jan Miller contacted Dr. David Schwab of the Great Lakes Environmental Research Laboratory (a division of NOAA) in Ann Arbor, Michigan. With Schwab's assistance, Miller gathered century-old weather data from several sources, particularly the National Climatic Weather Center. The old weather records documented the storm that sank the *Chicora,* detailing the wind speeds and directions throughout the storm's life cycle as it grew in power and then blew itself out.

Schwab used the data to generate a wind, wave, and current animation which he presented to Arthur Allen. Allen plugged this information into his drift analysis program, dropped pieces of wreckage—on his computer screen—into Lake Michigan, and followed them as wind and waves carried them to shore. The computer model tracked the wreckage from January 21 until late in the evening of

January 22. Contemporary accounts of the disaster often noted where pieces of the wreck had washed ashore; the computer model demonstrated that these bits of flotsam probably originated in a particular area of the lake farther west than the region previously had been searched. Had the bits of wreckage originated farther to the north or south, they would not have come ashore in the areas where they did; much closer to the shore or farther from it and they would have been found in a narrower or wider range along the coast.

In the end, the search team came away with a probable area in which to concentrate their efforts. Due to a variety of circumstances, the team had only a ten-day search window in the spring of 2001. They nevertheless hoped that the newly defined area gave them a realistic possibility of success.

On March 25, David Trotter's side-scan sonar picked up the image of wreckage on the bottom of the lake, almost in the center of the targeted search area. After making several passes over the spot to get the best possible print-out, the team found themselves staring at a clear image of a 200-foot vessel—nearly identical to the *Chicora's* 209-foot length. Back on shore, they compared the sonar profile to a profile of the ship from the original plans and found that it was a spot-on match. The search team returned to the site on May 25 with an underwater video camera. They only managed to secure about two minutes of videotape, but the pictures showed a railing, fender and side cargo openings, all of which matched those of the *Chicora*. Later in the summer, using a camera system of their own design, the team obtained three full hours of videotape of the wreck that again showed many details consistent with the *Chicora*. The elated members of SWMUP felt certain that they had found the *Chicora's* grave.

The wreck was located about fifteen miles off Saugatuck in about three hundred feet of water. The hull lay upright with the bow pointed to the northwest. Although the upper works were missing—probably ripped away on the surface as the ship went down—the wreck appeared remarkably intact.

Since the site lay well outside the boundaries of the Southwest Michigan Underwater Preserve, the search team decided to form a new organization to further study the site: Michigan Shipwreck Associates (MSRA), initially doing business as the Chicora Preservation Society. The initial mission of MSRA planned to use more advanced videotaping equipment to obtain better images of the wreck and confirm its identity.

Archaeologists hold to an old adage that no artifact or site can be found until it wants to be found. During the summer of 2002, MSRA learned that the *Chicora* does not yet want to be found. When divers descended on the wreck site, they located the ship's engine and found that it was not the type of triple-expansion engine that had powered the *Chicora;* moreover, it had been mounted in the vessel's stern, whereas the *Chicora's* engine was located near the center of the ship. The divers also found that the sunken ship had the large side-by-side hatches of a top-loader, whereas the *Chicora* was a side-loader. In all probability, the SWMUP search had located the *H. C. Akeley*—in many ways an even more historically significant wreck, but not the elusive *Chicora*. At this writing, the search for the Graham & Morton steamer continues.[12]

The thousands of shipwrecks lying on Michigan's Great Lakes bottomlands remained largely untouched and—because of the cold, dark, freshwater environment—in an excellent state of preservation. Few wrecked ships had carried cargo worth salvaging after submersion in water, so commercial salvers left most of them alone. The invention of scuba (self-contained underwater breathing apparatus) gear, however, put many wrecks within reach of sport divers. While the overwhelming majority of these divers held the wrecks in high regard and (to use their own parlance) "took nothing but pictures and left nothing but bubbles," a few found the taking of souvenirs an irresistible temptation. In addition, romantic notions about shipwrecks fueled a collectors' market for recovered items. Commercial salvagers who saw the wrecks as an opportunity for financial gain stripped them of historically valuable artifacts to sell as restaurant decor, furniture wood, museum pieces, or simply as curiosities. As a result, Michigan's shipwreck heritage began to disappear.[13]

With the fervent support of the sport-diving community, Governor William Milliken signed into law Public Act 184 of 1980. The new law gave Michigan's Department of Natural Resources and Department of State responsibility and authority for bottomland shipwreck management. In particular, the law set up a plan for a revised salvage permit program and mandated the establishment of Great Lakes bottomlands as preserves. Public Act 452 of 1988 strengthened the original law by, among other things, better defining salvage regulations and increasing the penalty for breaking the law from a mere misdemeanor to a felony.[14] In November 1999, the Southwest Michigan Underwater Preserve joined nine other existing Michigan Bottomland Preserves and two more proposed preserves. This latest preserve covers about 370 square miles of bottomland off the coast of southwest Michigan from the Michigan-Indiana state line to Holland and includes all of the Berrien County coastline.

The schooners and elegant passenger steamers disappeared from the Great Lakes long ago. Improved safety standards, navigational equipment, ship maintenance, and even the decline in numbers of merchant vessels have combined to reduce the number of ships lost each year to a negligible number. The stories of those ships lost on the lakes survive in archives, museums, and the memories of the few people who can still remember the golden age of Michigan's maritime history.

---

1. Robert Grimm, interim harbormaster, to Frank Walsh, St. Joseph City Manager, n. d. (January 2002), St. Joseph City Hall, St. Joseph, Michigan; John Kinney, Consumers Asphalt Company, interview by author, February 28, 2002.

2. Robert Grimm to Frank Walsh, n. d. (January 2002).

3. Ibid.; James LaVanway, Lafarge North America, interview by author, February 4, 2002.

4. Elliott, 256–64; *Benton Harbor Palladium,* October 16, 1924.

5. Elliott, 276–82.

6. Petition for Probate of Will, February 26, 1932, Bill of Oscar C. Hoffman, March 21, 1932, Petitions of H. W. Whitney, March 26, 1932 and April 6, 1932, all in Berrien County Probate Court, Deceased Files, File No. 10364, William L. Stevens, Berrien County Historical Association, Berrien Springs, Michigan; *The Herald-Press* (St. Joseph, Michigan), January 27, 1932.

7. Mrs. Dora Boneta Whitney to Judge Malcolm Hatfield, October 11, 1941, in Berrien County Probate Court, Deceased Files, File No. 10364; *The Herald-Press,* February 1, 1932.

8. *The Herald Palladium,* November 5, 1983, October 30, 1984, and August 16, 1988.

9. Steve Harrington, *Divers Guide to Michigan* (Mason, MI: Maritime Press, 1990), 31 and 108.

10. *The Herald Palladium,* June 7, 1998; Valerie van Heest, interview by author, January 12, 2002.

11. Valerie van Heest, Michigan Shipwreck Associates, interview by author, January 12, 2002. The following account of the search for the *Chicora* is from this interview.

12. *The Holland Sentinel,* July 1, 2002; Valerie van Heest, Michigan Shipwreck Associates, interview by author, July 3, 2002.

13. John R. Halsey, "Shipwrecks: A Unique and Undervalued Resource," *Michigan History* 83 (July-August 1999): 80.

14. Ibid., 81.

Appendix

List of Ships

Griffin, 1679

Other names: *"Griffin"* is Anglicized French for *"Le Grifon"*
Official No.: none
Type at loss: bark, exploration and trading; wood; two-mast
Built: 1679; Moise Hillaret for Sieur de La Salle; Cayuga Creek,
    Niagara
Specifications: 45–60 tons
Loss: September 1679
Cause: storm (probably)
Lives lost: six (all)
Cargo: furs

Pioneer, 1834

Other names: none
Official No.: none
Type at loss: sidewheel steamer; wood
Built: 1825; Benjamin Winslow; Black Rock [Buffalo], New York
Specifications: 96' x 16' 9" x 8'; 124 tons
Loss: July 9, 1834, at St. Joseph
Cause: storm
Lives lost: none
Cargo: unknown

Chance, 1835

Other names: none
Official No.: none
Type at loss: schooner, wood
Built: unknown
Specifications: unknown
Loss: November 10, 1835, near St. Joseph
Cause: storm
Lives lost: seven
Cargo: unknown

Swan, 1835

Other names: none
Official No.: none
Type at loss: schooner, wood
Built: unknown
Specifications: unknown
Loss: November 10, 1835, near New Buffalo
Cause: storm
Lives lost: unknown
Cargo: "freight"

Bridget, 1835

Other names: none
Official No.: none
Type at loss: schooner, wood
Built: 1834; David Crocket; Mt. Clemens, Michigan
Specifications: 77' 6" x 22' 6" x 7' 10"; 119 tons, old measure
Loss: November 10–11, 1835, eighteen miles north of St. Joseph
Cause: storm
Lives lost: fifteen (all)
Cargo: none

Delaware, 1836

Other names: none
Official No.: none
Type at loss: sidewheel steamer; wood; passenger and package freight

Built: 1834; Huron, Ohio
Specifications: 105' x 25' x 7' 6"; 178 tons
Loss: June 19, 1836, west of Michigan City, Indiana
Cause: storm
Lives lost: none
Cargo: passengers and general merchandise

Davy Crockett, 1836

Other names: none
Official No.: none
Type at loss: sternwheel riverboat; wood; package freight
Built: 1834; Stephen Jenkins; Erie, Pennsylvania
Specifications: 35 tons
Loss: August 1836, on the St. Joseph River
Cause: grounding
Lives lost: none
Cargo: unknown

Post Boy, 1841

Other names: none
Official No.: none
Type at loss: schooner; wood; two-mast
Built: 1832; Portland Harbor, New York
Specifications: 59' 3" x 18' x 6' 1"; 56 tons, old measure
Loss: October 1841, at Buffington Harbor, near Chicago
Cause: explosion
Lives lost: ten (all)
Cargo: general merchandise, gunpowder

Edward Bancroft, 1842

Other names: none
Official No.: none
Type at loss: schooner; wood
Built: 1836; Point Peninsula, New York
Specifications: 79' 9" x 20' 2" x 8'; 114 tons
Loss: November 19, 1842, at St. Joseph
Cause: storm

Lives lost: none
Cargo: salt, apples, general merchandise

Jefferson, 1844

Other names: none
Official No.: none
Type at loss: schooner; wood; two-mast
Built: 1834; French Creek, New York
Specifications: 76' x 20' 3" x 8'; 109 tons (old measure)
Loss: March 17, 1844
Cause: storm
Lives lost: none
Cargo: stone

Experiment, 1855

Other names: none
Official No.: 7523
Type at loss: schooner; wood; two-mast
Built: 1854; Aurelius McMillan; St. Joseph, Michigan
Specifications: 64' 6" x 17' x 5' 4"; 52 gross tons, 47 net tons
Loss: June 1, 1855
Cause: storm
Lives lost: all crew but one; one passenger
Cargo: unknown

Thomas Bradley, 1856

Other names: none
Official No.: none
Type at loss: schooner; wood
Built: probably Massachusetts
Specifications: unknown
Loss: about November 4, 1856, seven miles south of St. Joseph
Cause: storm
Lives lost: none
Cargo: steam engines and machinery

Antelope, 1857

Other names: none
Official No.: none
Type at loss: schooner; wood
Built: 1854; J. and J. Abbey; Port Robinson, Ontario
Specifications: 220 tons
Loss: November 20, 1857, near St. Joseph
Cause: storm
Lives lost: five
Cargo: wheat

Sunshine, 1859

Other names: none
Official No.: none
Type at loss: bark; wood
Built: 1854; M. Smith; East Saginaw, Michigan
Specifications: 157' x 29' 6" x 11' 8"; 594 gross tons
Loss: July 2, 1859, on Lake Erie
Cause: storm
Lives lost: six of sixteen
Cargo: general merchandise

Hurricane, 1860

Other names: none
Official No.: none
Type at loss: schooner; wood
Built: 1854; George S. Weeks; Buffalo, New York
Specifications: 120' x 26' x 11'; 331 tons
Loss: November 24, 1860, twelve miles south of St. Joseph
Cause: storm
Lives lost: nine (all)
Cargo: 14,000 bushels of rye

L. B. Britton, 1861

Other names: also listed as *L. L. Britton*
Official No.: none
Type at loss: propeller steamer

Built: 1854; Amity Springs, New York
Specifications: 115 tons
Loss: July 9, 1861, near the Calumet River, Illinois
Cause: storm
Lives lost: none
Cargo: railroad ties and fish

Whip, 1865

Other names: none
Official No.: none
Type at loss: schooner; wood; two-mast
Built: 1849; Luther Moses; Ohio City, Ohio
Specifications: 78' 8" x 17' 7" x 6' 6"; 77 tons
Loss: March 22, 1865, at St. Joseph, Michigan
Cause: storm
Lives lost: one
Cargo: lumber

Anna, 1865

Other names: none
Official No.: none
Type at loss: scow schooner; wood; two-mast
Built: 1852; Charles Rose; Swan Creek, Michigan
Specifications: 61' 2" x 19' 7" x 4' 9"; 48 tons
Loss: October 13, 1865, near St. Joseph, Michigan
Cause: storm
Lives lost: at least two
Cargo: unknown

Hippocampus, 1868

Other names: none
Official No.: 11819
Type at loss: propeller; wood; passenger and package freight
Built: 1867; George Hanson; St. Joseph, Michigan
Specifications: 82' x 18' x 7'; 153 tons
Loss: September 8, 1868, between St. Joseph and Chicago
Cause: storm and overloading

Lives lost: twenty-six
Cargo: peaches

A. P. Dutton, 1868

Other names: none
Official No.: 376
Type at loss: schooner; wood; two-mast
Built: 1856; Racine, Wisconsin
Specifications: 60' 6" x 14' 7" x 5' 6"; 30.74 tons; (43.6 tons old measure)
Loss: December 8, 1868, between Chicago and St. Joseph
Cause: storm
Lives lost: four (all)
Cargo: school furniture

William Tell, 1869

Other names: none
Official No.: 26348
Type at loss: scow schooner; wood; two-mast
Built: 1861; Charles Rose; New Baltimore, Michigan
Specifications: 33 gross tons (44 tons old measure)
Loss: August 20, 1869, off St. Joseph
Cause: fire
Lives lost: none
Cargo: barreled lime and salt

Union, 1870

Other names: none
Official No.: 25138
Type at loss: scow schooner; wood; two-mast
Built: 1857; F. H. Revell; Holland, Michigan
Specifications: 82.2' x 22.4' x 7.4'; 72 gross tons
Loss: October 31, 1870, in the St. Joseph harbor
Cause: striking sunken pilings
Lives lost: none
Cargo: unknown

Emma, 1871

Other names: none
Official No.: unknown
Type at loss: schooner; wood; two-mast
Built: 1859; Elery & Spaulding; Port Huron, Michigan. Rebuilt from
    the sloop Emma, originally constructed by Jacob H. Randall
Specifications: 48' 3" x 17' 6" x 5' 10"; 40 gross tons
Loss: March 20, 1871, off St. Joseph
Cause: storm
Lives lost: four (all)
Cargo: fish

J. Barber, 1871

Other names: sometimes seen as *Joe Barber*
Official No.: 12981
Type at loss: propeller; wood; passenger and package freight
Built: May 1856; Luther Moses and Thomas Quayle; Cleveland, Ohio
Specifications: 125.95' x 26.35' x 8.45'; 302 gross tons
Loss: July 19, 1871, ten miles off Michigan City, Indiana
Cause: fire
Lives lost: two
Cargo: peaches

Magnolia

Other names: none
Official No.: 90047
Type at loss: sidewheel riverboat; wood
Built: 1867; Lorenzo P. Maxfield; Pentwater, Michigan
Specifications: 56' x 12' x 3'; 27.93 tons
Loss: unknown, on St. Joseph River near Berrien Springs
Cause: wrecked on a sandbar
Lives lost: unknown
Cargo: unknown

E. B. Perkins, 1875

Other names: unknown
Official No.: unknown

Type at loss: fishing boat; wood
Built: unknown
Specifications: unknown
Loss: April 29, 1875, near St. Joseph
Cause: storm
Lives lost: four (all)
Cargo: fish

Sea Gull, 1875

Other names: unknown
Official No.: unknown
Type at loss: fishing boat; wood
Built: unknown
Specifications: unknown
Loss: April 29, 1875, near St. Joseph
Cause: storm
Lives lost: three (all)
Cargo: fish

St. Joe Doll, 1875

Other names: unknown
Official No.: unknown
Type at loss: fishing boat; wood
Built: unknown
Specifications: unknown
Loss: April 29, 1875, near St. Joseph
Cause: storm
Lives lost: four (all)
Cargo: fish

Grace Greenwood, 1876

Other names: none
Official No.: 10196
Type at loss: schooner; wood (three-mast); built as a bark
Built: 1853; G. R. Rogers; Oswego, New York
Specifications: 134' x 25' 6" x 14' 6"; 306 tons; built as 337-ton bark
Loss: October 5, 1876, near the north pier, St. Joseph

Cause: storm
Lives lost: none of six
Cargo: iron ore

L. Painter, 1877

Other names: none
Official No.: 15441
Type at loss: scow schooner; wood
Built: 1867; South Haven, Michigan
Specifications: 93.74 tons
Loss: October 10, 1877, near the north pier, St. Joseph
Cause: storm
Lives lost: none
Cargo: cordwood

City of Tawas, 1877

Other names: none
Official No.: 4391
Type at loss: sloop; wood; three-mast
Specifications: 135' x 28' x 10'; 291 tons, old measure
Loss: October 30, 1877
Cause: storm
Lives lost: none
Cargo: iron ore

Col. H. C. Heg, 1877

Other names: none
Official No.: 5398
Type at loss: schooner; wood; two-mast
Built: 1868; Sanford; De Pere, Wisconsin
Specifications: 149.47 tons
Loss: November 9, 1877, off St. Joseph
Cause: storm
Lives lost: none
Cargo: unknown

Mary, 1878

Other names: none
Official No.: 16416
Type at loss: schooner; wood, two-mast
Built: 1865; Sheboygan, Wisconsin
Specifications: 82 tons (94 tons, old measure)
Loss: September 10–11, 1879, two miles north of New Buffalo
Cause: storm and damage in loading
Lives lost: four of six
Cargo: lumber

Ithaca, 1879

Other names: none
Official No.: 12081
Type at loss: schooner; wood
Built: 1847; Henry Kelley; Milan, Ohio
Specifications: 144 tons
Loss: November 2, 1879, near the north pier at St. Joseph
Cause: storm
Lives lost: none of seven
Cargo: lumber

Alpena, 1880

Other names: none
Official No.: 404
Type at loss: sidewheel steamer; wood; passenger and package freight
Built: 1867; Arnold and Gallagher; Marine City, Michigan
Specifications: 170' x 35' x 12'; 653 gross tons
Loss: October 15, 1880, somewhere off Holland, Michigan
Cause: storm
Lives lost: between sixty and one hundred (all)
Cargo: passengers and package freight

Nina Bailey, 1880

Other names: none
Official No.: 18767
Type at loss: schooner; wood

Built: 1873; Collins; Ludington, Michigan
Specifications: 52' x 16' x 5'; 35 tons
Loss: November 1, 1880, at St. Joseph
Cause: storm
Lives lost: none
Cargo: none

W. H. Willard, 1880

Other names: none
Official No.: 26231
Type at loss: schooner; wood
Built: 1856; Charles Harman; Black River, Ohio
Specifications: 91' 9" x 22' 6" x 9' 1"; 168 tons
Loss: November 6, 1880, off the north pier at St. Joseph
Cause: storm
Lives lost: none of four
Cargo: lumber

Industry, 1882

Other names: none
Official No.: (12083?)
Type at loss: schooner; wood; two-mast
Built: 1847; Michigan City, Indiana
Specifications: 63' 2" x 14' 8" x 5' 3"; 44 tons
Loss: June 1, 1882, just off South Haven
Cause: storm
Lives lost: three (all)
Cargo: lumber

R. G. Peters, 1882

Other names: none
Official No.: 110424
Type at loss: propeller; wood; bulk freight steambarge
Built: 1880; Milwaukee Ship Yard Co.; Milwaukee, Wisconsin
Specifications: 175.4' x 31.0' x 10.5'; 386 tons
Loss: December 2, 1882, about forty miles off Milwaukee
Cause: storm and fire

Lives lost: fourteen (all)
Cargo: in ballast

Arab, 1883

Other names: none
Official No.: 311
Type at loss: schooner; wood; lumber
Built: 1854; Moses Lavayea; Buffalo, New York
Specifications: 100' x 23' 2" x 9' 6"; 158 gross tons
Loss: November 13, 1883, well off Arcadia, MI
Cause: storm
Lives lost: one
Cargo: lumber

H. C. Akeley, 1883

Other names: sometimes seen as *H. C. Ackley*
Official No.: 95639
Type at loss: propeller; wood; bulk freight
Built: 1881; Kirby and Akeley, Mechanic's Dry Dock Co.; Grand
    Haven, Michigan
Specifications: 231.6' x 35.1' x 18.7'; 1,187 gross tons, 794 net tons
Loss: November 13, 1883, off Holland, Michigan
Cause: storm
Lives lost: five
Cargo: corn

Protection, 1883

Other names: none
Official No.: 20471
Type at loss: propeller steam tug; wood
Built: 1873; John Gregory; Chicago, Illinois
Specifications: 60 gross tons, 30 net tons
Loss: November 14, 1883, near Holland, Michigan; recovered and
    rebuilt
Cause: storm
Lives lost: one
Cargo: none

Regulator, 1883

Other names: none
Official No.: 21186
Type at loss: schooner; wood
Built: 1866; Frederick Nelson Jones; Buffalo, New York
Specifications: 121 tons
Loss: November 16, 1883, nineteen miles south of St. Joseph
Cause: storm
Lives lost: one
Carrying: lumber

Havana, 1887

Other names: none
Official No.: 95116
Type at loss: schooner; wood; two-mast
Built: August 1871; A. Miller and Co.; Oswego, New York
Specifications: 141' 6" x 26' 1" x 11' 5"; 306 gross tons, 290 net tons
Loss: October 3, 1887, one mile north of St. Joseph
Cause: storm
Lives lost: three of seven
Cargo: 551 tons of iron ore

Myosotis, 1887

Other names: none
Official No.: 90764
Type at loss: schooner; wood; bulk freight
Built: 1874; Milwaukee Shipyard Company, Milwaukee, Wisconsin
    (begun by Allen and McClelland, Milwaukee)
Specifications: 137' x 26' x 11'; 333 gross tons, 316 net tons
Loss: November 11, 1887, near the harbor mouth at St. Joseph
Cause: storm
Lives lost: none
Cargo: iron ore

Joseph P. Farnam, 1889

Other names: also listed as *Joseph P. Farnan* and *Joseph P. Farman*
Official No.: 76691

Type at loss: propeller; wood; bulk freight "steambarge"
Built: 1887; William R. Radcliffe; Cleveland, Ohio
Specifications: 151.4' x 33.6' x 9.6'; 409 gross tons, 346 net tons
Loss: July 20, 1889, northwest of Benton Harbor
Cause: fire
Lives lost: none of twelve
Cargo: light

Thomas Hume, 1891

Other names: built as the schooner *H. C. Albrecht,* renamed in 1883
Official No.: 95135
Type at loss: schooner; wood
Built: 1870; Hansen and Scove; Manitowoc, Wisconsin
Specifications: 131.6' x 26.3' x 8.4'; 210 gross tons, 199 net tons
Loss: May 21, 1891, along the Chicago-Muskegon route
Cause: went missing
Lives lost: six (all)
Cargo: light

Chicora, 1895

Other names: none
Official No.: 126902
Type at loss: propeller; wood; passenger and package freight
Built: 1892; Detroit Dry Dock, hull no. 111; Wyandotte, Michigan
Specifications: 209' x 35' x 15' 3"; 1,122.92 gross tons, 708.15 net
   tons
Loss: January 21, 1895, somewhere off St. Joseph
Cause: storm
Lives lost: twenty-three (all)
Cargo: flour

City of Duluth, 1898

Other names: none
Official No.: 125278
Type at loss: propeller; wood; passenger and package freight
Built: 1874; Philander Lester; Marine City, Michigan, as a passenger
   vessel
Specifications: 202' x 36' x 13'; 1,310 gross tons, 912 net tons

Loss: January 26, 1898, at St. Joseph harbor
Cause: storm
Lives lost: none
Cargo: corn, flour, general merchandise

Tourist, 1898

Other names: none
Official No.: 145742
Type at loss: sternwheel riverboat; wood; passenger and package freight
Built: 1897; Logan Drake and Louis Wallace; St. Joseph
Specifications: 87.1' x 17' x 4.4'; 66 gross tons, 45 net tons
Loss: September 6, 1898, St. Joseph River at St. Joseph
Cause: fire
Lives lost: none
Cargo: none

Lena M. Neilson, 1898

Other names: none
Official No.: unknown
Type at loss: schooner; wood; lumber
Built: 1896; Ludington, Michigan
Specifications: 86 tons
Loss: November 10, 1898, near Lakeside, Michigan
Cause: storm
Lives lost: none
Cargo: lumber

Experiment, 1902

Other names: none
Official No.: 7523
Type at loss: schooner; wood; two-mast
Built: 1854; Aurelius McMillan; St. Joseph, Michigan
Specifications: 64.6' x 17.6' x 5.3'; 52 gross tons, 47 net tons
Loss: September 12, 1902, just north of the St. Joseph harbor
Cause: storm
Lives lost: none of six
Cargo: firewood

Emily and Eliza, 1910

Other names: none
Official No.: 36582
Type at loss: scow schooner; wood; two-mast
Built: 1878; Anspaugh Brothers; Oak Harbor, Ohio
Specifications: 78' x 21' x 5'; 63 gross tons, 60 net tons
Loss: September 9, 1910, in Platte Bay near the mouth of Otter
    Creek, Sleeping Bear Dunes National Shoreline
Cause: overloading
Lives lost: none
Cargo: cedar posts

Evening Star, 1911

Other names: none
Official No.: 201984
Type at loss: propeller steam fishing tug; wood
Built: 1905; Chicago, as a passenger steamer
Specifications: 70' x 14' x 5'; 31 gross tons, 26 net tons
Loss: November 13, 1911, off St. Joseph
Cause: storm
Lives lost: none of seven
Cargo: none

Hattie Wells, 1912

Other names: none
Official No.: 11609
Type at loss: schooner; wood; three-mast
Built: 1867; Stewart and Fitzgerald; Port Huron, Michigan
Specifications: 164' x 28' x 11'; 376 gross tons, 357 net tons; original-
    ly 135' x 26' x 11', enlarged and rebuilt in 1895
Loss: November 6, 1912, off St. Joseph
Cause: storm
Lives lost: none
Cargo: lumber

City of Chicago, 1914

Other names: renamed *City of St. Joseph* in 1915
Official No.: 126627
Type at loss: sidewheel steamer; steel; passenger and package freight
Built: 1890; Frank W. Wheeler; West Bay City, Michigan, hull no. 68
Specifications: 226' x 34'; 1,164 gross tons; later rebuilt to 254' x 34'
    x 14', 1,439 gross tons
Loss: September 1, 1914, off Chicago
Cause: fire
Lives lost: none
Cargo: passengers and fruit

Eastland, 1915

Other names: rebuilt as USS *Wilmette*
Official No.: 20031
Type: propeller steamer; steel; passenger
Built: 1903; Jenks Shipbuilding Co., hull no. 25; Port Huron,
    Michigan
Specifications: 265' x 38' x 19' 6"; 1,961 gross tons, 1,218 net tons
Loss: July 24, 1915, in the Chicago River, Chicago, Illinois
Cause: capsized at pier
Lives lost: 844
Cargo: none

Rising Sun, 1917

Other names: built as the *Minnie M.,* renamed in 1913
Official No.: 91764 (107889 Canadian)
Type at loss: propeller; wood; passenger and package freight
Built: 1884; John Oades; Detroit, Michigan
Specifications: 133.3' x 26.0' x 10.8'; 448 gross tons, 296 net tons
Loss: October 29, 1917, just south of Pyramid Point, seven miles
    south of Sleeping Bear Point
Cause: storm
Lives lost: none
Cargo: fence posts, farm produce

Rosa Belle, 1921

Other names: also seen as the *Rosabelle*
Official No.: 21302
Type at loss: schooner; wood; two-mast
Built: 1863; L. H. Boole; Milwaukee
Specifications: 100' x 26' x 8'; 132 gross tons, 125 net tons
Loss: October 30, 1921, on Lake Michigan about forty miles off
    Milwaukee
Cause: collision (probably)
Lives lost: fourteen (all)
Cargo: lumber

Forelle, 1923

Other names: none
Official No.: 205777
Type: gasoline propeller; steel; steam fishing tug
Built: 1908; Johnston Brothers; Ferrysburg, Michigan
Specifications: 54.5' x 15.66' x 7.42'; 46 gross tons, 31 net tons
Loss: September 20, 1923, off Milwaukee, Wisconsin
Cause: storm
Lives lost: five (all)
Cargo: grapes

Isabell K., 1937

Other names: none
Official No.: 215600
Type at loss: gasoline/oil fishing tug; wood
Built: 1917; Charlevoix, Michigan
Specifications: 38' x 10' x 4'; 13 gross tons
Loss: June 27, 1937, in the St. Joseph harbor
Cause: collision at the dock
Lives lost: none
Cargo: none

City of Cleveland III, 1950

Other names: built as the *City of Cleveland,* renamed in 1912
Official No.: 204080

Type: sidewheel steamer; steel; passenger
Built: 1907; Detroit Shipbuilding Company; Wyandotte, Michigan
Specifications: 390' x 54' x 23'; 4,568 gross tons, 2,403 net tons
Loss: June 25, 1950, off Harbor Beach, Michigan
Cause: collision
Lives lost: five
Cargo: none

Bibliography

Primary Sources

Annual Corporation Reports of the Great Waters Transportation Company. 1910–1921. Berrien County Historical Association, Berrien Springs, Michigan.

Around the Lakes. Cleveland, OH: Marine Review Print, 1894.

Atlas of Berrien County, Michigan. Chicago: Rand, McNally & Company, 1887.

Atlas of Berrien County, Michigan. Philadelphia: C. O. Titus, 1873.

Berrien County Circuit Court. Marriage Records. 1875, certificate no. 392, W. Grönke to Robert Miller; 1901, certificate no. 40, Logan J. Drake to Maude Slanker; and 1907, certificate no. 1594, Louis D. Wallace to Laura Slanker. Berrien County Historical Association, Berrien Springs, Michigan.

Berrien County Probate Court. Deceased Files. File No. 236, Cornelius McNeil; File No. 484, James Campbell; File No. 1815, Wilhelmina Groenke; and File No. 10364, William L. Stevens. Berrien County Historical Association, Berrien Springs, Michigan.

Blue Book of American Shipping. Cleveland, OH: Marine Review, 1897.

Bureau of the Census. *Ninth Census of the United States.* Washington, DC: 1870.

Bureau of the Census. *Twelfth Census of the United States.* Washington, DC: 1900.

Calvert, Gwalter C. to Capt. Merwin S. Thompson. February 13, 1967, "Ships and Shipwrecks" file. Michigan City Public Library, Michigan City, Indiana.

Carter, Clarence Edwin, comp. and ed. *The Territorial Papers of the United States.* Vol. 12, *The Territory of Michigan, 1829–1837.*

Washington, DC: United States Government Printing Office, 1945.

Classification, Association of Lake Underwriters. Buffalo, NY: Printing House of Matthews & Warren, 1876.

Classification of Lake Vessels and Barges. Buffalo, NY: Warren, Johnson, & Co., 1871.

DeLand, Charles J., comp. *Michigan Official Directory and Legislative Manual for the Years 1921 and 1922.* N.p., 1921.

Hennepin, Louis. *A New Discovery of a Vast Country in America.* Trans. and ed. by Reuben G. Thwaites, 2 vols. London: 1698. Reprint. Cambridge, MA: John Wilson & Son, University Press, 1903.

Keeper's Log of the Light House Station at South Haven, 1872–1889. A-318, Regional History Collections. Western Michigan University, Kalamazoo, Michigan.

Lake Hull Registration of Lake Underwriters. Detroit: Free Press Book and Job Printing House, 1879.

Laws of the Territory of Michigan. 3 vols. Lansing: W. S. George & Co., 1874.

Martineau, Harriet. *Society in America.* 2 vols. New York: Saunders and Otley, 1837.

Merchant Vessels of the United States. Washington, DC: Government Printing Office, 1868–1912.

Morton, James Stanley to Mary A. Raymond. December 8, 1903. Josephine Morton Memorial House, Benton Harbor, MI.

Osmun, Gilbert R. *Official Directory and Legislative Manual of the State of Michigan for the Years 1887–8.* Lansing: Thorp & Godfrey, 1887.

Raymond, Mary A. to James Stanley Morton. November 30, 1903. Josephine Morton Memorial House. Benton Harbor, MI.

Records of the Graham-Morton Steamship Co. and Family Papers of the Morton Family, 1872–1936. A-1641, Regional History Collections. Western Michigan University, Kalamazoo, Michigan.

Relation of the Discoveries and Voyages of Cavalier de La Salle from 1679 to 1681. Trans. by Melville B. Anderson. 1682. Reprint. Chicago: The Caxton Club, 1901.

Thomas, Robert. *Register of the Ships of the Lakes and River St. Lawrence.* Buffalo, NY: Wheeler, Matthews & Warren, 1864.

Tipton, John. *The John Tipton Papers.* Comp. and ed. Glen A. Blackburn, Nellie A. Robertson, and Dorothy Riker. 3 vols. Indianapolis: Indiana Historical Bureau, 1942.

Tonty, Henri de. *The Journeys of Rene Robert Cavelier Sieur de La Salle.*

Trans. and ed. by Isaac Joslin Cox. 2 vols. New York: Allerton Book Co., 1922; reprint, New York: AMS Press, 1973.

Turner, T. G. *Gazetteer of the St. Joseph Valley, Michigan and Indiana*. Chicago: Hazlitt & Reed, 1867.

United States Coast Guard Casualty and Wreck Reports, 1913–1939. Record Group 26, Microfilm T 925. National Archives and Records Administration, Great Lakes Region (Chicago).

United States Coast Guard. Log of the No. 261 Coast Guard Station, Record Group 26. National Archives and Records Administration— Great Lakes Region (Chicago).

United States Coast Guard. "Report of the Marine Board of Investigation on the collision involving the SS *City of Cleveland III* and SS *Ravneffell* on June 25, 1950," September 21, 1950. United States Coast Guard Headquarters, Washington, DC.

United States Department of Commerce. *United States Coast Pilot 6*. 24th ed. Washington, DC: U.S. Dept. of Commerce, National Oceanic and Atmospheric Administration, 1994.

United States Land Sales Tract Book. Berrien County Register of Deeds Office, St. Joseph, Michigan.

United States Life-Saving Service, *Annual Report of the Operations of the United States Life-Saving Service for the Fiscal Year Ending June 30, 1881*. Washington, DC: Government Printing Office, 1882.

United States Life-Saving Service. *Annual Report of the Operations of the United States Life-Saving Service for the Fiscal Year Ending June 30, 1884*. Washington, DC: Government Printing Office, 1885.

United States Life-Saving Service. *Annual Report of the Operations of the United States Life-Saving Service for the Fiscal Year Ending June 30, 1898*. Washington, DC: Government Printing Office, 1899.

United States Life-Saving Service. Life-Saving Station Logs, Chicago District, St. Joseph Station, Record Group 26. National Archives and Records Administration—Great Lakes Region (Chicago).

United States Lighthouse Board. "Description of Buildings, Premises, Equipment, etc., at Front and Rear Range Lights, St. Joseph Pierhead Light-station, St. Joseph, Michigan," June 8, 1909. Lighthouse file, Maud Preston Palenske Memorial Library, St. Joseph, Michigan.

Western Division of Michigan. Southern Division at Grand Rapids, Admiralty Records, Admiralty Case Files, Record Group 21. National Archives and Records Administration—Great Lakes Region (Chicago).

Interviews

Kinney, John. Consumers Asphalt Company. Interview by author, February 28, 2002.

LaVanway, James. Lafarge North America. Interview by author, February 4, 2002.

van Heest, Valerie. Michigan Shipwreck Associates. Interview by author, January 12 and July 13, 2002.

Secondary Sources

Abbott, Jacob. "Some Account of Francis's Life-boats and Life-cars." *Harper's Magazine,* 1851. Reprint. *The United States Life-Saving Service—1880.* Grand Junction, CO: Vistabooks, 1989.

Adkin, Clare E., Jr. *Brother Benjamin: A History of the Israelite House of David.* Berrien Springs, MI: Andrews University Press, 1990.

_____. "Island Israelites," in Florence C. Frank, ed., *The Journal of Beaver Island History.* Vol. 4. Beaver Island, MI: Beaver Island Historical Society, 1998.

Armstrong, William John. "The Bung Town Canal." *Michigan History Magazine* 76 (January/February 1992): 14–22.

Badger, Reid. *The Great American Fair: The World's Columbian Exposition and American Culture.* Chicago: N. Hall, 1979.

Boyer, Dwight. *Ghost Ships of the Great Lakes.* New York: Dodd, Mead & Company, 1968.

Brands, H. W. *The Reckless Decade: America in the 1890s.* New York: St. Martin's Press, 1995.

Caesar, Pete. *Chicora.* Green Bay, WI: Great Lakes Maritime Research, 1982.

Clifford, Mary Louise, and J. Candace Clifford. *Women Who Kept the Lights: An Illustrated History of Female Lighthouse Keepers.* Williamsburg, VA: Cypress Communications, 1993.

Coolidge, Orville W. *A Twentieth Century History of Berrien County, Michigan.* Chicago: The Lewis Publishing Company, 1906.

Cowles, Edward B. *Berrien County Directory and History.* Buchanan, MI: Record Steam Printing House, 1871.

Cozzens, Peter. *This Terrible Sound.* Urbana: University of Illinois Press, 1992. Reprint, Illini Books, 1996.

Devendorf, John F. *Great Lakes Bulk Carriers, 1869–1985.* Niles, MI: By the author, 1996.

Donahue, James L. *Schooners in Peril*. Cass City, MI: Anchor Publications, 1995. Reprint. Holt, MI: Thunder Bay Press, n.d.

_____. *Steaming Through Smoke and Fire 1871*. Holt, MI: Thunder Bay Press, 1990.

Dunbar, Willis F. *Michigan: A History of the Wolverine State*. 1965. Rev. and ed. by George S. May. Grand Rapids, MI: Eerdmans Publishing Co., 1980.

Dupré, Céline. "René-Robert Cavalier, De La Salle." *Dictionary of Canadian Biography*, 12 vols. Toronto: University of Toronto Press, 1866. Reprint, 1979.

Elliott, James L. *Red Stacks over the Horizon: The Story of the Goodrich Steamboat Line*. Grand Rapids, MI: William B. Eerdmanns Publishing Co., 1967.

Ellis, Franklin. *History of Berrien and Van Buren Counties, Michigan*. Philadelphia: D. W. Ensign & Co., 1880.

Fogarty, Robert S. *The Righteous Remnant: The House of David*. Kent, OH: The Kent State University Press, 1981.

Franz, Harvey. "Lumber Piers of Southwestern Michigan." Berrien County Historical Association, Berrien Springs, MI. Photocopy.

Fuller, George N. *Historic Michigan*. Vol. 3: *Southwest Michigan and Berrien County*. Ed. by Charles A. Weissert. N.p.: National Historical Assn., n.d.

Gebhart, Richard. "The Chaptered Loss of the H. C. Akeley," *Soundings* (Spring 1994): 3–14.

Greenwood, John Orville. *Namesakes, 1930–1955*. Cleveland, OH: Freshwater Press, 1978.

Halsey, John R. "Shipwrecks: A Unique and Undervalued Resource." *Michigan History* 83 (July-August 1999): 80–85.

Harold, Steve. *Shipwrecks of the Sleeping Bear*. Traverse City, MI: Pioneer Study Center, 1984.

Harrington, Steve. *Divers Guide to Michigan*. Mason, MI: Maritime Press, 1990.

Harris, Patricia Gruse. *New Buffalo, MI, Lighthouse, 1839–1859*. Michigan City, IN: Gen-Hi-Li, 1992.

Haswell, John. "History of Aral." Benzie Shores District Library, Frankfort, MI, n.d.

Hemming, Robert J. *Gales of November: The Sinking of the* Edmund Fitzgerald. N.p.: Thunder Bay Press, 1981.

Hilton, George W. Eastland: *Legacy of the Titanic*. Stanford, CA:

Stanford University Press, 1995.

Hood, Phil, ed. *Artists of American Folk Music.* New York: William Morrow, 1986.

House, Jan H., and Robert C. Myers. "The Berrien County Courthouse Square: A Sesquicentennial History." *Michigan History* 70 (November/December 1986): 21–27.

Idle, Dunning. "The Post of the St. Joseph River during the French Regime, 1679–1761." Ph.D. diss., University of Illinois, 1946.

Johnson, Rossiter. *A History of the World's Columbian Exposition Held in Chicago in 1893.* 4 vols. New York: D. Appleton and Company, 1897–1898.

Knoblock, Otto M. *Early Navigation on the St. Joseph River.* Indianapolis: Indiana Historical Society Publications, 1925.

Kriehn, Ruth. "The Meyer-Tamms Families." Forelle folder, The Herman G. Runge Collection, Milwaukee Public Library, Milwaukee, WI.

Lamb, M. J. "The American Life-Saving Service." *Harper's New Monthly Magazine* 64 (December 1881-May 1882). New York: Harper & Brothers, 1882.

Lane, Kit. *The* Chicora: *Lost on Lake Michigan.* Douglas, MI: Pavilion Press, 1996.

_____. *Lake Michigan Shipwrecks, South Haven to Grand Haven.* Saugatuck Maritime Series, Book 4. Douglas, MI: Pavilion Press, 1997.

Lloyd, Timothy C., and Patrick B. Mullen. *Lake Erie Fishermen: Work, Identity, and Tradition.* Urbana: University of Illinois Press, 1990.

Lytle, William M., and Forrest R. Holdcamper, eds. *Merchant Steam Vessels of the United States, 1790–1868.* Rev. and ed.by C. Bradford Mitchell. Staten Island, NY: The Steamship Historical Society of America, 1979.

Mansfield, J. B. *History of the Great Lakes.* 2 vols. Chicago, IL: J. H. Beers & Co., 1899. Reprint. Cleveland, OH: Freshwater Press, 1972.

Martin, Jay C. Letter to the author, August 18, 1989.

Morton, James Stanley. *Reminiscences of the Lower St. Joseph River Valley.* Benton Harbor, MI: The Federation of Women's Clubs, n.d.

Myers, Robert C. *Historical Sketches of Berrien County.* Vol. 2. Berrien Springs, MI: Berrien County Historical Association, 1989.

_____. *Millennial Visions and Earthly Pursuits: The Israelite House of*

David. Berrien Springs, MI: Berrien County Historical Association, 1999.

Nelson, Ramon. *The House of David on High Island.* Ann Arbor, MI: Sarah Jennings Press, 1990.

Oleszewski, Wes. *Keepers of Valor, Lakes of Vengeance: Lakeboats, Lifesavers & Lighthouses.* Gwinn, MI: Avery Color Studios, 2000.

_____. *Mysteries and Histories: Shipwrecks of the Great Lakes.* Marquette, MI: Avery Color Studios, 1997.

Pender, James. *History of Benton Harbor and Tales of Village Days.* Chicago: The Braun Printing Company, 1915.

Pitz, Herbert. *Lake Michigan Disasters.* Manitowoc, WI: n.p., 1925. Reprint. Manitowoc, WI: Manitowoc Maritime Museum, n.d.

Portrait and Biographical Record of Berrien and Cass Counties, Michigan. Chicago: Biographical Publishing Company, 1893.

Quimby, George Irving. *Indian Culture and European Trade Goods.* Madison: The University of Wisconsin Press, 1966.

Ratigan, William. *Great Lakes Shipwrecks & Survivals.* Grand Rapids, MI: William B. Eerdmans Publishing Co., 1960; rev. ed., 1977.

Romig, Walter. *Michigan Place Names.* Detroit: Wayne State University Press, 1986.

Schultz, Alan. "Silver Beach: A Scrapbook of Summers Past." *Michigan History* 63 (July/August 1979): 8–19.

Ship Reference Files. Central Humanities Marine Collection. Milwaukee Public Library, Milwaukee, WI.

Stonehouse, Frederick. *Went Missing, II.* Au Train, MI: Avery Color Studios, 1984.

_____. *Wreck Ashore: The United States Life-Saving Service on the Great Lakes.* Duluth, MN: Lake Superior Port Cities, 1994.

Thompson, Mark L. *Graveyard of the Lakes.* Detroit: Wayne State University Press, 2000.

Tolhuizen, James A. "History of the Port of St. Joseph-Benton Harbor." Master's thesis, Western Michigan University, Kalamazoo, MI, 1965.

Van der Linden, Peter J. *Great Lakes Ships We Remember.* Cleveland, OH: Freshwater Press, 1979, rev. ed. 1986.

_____. *Great Lakes Ships We Remember II.* Cleveland, OH: Freshwater Press, 1984.

Wade, Wyn Craig. *The Titanic: End of a Dream.* New York: Rawson, Wade Publishers, 1979. Reprint. New York: Penguin Books, 1980.

Internet Sites

Historical Collections of the Great Lakes. *Great Lakes Vessels Online Index.* January 11, 2001.
<http://www.bgsu.edu/colleges/library/hcgl/hcgl.html>

Lewis, Walter. *Maritime History of the Great Lakes.* June 6, 2001.
<http://www.hhpl.on.ca/GreatLakes/>

Macpherson, Ken R. *U. S. Great Lakes Vessel Enrolments to 1860.* n.d.
<www.halinet.on.ca/GreatLakes/scripts/enrolment/>

Milwaukee Public Library. *Great Lakes Ship Files.* October 2, 2000.
<http://www.mpl.org/file/hum_marine_shipfile.htm>

Parker, Martha. *Curran Family of Ballyhalbert, Co Down.* August 9, 2001.
<http://geocities.com/Heartland/Meadows/1725/curran.htm>

Swayze, David. *The Great Lakes Shipwreck File.* January 17, 2002.
<http://greatlakeshistory.homestead.com/home.html>

Townsend, Peggy Jean, and Charles Walker Townsend III, eds. "Sara Jane Clarke (Grace Greenwood)." *Milo Adams Townsend and Social Movements of the Nineteenth Century.* January 1994.
<http://www.bchistory.org/beavercounty/booklengthdocuments/A Milobook/chapters.html>

U. S. Coast Guard, "Gold Lifesaving Medal Awardees," *United States Coast Guard Historian's Office,* January 2002.
<http://www.uscg.mil/hq/g%2Dcp/history/gold%20medal%20index.html>

University of Wisconsin Sea Grant Institute and Wisconsin Historical Society. *Wisconsin's Great Lakes Shipwrecks.* January 4, 2002.
<http://seagrant.wisc.edu/shipwrecks/>

Newspapers

Allegan (Michigan) *Journal*
Benton Harbor (Michigan) *Palladium*
Benton Harbor (Michigan) *The Daily Palladium*
Benton Harbor (Michigan) *The News-Palladium*
Benton Harbor (Michigan) *The Palladium*
Berrien Springs (Michigan) *Era*
Black Rock (New York) *Gazette*
Buchanan (Michigan) *Berrien County Record*
Buffalo (New York) *Whig and Journal*
Chicago Daily News
Chicago Democrat

Chicago Tribune
Chicago (Illinois) *The Daily Inter Ocean*
Chicago (Illinois) *The Inter Ocean*
Detroit Democratic Free Press
Detroit Free Press
Detroit Gazette
Detroit Post
The Grand Haven (Michigan) *Evening News*
Grand Rapids (Michigan) *Daily Morning Times*
Holland (Michigan) *City News*
Holland (Michigan) *Sentinel*
Kenosha (Wisconsin) *Evening News*
The Michigan City (Indiana) *News*
Milwaukee Daily Sentinal
Milwaukee Sentinal
Niles (Michigan) *Gazette and Advertiser*
Niles (Michigan) *Republican*
Oswego (New York) *Advertiser & Times*
Oswego (New York) *Daily Times*
Pentwater (Michigan) *News*
St. Joseph (Michigan) *The Daily Evening Herald*
St. Joseph (Michigan) *Daily Press*
St. Joseph (Michigan) *Evening Herald*
St. Joseph (Michigan) *The Herald-Palladium*
St. Joseph (Michigan) *Herald-Press*
St. Joseph (Michigan) *The Herald-Press*
St. Joseph (Michigan) *Saturday Herald*
St. Joseph (Michigan) *Traveler-Herald*
Saugatuck (Michigan) *Commercial*
South Bend (Indiana) *St. Joseph Valley Register*
Traverse City (Michigan) *Record-Eagle*

Index